NEW

CUTTING EDGE

UPPER INTERMEDIATE

STUDENTS' BOOK

sarah cunningham   peter moor

PEARSON

Longman

CONTENTS

Past and present

- ▶ Revision of verb forms
- ▶ Uses of auxiliaries
- ▶ **Task:** Talk about your life circles
- ▶ **Reading:** *The family that plays together …*
- ▶ **Vocabulary:** Past and present time phrases
- ▶ **Writing:** Planning and drafting a biography
- ▶ **Wordspot:** *get*
- ▶ **Pronunciation:** Strong and weak auxiliaries, Sounding polite
- ▶ **Real life:** Making conversation

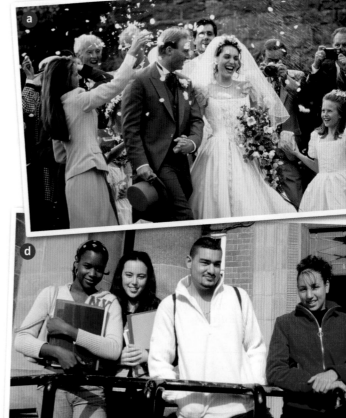

Task: Talk about your life circles
Preparation: listening

1 What can you see in the photos? Why might these photos have sentimental value for the owners? Do you keep many old photos? Which do you treasure most?

2 a T1.1 You will hear people talking about ten important names, dates and places in their past and present. Listen and say what or who the person, place or day is.

1   Park Hill   *grandparents' house*
2   Miss Brown
3   Monday
4   6th June
5   Glengareth
6   Emma
7   3042
8   4th September
9   Tony
10 Berlin

b Look at the life circles. Then listen again. Which life circle is each person speaking about? (Some people talk about the same life circle.)

3 Listen again. What else do you learn about these people, places and days?

1 An important person when you were growing up

2 An important date

3 An important person you haven't seen for several years

Your Past

4 An interesting town or city you've visited

5 The name of a teacher you remember

6 An important place in your family history

b

c

f

e

Task: speaking

1 a Complete the life circles with important names, dates, etc. from your life.

b Decide what to tell other students about your life circles. Ask your teacher for any important words or phrases you need.

▶ Useful language a

2 Work in pairs. Explain your life circles to each other and answer any questions your partner has.

▶ Useful language b

3 What were the most interesting things you learnt about your partner? Tell the class.

7
The number of a house or apartment that is important for you

8
An important birthday

9
The name of a person you see most days

Your Present

10
Your favourite day of the week

11
The number of people living in your house / apartment

12
Someone you met for the first time recently

Useful language

a Explaining your life circles

I put ... because ...

... is important to me because ...

... is a woman / a boy who ...

... is the place where ...

That's when I ...

The last time I ... was ...

I haven't seen ... for ...

b Asking about life circles

Why did you put ...?

Why is/was ... important for you?

Who/Where exactly is ...?

Can you tell me a bit more about ...?

When did you last ...?

Reading

1 Which of these types of music do you like most? Are there any that you don't like? Why not?

folk	jazz	rock
disco	dance	pop
electronic	hip-hop	rap

2 Look at the photos in the text of musicians from different decades. Do you know any of them? What do you think they have in common?

3 Read the text quickly and answer as many of the questions as you can about the people in each photo.

a Where are they from?
b In which period were they successful?
c What are the names of their hit songs/albums?

4 According to the text, who ...

a admits that they argue from time to time?
b ceased to exist when one member died?
c are as well known for their bad behaviour as for their music?
d implies that family matters are more important than fame and money?
e expresses different views about how well they get on?
f is very grateful to her parents?
g seems to be very ambitious?

5 Discuss the following questions in small groups.

• What are the advantages and problems of working with other members of your family? Would you ever do it? Why / Why not?
• Do you think that the parents of talented children push them to be successful? Do you know of other cases like this? What has happened to the children?

The family that plays

'The family that plays together,' goes the old saying, 'stays together.' While fashions and groups come and go in the world of pop music, acts featuring brothers and sisters seem to have a consistent appeal.

Back in the 1970s, all-singing, all-dancing groups like the Jackson 5 and the Osmond Brothers were the equivalent of today's boy bands – although **in those days** the term had not been invented. But the Gibb brothers, known all over the world as The Bee Gees, outlasted them all, with major hits through four decades, reaching their peak in the disco years of the late 1970s. **At one time**, their album *Saturday Night Fever* was Number One for 24 consecutive weeks in the US, and it is still the best-selling soundtrack album of all time. Their existence as a group ended only with the death of brother Maurice in 2003, and there are **currently** no plans for them to record again under the Bee Gees' name. And what was the secret of their success? 'We are brothers first, a group second,' said eldest brother Barry in 1997.

During the 1990s, it was the turn of three sisters and a brother from Ireland to become the world's favourite family act. Playing a blend of pop, rock and Irish traditional music, The Corrs became a truly global phenomenon – their album *In Blue* went to Number One in no fewer than eighteen countries. As with many musical families, they started early. At the age of fifteen, eldest brother Jim used to perform folk songs with his parents – **at that time**, the

younger sisters were all attending primary school. For a number of years, the siblings performed in pubs and clubs in their local area. They were playing in a Dublin pub when the US ambassador to Ireland, Jean Kennedy Smith heard them and was so impressed that she arranged for them to play at the opening celebrations for the World Cup in New York. After that world-wide success soon followed.

But how do the four get on? According to middle sister and drummer Caroline, 'Oh, we do fight. We have spectacular fights, you wouldn't believe it.' But eldest sister and violinist Sharon takes a different view: '**Over the last few years**, we've grown up, and we rarely argue **nowadays**. As for jealousy, that doesn't come into it. Unless we're having a photo shoot and one of us is feeling particularly ugly.'

More recently the northern English city of Manchester has been home to the Gallagher brothers – founders of the rock group Oasis whose *What's the Story Morning Glory?* was the biggest-selling UK album of the 90s, and whose very public rows and outrageous behaviour often attracted more attention than their music.

together ...

So how is the face of family groups changing as we move into the 21st Century? Celebrities move easily between the worlds of pop and movies **these days**, and one duo from the USA who reflect this are Taryn and Kellin Manning, better known as BoomKat. After film roles alongside Britney Spears and Eminem, Taryn teamed up with her elder brother to launch a musical career. Their **latest** album *Boomkatalog 1* is a mixture of hip-hop, electronic and pop.

Or could the future **now** lie with dads and daughters rather than brothers and sisters? At the end of 2003, Ozzy Osbourne – **former** singer with heavy metal band Black Sabbath – and daughter Kelly teamed up for a duet on the hit single *Changes*. Kelly makes it quite clear who she owes her fame to: 'My parents have been so supportive. Everything I know about the industry is from them.'

Whether or not BoomKat and the Osbournes have the staying power of The Bee Gees or The Corrs remains to be seen. But they prove the fact that families can work and play together happily ... for a while at least.

Vocabulary
Past and present time phrases

1 Look back at the time phrases highlighted in bold in the text. Which of them refer to the past? Which of them refer to the present?

2 Read the sentences about the British rock group, Queen. Complete the sentences with the words and phrases in the box.

days
during
nowadays
those days
that time
former
the last few years
one time
now
currently
latest
back

a Queen were formed _____ in 1971 by Brian May and Freddie Mercury. At _____ they were known as Smile.

b Mercury wasn't always a singer – at _____ he worked as a dishwasher at Heathrow Airport!

c One thing that helped make them famous was their video for *Bohemian Rhapsody* – promotional videos weren't common in _____ .

d Queen reached the peak of their popularity _____ the 1980s, and played at the Live Aid concert in 1985.

e Mercury died in 1991. Over _____ , his house in London has become a popular visiting place for Queen fans from all over the world.

f A musical show based on their songs – entitled *We Will Rock You* – is _____ showing in London.

g _____ Queen guitarist Brian May doesn't play many concerts these _____ .

h However, he makes an album from time to time. The _____ one is called *Furia*, and it was released in 2000.

i The chances are that there is a Queen song playing on the radio right _____ somewhere around the world! It seems that Queen are just as popular _____ as they were thirty years ago!

3 **a** Think of a favourite musician or group, past or present. Use these ideas to make notes about them.

– name of the group – any changes in the group / their music
– type of music – current activities/albums
– early career – your favourite album / why you like them

b Tell a partner about them, using the time phrases in exercise 2.

9

Language focus 1
Revision of verb forms

a Are you a grammar genius? Find out how good your knowledge of English verbs is by doing this test with a partner.

b Then check your answers on page 138 and find out your 'grammar genius rating'.

Nine things you should know about English verbs

1 Underline the verb forms in the sentences adapted from the text on pages 8 and 9. Match the forms to the names in the box. **(6 marks)**

> Present simple   Present continuous   Past simple
> Past perfect   Past continuous   Present perfect

a At the end of 2003, Ozzy Osbourne and daughter Kelly teamed up for a duet on the hit single *Changes*.

b Back in the 1970s, the term 'Boy Band' had not been invented.

c At that time, the younger Corrs were attending primary school.

d Over the last few years they have grown up.

e There's no jealousy ... unless we're having a photo shoot and one of us is feeling particularly ugly.

f The family that plays together, stays together.

2 Look at the picture and answer the questions. **(2 marks)**

a Which job does the man on the left see as his permanent job?

b What does he see as his temporary job?

Of course, I really drive Formula One cars. I'm only doing this job to get a bit of extra money!

3 Two of the sentences below contain incorrect verb forms. Cross out the incorrect sentences. **(2 marks)**

a Do you like this soup?

b Are you liking this soup?

c What do you think?

d What are you thinking?

e Her brother's being very unfriendly.

f Her brother's very unfriendly.

g I know the answer to that question.

h I'm knowing the answer to that question.

i I don't have any coffee.

j I'm not having any coffee.

4 Underline the best verb form in the two sentences below. **(2 marks)**

a Hannah broke / was breaking her leg while she ice-skated / was ice-skating.

b We sat / were sitting watching the television when suddenly the lights went out / were going out.

5 Which diagram represents each sentence most accurately? **(2 marks)**

a She's worked in television for three years.

b She worked in television for three years.

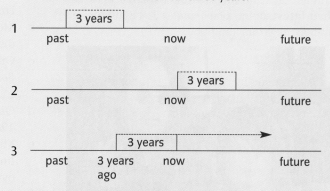

6 You meet a friend in the street and notice she has a new hairstyle. What do you say? **(1 mark)**

a You're changing your hair – it looks really good!

b You've changed your hair – it looks really good!

c You were changing your hair – it looks really good!

7 Tick the most logical way to complete each sentence. (2 marks)

a They'd known each other for a long time
… before they started going out.
… and they're really good friends.

b They've known each other for a long time
… before they decided to get married.
… but they don't get on very well.

8 Which of the sentences below refer to the past only? (1 mark)

a They used to phone each other every day.
b They've always phoned each other every day.
c They phoned each other every day.

9 All the verbs in bold are past forms, but which of them really refer to the past? (2 marks)

a If only I **had** all the time to do the things I'd like to!
b As a child, he always **had** plenty of friends.
c I **knew** at once that he was lying.
d If I **knew** what you wanted, maybe I could help you.

▶ Look at Language summary A on page 144.

Practice

1 a Read about Keema's experience of growing up as a British Asian, and choose the best verb forms.

b **T1.2** Listen and check.

2 a Write eight sentences about your childhood and family background. Include details about some of these things.

birthplace	different homes and how long you were there
first school	what it was like growing up in your family
holidays	people who influenced you

Pay attention to the tenses you use.

b Change three pieces of information to make them false. Read your sentences to another student. Can he/she guess which are false?

Mmm, I don't think you were born in the country.

No, that's true, really!

Growing up a British Asian

'I (1) am born / have been born / was born in a town called Blackburn, in the north-west of England, and (2) have lived / lived / was living there till I (3) had left / left / was leaving home at the age of eighteen. My parents (4) had moved / have moved / used to move to England from India during the 70s.

As a child, I (5) have been / had been / went to my local school and, of course I (6) have spoken / spoke / had spoken English with a local accent, just like all the other kids. But home was very different: we (7) have lived / had lived / lived in a kind of 'little India', with a huge extended family of uncles and aunts. I (8) remember / am remembering / have remembered feeling part of this big thing called 'family', and an even bigger thing called 'India'. I suppose my family really (9) have influenced / influenced / were influencing me while I (10) had grown up / used to grow up / was growing up. They often (11) had talked / have talked / used to talk about India as 'home' – even though at that time I (12) had never been / was never going / have never been there!

To me, it (13) doesn't seem / isn't seeming / wasn't seeming at all strange to grow up as part of two cultures. I (14) am always thinking / 've always thought / was always thinking that growing up with two cultures is a gift, not a disadvantage. Now that I (15) have / am having / had a child of my own, I (16) am wanting / have wanted / want her to get in touch with her Indian roots too, so we (17) 're planning / plan / used to plan a visit there later this year. All her Indian cousins (18) are looking forward / looks forward / looked forward to meeting her!'

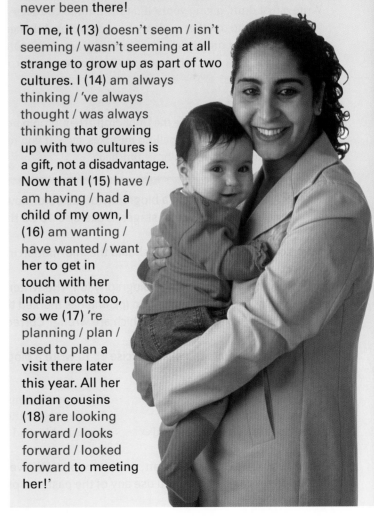

Writing
Planning and drafting a biography

1 **a** When you write an important letter or composition, do you plan it before you write the final draft? What do you do?

b Read the ideas below for planning and drafting a piece of writing. Which do you find most useful?

Four steps to better writing

1 Preparing and gathering information
Give yourself a time limit to brainstorm all the topics you might include, and to check information. Make brief notes by each topic. Get as much information as you can on paper (a quick search on the Internet may help you here). Don't worry too much about the organisation of your ideas at this point – you can always change things later.

2 Structuring
Think about the order in which you will present the information. If possible, check with another student or your teacher to see if they think your order is clear and logical.

3 First draft and feedback
Write a first draft, giving yourself a time limit to complete the text. Show your first draft to another student or your teacher. Ask them to tell you about things that are unclear, or if there are any important mistakes. Read the draft yourself. Are there better words or phrases you could use to express your ideas?

4 Final draft
Use the feedback to prepare the final draft. Then proofread your work (check it for simple errors, spelling mistakes, etc.). If you're happy with what you have written, you have finished!

2 **a** A student is writing a biography of the actor Rowan Atkinson. Look at notes A and B. Which stages in exercise 1b do they illustrate?

b Into which paragraphs in B should the information in A go?

3 Read the first draft of the biography (C). The writer is checking spelling (sp) and punctuation (p), and has marked the points he/she is unsure of. Which are correct? Which are wrong? Correct them.

4 **a** Use the 'four steps' in exercise 1b to write a biography of one of the people below.

– My sporting hero
– My grandfather/mother
– My oldest and dearest friend

– My favourite filmstar/entertainer
– The most eccentric person I know
– A musical legend

b As you check your first draft, pay attention to the verb forms you studied on page 10. Can you use any of the past and present time phrases from page 9?

A

a Married to Sunetra Sastry, a make-up artist, two children Ben and Lily.
b Rarely seen in public, almost never gives interviews.
c Attended Newcastle and Oxford Universities, where he appeared in several student productions.
d Born in north-east of England, 1955.
e Shy at school – had ability to make other students laugh.
f Is the fourth most recognised British person in the world.
g First film appearance 1983 – 'Never Say Never Again'.
h Developed character of Mr Bean in early 1990s.
i World-famous as Mr Bean.
j Many film roles including 'Johnny English' and 'Four Weddings and a Funeral'.

B

Paragraph 1: what he's famous for
Paragraph 2: early life and education
Paragraph 3: early career and development of Mr Bean character
Paragraph 4: personal life today

C

Rowan Atkinson: a Comic Legend

He was recently voted the fourth^sp? most-recognised british^p? person in the world – but while millions know him as the rubber-faced mr Bean^p? much less is known about the life of Rowan Atkinson, the actor who created the character, and who has played many other TV and film roles including the nervous preist^sp? in 'Four Weddings and a Funeral'^p? and the inept secret agent, Johnny English.

Born in the north-east of England in 1955^p? Atkinson was always shy at school, but he soon discovered that he could make his classmates laugh by pulling grotesque faces, which got him the nickname 'Moonman'. At this stage in his life, he had few thoughts of a career in entertainment, however:^p? after leaving school, he studyed^sp? electrical engineering at Newcastle University^p? and then went on to Oxford to do a masters degree. There, he began to take comedy more seriously, appearing in a number of comedy productions and at the Edinburgh Festival.

His appearances on TV in the popular comedy series 'Not the Nine O'Clock News' helped him to get his first film role in 1983 in the James Bond film 'Never Say Never Again'. But he was unknown outside the UK until he developed the character of Mr Bean who, he says, is based on himself at the age of ten. The TV programmes have been shown in eighty countrys^sp? and in 1997 the feature film 'Bean: The Movie' became the second biggest-earning^p? British film ever.

Despite his worldwide fame, Atkinson avoids publicity, rarely appearing in public and almost never giveing^sp? interviews. He lives quietly^sp? with his wife Sunetra and their two children, and little is known of his private life – apart from his love of classic racing cars. As he says about himself, 'I am essentially a rather quiet, dull person who just happens to be a performer.'/'^p?

Wordspot
get

1 Match the meanings of *get* with the examples in the diagram below.

arrive	become	catch
obtain/receive	phrasal verbs	understand

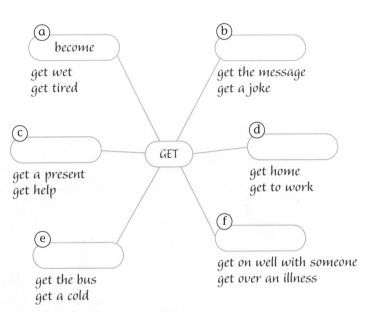

(a) become
get wet
get tired

(b)
get the message
get a joke

(c)
get a present
get help

GET

(d)
get home
get to work

(e)
get the bus
get a cold

(f)
get on well with someone
get over an illness

2 Add these phrases to the diagram above.

get a better job	get better/worse	get angry
get an early flight	get €50,000 a year	get lost
get on with your work	get there	get a shock
I don't get what you mean	get into trouble	get stuck

3 Work in pairs. Student A: Look at page 138. Student B: Look at page 141.

4 Can you find someone in the class who …

a   got home late last night?
b   got stuck in bad traffic on their way to work/school?
c   gets a lot of colds?
d   doesn't get on very well with their next door neighbours?
e   got a really special present for his/her last birthday?
f   got lost the first time they came to this school?
g   is getting the bus home today?
h   often gets tired in the middle of the afternoon?
i   rarely gets angry?
j   got into trouble a lot at primary school?

Decide what questions you will ask before you begin, and speak to as many students in the class as you can.

Language focus 2
Uses of auxiliaries

1 Look at the two women in the photo below. Who or what do you think they are talking about?

2 **a** [T1.3] Listen to the conversation, without reading. What are they gossiping about?

b Choose the correct auxiliary in the conversation below. Then listen again and check.

c In this kind of conversation, how do people show interest in what the other person is saying?

LIZ: I suppose you've heard the latest about Ian and Patsy?
KATE: No, what's happened?
LIZ: Oh, haven't you heard? They've split up!
KATE: (1) Are they? / Do they? / Did they? / Have they?
LIZ: Yeah, I thought everyone knew.
KATE: Hmm … well, I suppose it's not really surprising, (2) does it? / doesn't it? / is it? / isn't it? I mean they never really seemed to have that much in common.
LIZ: How do you mean?
KATE: Well, their interests for a start; he's really into his computers and computer games and things like that, but she (3) does / doesn't / is / isn't. She prefers something a bit livelier, going out to clubs and things, having a good time …
LIZ: Yeah. She (4) does / is / isn't / was like going out more than him, that's true.
KATE: Has she told you anything about it?
LIZ: Yes, (5) she did / she has / she is / she was, actually. She phoned me on Friday. It seems that it all came to a bit of a crisis when they …

Analysis

Where is the auxiliary verb in the conversation in exercise 2 used:
a to add emphasis?
b to form a tag question?
c to show interest?
d to form a short answer to a question?
e to avoid repeating words or phrases?

▶ Look at Language summary B on page 144.

Practice

1 [T1.4] Listen, pause the recording and tick the correct response. Then listen and check.

a 1 Of course I am!
  2 Of course I do!
  3 Of course I have!

b 1 I am listening, darling.
  2 I do listen, darling.
  3 I did listen, darling.

c 1 No, to be honest, it isn't.
  2 No, to be honest, it didn't.
  3 No, to be honest, it wasn't.

d 1 I think I am, she hasn't phoned yet.
  2 I think I do, she hasn't phoned yet.
  3 I think I can, she hasn't phoned yet.

e 1 Really, are they?
  2 Really, have they?
  3 Really, did they?

f 1 Oh no, had you?
  2 Oh no, have you?
  3 Oh no, were you?

g 1 I am believe you!
  2 I do believe you!
  3 I can believe you!

h 1 No, I can't.
  2 No, I don't.
  3 No, I'm not.

i 1 I did, didn't I?
  2 I was, wasn't I?
  3 I do, don't I?

j 1 Oh dear, had you? Why?
  2 Oh dear, did you? Why?
  3 Oh dear, have you? Why?

2 a Complete the sentences with an appropriate auxiliary verb.

1 I _____ like your shoes. Where did you get them?
2 Everyone else seemed to like it, but I _____ .
3 You don't care about what I want, _____ you?
4 Things have definitely got worse round here, _____ they?
5 You _____ remember to lock the back door when you left the house, _____ you?
6 Thanks for a lovely evening, we really enjoyed it, _____ we George?
7 Alex can't come on the 14th, but everyone else _____ .
8 But you're feeling better now, _____ you?

b Work with a partner. Choose at least three sentences and develop each one into a short dialogue of four to eight lines. Think about the following.

– the context
– who is speaking to whom and how they feel
– what happens, if anything

c Practise the dialogues, paying attention to the pronunciation of the auxiliaries. Choose the best dialogue to act out for the class.

Real life
Making conversation

1 Discuss the following questions in small groups.

- When people meet for the first time, what kind of things do they usually talk about?
- Do you ever find it difficult to keep a conversation going in these circumstances? Why?

2 a T1.7 Sean and Fiona are meeting for the first time at the reception desk of a hotel. Listen and tick the topics they talk about from the list below.

– where Fiona is from
– the purpose of Fiona's visit
– details of Fiona's journey
– how long Fiona will stay at the hotel
– Fiona's job
– where Sean is from
– Sean's job
– Sean's plans for tomorrow
– the purpose of Sean's visit

b Do you notice any difference in the attitude of the two speakers?

3 Listen again and answer the following questions.

a How does Sean begin the conversation?
b How many questions does Sean ask Fiona?
c What kind of answers does Fiona give?
d How many questions does Fiona ask Sean?
e What words/phrases tell you that Fiona wants to finish the conversation?
f Do you think she was rude?

4 **a** Mark the sentences S if they are useful for starting a conversation and E if they are useful for ending a conversation.

1 Nice to meet you. Did you have a comfortable flight?
2 Leave me alone, will you?
3 Hi! What are you doing here?
4 OK, I'll let you get on.
5 Well, I'd better be off.
6 Excuse me, could you help me?
7 Anyway, it's been nice seeing you again.
8 Sorry to disturb you.
9 Welcome to Canada ... is this your first visit here?
10 Right, I'd better get back to work.

b **T1.8** Listen and mark the sentences P if they sound polite, C for casual but friendly, and R for rude.

Pronunciation

1 Intonation is important if you want to sound polite. When people are being polite, they generally start high and use a wide range of intonation. When they are not being polite, they use a narrower range of intonation.

2 Listen again to exercise 4b and copy the intonation on the recording.

---

5 One way to maintain a conversation is to ask questions to find out more. What questions could you ask someone who said these things?

a I only got here yesterday.
b I'm a teacher.
c My name's Amazon.
d We're just on our way to the cinema.

Example:

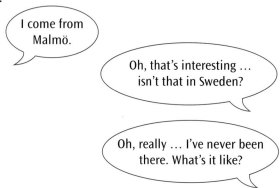

I come from Malmö.

Oh, that's interesting ... isn't that in Sweden?

Oh, really ... I've never been there. What's it like?

6 **a** Work in pairs. Choose a situation and a relationship from the list.

Situation	Relationship
• at an airport	• old friends who haven't met up for a while
• in a hotel lounge	• acquaintances who meet unexpectedly
• in an office	• new work colleagues
• in a café or bar	• complete strangers
• at a tourist attraction	• good friends

b Discuss your roles, then act out your conversation using sentences from exercise 4. Keep the conversation going for at least two minutes.

STUDY...

Using the mini-dictionary

The mini-dictionary helps you with new words and phrases in *New Cutting Edge Upper Intermediate*. It tells you about:

①   ②   ③

eccentric/ɪkˈsentrɪk/ *adj* someone who is **eccentric** behaves in an unusual or strange way that is different from most people: *They have always been a very eccentric family.*

④

① Pronunciation and stress
You can check the pronunciation using the phonemic alphabet (there is a key to this in the mini-dictionary). The symbol ˈ shows the main stress.

② Part of speech
You can check the 'word class', e.g. noun (*n*), adjective (*adj*), etc.

③ Meaning / ④ Example sentence
The mini-dictionary gives a definition and an example sentence.

Extra information
In some cases, the mini-dictionary gives you extra information, e.g.

• UK/US equivalents
• if a word/phrase is formal or informal
• opposites
• the grammatical pattern / preposition which follows a word
• if nouns are countable or uncountable
• if verbs are transitive (take an object) or intransitive (do not take an object)
• past tense and past participle of irregular verbs

How and when to use the mini-dictionary

• Use the context to work out the meaning of new words. Then check by looking the word up in the mini-dictionary.
• Make a note of new words and phrases in each module.
• Do the exercises in the Workbook to prepare yourself for the Mini-check.

PRACTISE...

1 Continuous forms ☐

Can the underlined verb be changed into the continuous form? How does this change the meaning?

a He <u>worked</u> in a hotel during the summer holidays.

b I've <u>thought</u> about what you said yesterday.

c When I saw him, Ben <u>looked</u> down at his magazine.

d I <u>don't like</u> the rainy weather.

e Susan <u>has had</u> a lot of problems with her car recently.

f While Fred <u>sat</u> at home, his wife was out looking for work.

g I don't know why Juliette <u>is</u> so difficult.

h <u>Does</u> this umbrella <u>belong</u> to you?

▶ **Need to check? Language summary A3, page 144.**

2 Past and present verb forms ☐

Look at the sentences below. Are the statements True (T), False (F) or Not Sure (NS)?

a *We used to go to Spain for our holidays.*

• We went to Spain once. ___

• We went to Spain more than once. ___

• We go to Spain now. ___

b *If my parents lived nearby, we could see them more often.*

• My parents live nearby. ___

• My parents used to live nearby. ___

• My parents don't live nearby now. ___

c *They'd started dinner when we arrived.*

• When we arrived, they began eating. ___

• When we arrived, they were eating. ___

• When we arrived, the meal was finished. ___

d *I worked as a travel courier for several years.*

• I'm a travel courier now. ___

• I used to be a travel courier. ___

• I was a travel courier at one time. ___

▶ **Need to check? Language summary A, page 144.**

3 Auxiliary verbs ☐

a Write an auxiliary verb in the correct position in each sentence.

1 The test wasn't as difficult as we expected, it?

2 I want to go to the shopping centre with you, honestly!

3 Kate wasn't keen on sport before, but she now.

4 'Steve's decided to look for a new job.'
'he? What made him want to leave?'

5 'Did you see anything unusual in the park, Mr Ball?'
'Yes, I. There was a group of young men acting suspiciously.'

b In which sentence is the auxiliary verb used:

• to add emphasis?   • to form a tag question?

• to show interest?   • to form a short answer?

• to avoid repeating a phrase?

▶ **Need to check? Language summary B, page 144.**

4 Time phrases ☐

Complete the sentences with the time phrases.

> currently   during   former   in the 1980s
> that time   now   these

a He lived there back _____ .

b At _____ , he was a very rich man.

c The city continued to grow _____ the 1990s.

d I don't see my cousin much _____ days.

e They are _____ recording a new album in Paris.

f The _____ President still has a lot of influence.

g I'm very busy right _____ . Could you call back in half an hour?

▶ **Need to check? Vocabulary, page 9.**

5 Phrases with *get* ☐

What does *get* (or *get* + particle) mean in the sentences?

a The situation is going to get worse.

b It took her a long time to get the joke.

c We decided not to get the bus.

d I got a phone call from Carol last night.

e What time did you get home last night?

▶ **Need to check? Wordspot, page 13.**

Pronunciation spot

Word stress

a **T1.9** **Match the words from Reading, page 8 to the stress pattern. Then listen and check.**

> global   nowadays   success   supportive
> traditional

1 ● ● _____   4 ● ● _____

2 ● ● ● _____   5 ● ● ● _____

3 ● ● ● ● _____

b **Look back at the text again and find another word for each stress pattern.**

REMEMBER!

Look back at the areas you have practised. Tick the ones you feel confident about. Now try the MINI-CHECK on page 158 to check what you know!

MODULE 2

Life's ups and downs

- ► Forming nouns and gerunds
- ► Forming adjectives
- ► **Reading and vocabulary:** *So you think you know what's good for you?*
- ► **Pronunciation:** Word stress in nouns, Sounding sympathetic
- ► **Real life:** Responding sympathetically
- ► **Task:** List the things that make you feel …
- ► **Wordspot:** *life*

Reading and vocabulary

1 a Read the title of the article. Do you know what is good for you (physically and psychologically)? In pairs, make two lists.

Good for you: *eating fruit and vegetables*
Bad for you: *stress*

b Discuss which list to add these things to. Which might go on both lists?

being single / being married	gentle/strenuous exercise
belonging to a community	high blood pressure
doing absolutely nothing	a low-fat diet
drinking coffee / tea	low self-esteem
eating chocolate	playing computer games
feeling out of control	watching soap operas

2 Work in pairs. Student A: Read Part A of the text. Then look at the questions and choose the correct alternative(s) according to the article. Student B: Do the same for Part B. Check the words in bold in your mini-dictionary, if necessary.

3 a Close your book and explain briefly to your partner what you learnt from the article.

b Which information do you find most/least surprising? Is there anything that you don't really believe?

4 Read your partner's text and then discuss the following questions.

- Has the article made you feel that you should make any changes to your own lifestyle (exercise, diet, etc.)?
- Is there anything else you could do to make your lifestyle healthier?

Questions for Part A

1 After strenuous exercise, people are often more / less active for the rest of the day.
2 Doing nothing for a couple of hours every day is the best way to **keep fit** / increase your **immunity**.
3 A low-fat diet will make you slimmer but more **aggressive** / fatter and less aggressive.
4 The chemicals in coffee / tea / chocolate **reduce the risk** of heart disease.
5 The chemicals in coffee / chocolate / tea **protect you from** coughs and colds.

Questions for Part B

1 Children who play a lot of computer games have better **social skills** / **behaviour** than children who don't.
2 Single / Married men are happier than single / married men.
3 Married women with children and a job have more / fewer **mental health** problems than other groups.
4 The biggest cause of backache is **depression** / **heavy lifting**.
5 People who watch soap operas have / do not have a sense of belonging to a community.

So you think you know what's good for you?

Part A

Exercise

Everyone nowadays knows the benefits of physical exercise – but scientists at the University of Maastricht in the Netherlands say the key to staying slim and keeping fit is to eat less and take gentle exercise such as walking or
5 cycling. 'People who take intensive exercise often reward themselves by spending the rest of the day in front of the TV,' says Professor Klaas Westertep. 'At the same time they have to eat more to give them energy for the next work-out. To avoid weight gain, it's better to take gentle exercise
10 over a longer period.' And health researcher Peter Axt believes that spending a couple of hours a day doing absolutely nothing is more effective than exercise in building immunity and prolonging life. 'We always think that we have to be achieving something but just
15 vegetating for half of your free time could be more healthy,' he claims.

A low-fat diet

A low-fat diet may be good for your waistline, but the latest research suggests that it is less beneficial psychologically. A team of volunteers at Sheffield
20 University asked to follow a diet consisting of just twenty-five percent fat (the level recommended by the World Health Organisation) reported increased feelings of depression and hostility towards others. One reason perhaps that people on low-fat diets are apparently more
25 likely to meet a violent death!

Drinking tea and coffee

Many of us already know that drinking coffee raises your blood pressure but according to the latest research, it can also make you bad-tempered. Mice who were given regular doses of caffeine by researchers were found to be
30 unusually aggressive! On the other hand, the chemicals found in tea can reduce the risk of heart attacks, and have a beneficial effect on cholesterol levels and high blood pressure. And tea doesn't keep you awake at night either!

Eating chocolate

Ever heard of the old saying 'A little of what you fancy
35 does you good'? Well, if you're a chocolate fan there's good news! Recent studies have revealed that chemicals found in chocolate can protect you from a variety of minor illnesses including colds, coughs, depression and even help reduce the risk of heart disease!

Part B

Playing computer games

40 Parents worried about their children spending hours on their PlayStation may have it all wrong – it could actually be time well spent. Researchers at Manchester University found that gamers who play up to eighteen hours a week seem able to focus on what they are doing better than
45 other people, have better co-ordination; and, far from being anti-social, 'computer nerds' find it easier to form friendships than children who prefer activities such as reading and watching TV. But scientists in Japan have found that gaming develops only vision and movement,
50 but not the parts of the brain associated with learning, emotion or behaviour. 'This might be a problem in our increasingly violent society,' says Professor Ryuta Kawashima of the Tohoku University.

Being married

'Every woman should marry – and no man' commented
55 one wit almost 150 years ago. But scientific evidence has tended to suggest that it's men who find happiness through marriage more than women. It has been shown that single men are the least happy social group, while married men are the happiest. But a new study from La Trobe University in
60 Melbourne reveals that women do benefit as well: twenty-five percent of single people were miserable, compared with only thirteen percent of married people. Among the women surveyed, those who were married with children and a job had the fewest mental health problems.

Low self-esteem

65 The feeling of being undervalued can damage your health. Research by the National Arthritis Council shows that employees who suffer constant criticism, or feel out of control at work, are much more likely to suffer from back problems. Depression, says one researcher, is actually
70 far more likely to cause backache than heavy lifting!

Watching soap operas on TV

Finally, a surprising piece of research that shows people who regularly watch soap operas are significantly happier than those who don't. Psychologists believe that this is because such programmes provide viewers with an
75 imaginary set of friends, and a sense of belonging to a community. 'It works in rather the same way as membership of a club, or a church,' says Professor Michael Argyle of Oxford Brookes University.

Language focus 1
Forming nouns and gerunds

a Some nouns from the article on pages 18 and 19 are missing from the dictionary definitions below. How many can you get without looking back at the article?

1 *happiness* n. [U] the quality of being happy (line 56)

2 _____ n. [C] a person who conducts research (line 10)

3 _____ n. [C,U] a feeling of sadness that makes you think there is no hope for the future (line 23)

4 _____ n pl. [C] people who work for someone else (line 67)

5 _____ n pl. [C] the relationships between friends (line 47)

6 _____ n pl. [C] people who are trained, or work, in science (line 2)

7 _____ n. [C] an act of moving your body (line 49)

8 _____ n. [U] facts that make you believe something is true (line 55)

9 _____ n. [C, U] people in general living in an organised group (line 52)

10 _____ n. [C, U] saying things that show you have a bad opinion of someone (line 67)

11 _____ n. [C] something that you feel, e.g. anger, happiness, etc. (line 65)

12 _____ n. [U] what you do; how you act (line 51)

b Look back at the article and check your answers.

Analysis

1 These are some of the most common suffixes (letters at the end of the word) which form nouns. Match the words above with the correct suffix.

-ness	-ion/-sion/-tion	-ity/-iety/-y	-ment
happiness			
-ance/-ence	-our/-iour	-ism	-ing
-ship	-ee	-er	-ist

2 Many nouns are exactly the same as the verb, e.g. *to benefit, a benefit, to damage, some damage,* etc.

3 Gerunds (verb + *-ing*) are used the same way as nouns, and can be the subject or the object of the sentence.
Feeling undervalued can damage your health.
I really enjoy *doing absolutely nothing*.

Look back at the paragraph about Exercise in the text on page 18 and find at least five gerunds.

▶ Read Language summaries A and B on page 145.

Pronunciation

1 **T2.1** Listen to the nouns from the article and mark the stress. Which suffixes, if any, are stressed?

•
happiness

2 Many of the unstressed syllables have schwa sounds. Mark where you think they are.

/ə/
happiness

3 Listen and check. Then practise saying the words, paying attention to stress and weak forms.

Practice

1 a What are the noun forms of these words?

active (adj)	hostile (adj)	psychological (adj)
aggressive (adj)	ill (adj)	suffer (v)
develop (v)	member (n)	violent (adj)

b Which of the noun forms are different to these verbs?

attack	cause	diet	exercise	increase
reduce	research	reward	risk	survey

2 **T2.2** Choose the correct alternative. Then listen and check.

According to experts, the way you spend your free time is vital to your general (a) happy / happiness and (b) healthy / health, and (c) get / getting the right (d) balance / balancing is very important. It goes without saying that physical (e) fit / fitness is the key, so everyone's leisure time should include some form of exercise, ideally something that you also find (f) enjoyable / enjoyment. Most people also gain (g) satisfied / satisfaction from (h) do / doing something (i) creative / creativity, such as (j) paint / painting, (k) cook / cooking or (l) garden / gardening. However, as Professor Michael Argyle points out, not all your free time activities should be (m) solitary / solitariness, or you may end up feeling (n) lonely / loneliness. (o) Companion / Companionship is also (p) important / importance to most people's sense of well-being. But you must find the right kind of social (q) interaction / interactive, argues the professor. (r) Member / Membership of some groups, such as (s) political / politician parties, can simply lead to (t) stressful / stress and (u) frustrated / frustration. (v) Join / Joining a (w) supportive / support (x) social / society group like a choir or a dance class is likely to be much more (y) benefit / beneficial.

3 a Look at the list of things that make you feel good and things that make you feel bad. Complete the noun/gerund forms.

What makes you feel good?

financial secur _ _ _
succ_ _ _ in your career/exams
be_ _ _ physically fit
sleep _ _ _ well
plenty of vari_ _ _ and excit_ _ _ _ _ in your life
spend_ _ _ time with your family
be_ _ _ in a good relation_ _ _ _
hav_ _ _ time to relax
keep_ _ _ busy
good friend _ _ _ _ s
go_ _ _ out a lot
be_ _ _ creative
intellectual stimula_ _ _ _
spend_ _ _ money
feel_ _ _ in control of your life

What makes you feel bad?

financial worr_ _ _
feel_ _ _ under too much press_ _ _
not sleep_ _ _
critic_ _ _ from your colleagues, family, etc.
anxi_ _ _ about work/college
lack of confid_ _ _ _ in what you're doing
eat_ _ _ badly
lonelin_ _ _
problems in your relation_ _ _ _
feel_ _ _ unfit
bore_ _ _

b Which things make you feel good/bad? Complete these sentences.

– The three most important things here that make me happy are …
– I also enjoy …
– … doesn't bother me much.
– The three worst things on the list are …
– I also hate …

c Compare your sentences with other students. What were the biggest differences between you?

Language focus 2
Forming adjectives

This text was posted on inspirations.com, a website offering advice and encouragement for life's ups and downs. Read the text and decide which word is blanked out. Then check on page 138.

inspirations

A ▮ costs nothing, but gives much. Those who receive it become richer, but it does not make the giver any poorer. It may last only a moment, but its **beneficial** effects can last a lifetime.

There is no one who is so **wealthy** or **powerful** that they can survive without one, but even a **penniless** beggar can afford to give one.

A ▮ transforms an **unhappy** home into a place of love, turns acquaintances into friends and brings hope to those who are **discouraged**. It can give a more **optimistic** outlook to those who see only darkness, and is nature's best cure for those who are **depressed**, **anxious** or **insecure**. Yet it cannot be bought, begged, borrowed or stolen. It is something which only becomes **valuable** when it is given freely. Some people are too **tired** to give you a ▮. Give them one of yours, as no one needs a ▮ more than the person who has no more to give.

Analysis 1

1 **Suffixes**
   a Many suffixes (letters added to the end of a word) are used to form adjectives.
   power + -ful = powerful   value + -able = valuable
   Underline the suffixes of the adjectives in **bold** in the text above.
   b Notice that many adjectives of feeling have two forms, ending with -ed and -ing.
   depress**ed**   depress**ing**
   Which describes the thing that makes you feel like this? Which describes the way you feel? Think of at least five more adjectives like this.

2 **Prefixes that mean 'the opposite of'**
   We can also add prefixes (letters added to the beginning of a word) to adjectives. Many of these mean 'the opposite of' or 'not'.
   *un*happy ≠ happy   *dis*courage ≠ encourage
   Find another prefix like this in the text above. Do you know any other prefixes that mean 'the opposite of'?

▶ Read Language summaries C and D on page 146.

Practice

1 Here are some more ideas from the same website. Complete the adjectives in bold with the correct prefix or suffix from the box.

| -able   -ed (x 3)   -ent   -ful (x 3)   -ic (x 3)   -ient   -ing (x 3) |
| -ive (x 2)   dis-   im-   un- |

inspirations

a Don't make the mistake of thinking that by running around you are at your most **effective** and **effic_____** . Sometimes the most **use_____** thing to do is to stop and think!

b Life can be an **excit_____** journey: but sometimes the journey is more **interest_____** than the destination.

c People who are **pessimist_____** about things have an advantage over those who are always **optimist_____** : they are never **disappoint_____** .

d Life gives us a series of **wonder_____** opportunities, which often come disguised as **unsolv_____** problems.

e A few people are **success_____** because they're **talent_____** : most succeed because they're **determin_____** .

f Tell the truth, even though it hurts: it is better to be **_____popular** than to be **_____honest**.

g As long as you are **enthusiast_____** and **persist_____** , nothing is **_____possible**!!

h Being **posit_____** has one very important side-effect: it's **catch_____** !!

2 a Which adjectives above describe a person's character? Make a list of positive and negative adjectives, adding ideas of your own.

b Which characteristics on your list do you most admire? Which do you find most annoying? Compare ideas with a partner.

> I really like people who are honest and say what they think.

> I can't stand people who are negative about everything!

Other prefixes

Prefixes don't always mean 'the opposite of'. They can alter meaning in other ways. Add a prefix from the box to complete the adjectives below.

anti-	non-	over-	pre-
post-	pro-	self-	under-

____paid = paid too much
____fed = not given enough food
____-stop = without stopping
____-war = after the war
____-arranged = arranged in advance
____confident = confident in yourself
____-American = in favour of America
____-government = against the government

▶ Read Language summary E on page 146.

3 **a** Think of examples for the following things.

1 A profession in which people are **underpaid**.
2 A profession in which people are often **overpaid**.
3 The name of a person or place that looks after **preschool** children.
4 A public place that is usually **non-smoking**.
5 A popular **postgraduate** degree course.
6 The name of a newspaper that is considered **pro-government**.
7 The name of someone you know who is very **anti-smoking**.
8 The name of a famous person who seems very **self-centred**.

b Compare your ideas in small groups.

> I wrote 'library' because libraries are usually non-smoking.

Real life
Responding sympathetically

1 Do you consider yourself to be generally sympathetic or not? Who do you turn to if you need a sympathetic listener?

2 **T2.3** Listen to three short conversations and answer the questions.

a What is the person's problem in each case?
b Is the listener very sympathetic, reasonably sympathetic or not very sympathetic? What suggestions does he/she make?

3 **a** Mark the sentences in the box: *** for very sympathetic, ** for fairly sympathetic and * for unsympathetic.

Calm down!	Never mind.
Come on! Pull yourself together!	That sounds awful!
Don't take any notice of him/her.	There's no point in getting upset about it.
Don't worry. It doesn't matter.	Try not to worry about it.
How annoying!	What a shame!
Just ignore him/her/it/them.	You must be really worried.

b Read the situations and choose one or two appropriate responses from the box for each.

1 A visitor to your house is embarrassed because he's spilled his drink.
2 A child tells you that his best friend said something unkind to him.
3 Your best friend phones because she's had a row with her boyfriend.
4 Your friend is in tears at the end of a sad film.
5 Your friend is worried because his mother is going into hospital.
6 Everyone is laughing at your friend's new hairstyle.
7 Your friend is too scared to go to the dentist by herself.

Pronunciation

1 **T2.4** Intonation is important if you want to sound sympathetic. Listen to some of the sentences from the box above. Which two do not sound sympathetic?

2 Practise saying all the sentences sympathetically.

4 Work in pairs. Choose one of the situations in exercise 3b and write a conversation similar to the ones you listened to.

5 Act out your conversation for the rest of the class. The others listen and say which situation you are acting out and whether or not the listener is sympathetic.

Task: List the things that make you feel ...

Preparation: listening

1 **T2.5** Listen to ten people answering one of the questions below. Match the speakers to the questions.

a   What makes you laugh?
b   What frightens you?
c   What makes you feel depressed?
d   What helps you to relax?
e   What do you really detest?
f   What makes you stressed?
g   What makes you feel embarrassed?
h   What makes you happy?

2 Listen again and make notes about what each speaker said.

3 Compare your notes with a partner. Do you have the same feelings about the things that were discussed?

4 **T2.6** Listen and complete the sentences from the recording.

a   One thing that always _____ _____ is I say the wrong thing at the wrong time.
b   There's only _____ _____ me.
c   It just _____ crazy.
d   I _____ all sorts of strange situations _____ .
e   The thing _____ horror films.
f   It just puts me _____ mood.
g   I _____ snakes.
h   I know you _____ , but I _____ laughing.

24

Task: speaking

1 a Make brief notes about your own answers to the eight questions. You can write one or several things. Miss out any questions you do not wish to answer.

b Ask your teacher about any words or phrases that you need to explain your ideas.

▶ Useful language a

2 Work in groups. Go through the questions, comparing and explaining your ideas. Make a list of the most interesting ideas for each question.

▶ Useful language b

3 *Either* explain your group's ideas to the class. *Or* work with a partner from a different group. Compare the ideas you discussed in exercise 2.

Useful language

a Describing your feelings

One thing/another thing that really frightens/embarrasses me is when …

I hate/love it when …

It really annoys me when …

I find … very embarrassing/ relaxing/annoying, etc.

… makes me very happy/relaxed/ depressed, etc.

I just can't stand/cope with …

b Comparing

Me too./So do I.

What about you?

Does anyone else feel the same way?

Yes, I find …very relaxing/ annoying, too.

Wordspot
life

1 a The word *life* has been omitted from the sentences below. Write it in the correct position. Use a dictionary, if necessary.

1 Since they won the lottery, the Powells have lived a ^life^ of luxury in Italy.
2 The actor Danny Mackay told the press that he would not answer any questions about his private.
3 Although there was no danger of the ship sinking, everyone had to put on their jacket as a precaution.
4 I wouldn't worry about Suzy. She's probably having the time of her.
5 The accused was given a sentence for the murder of two police officers.
6 Fortunately, there was a guard on duty at the beach – otherwise the child might've drowned.
7 I've been offered a place at Oxford University! It's the chance of a time!
8 Although he can't actually throw us out, our landlord is making very difficult for us.
9 At university, I had a very good social, and there was always plenty to do.
10 Despite his tough screen image, in real Brad Tom is a quiet, gentle man.
11 The wax models are so like that you almost feel you could talk to them!
12 It's disappointing that you didn't win the prize, but that's! There's nothing you can do about it!

b Underline the word or phrase with *life* in each sentence.

2 Complete the definitions with an appropriate word or phrase.

a 'In _____' means in reality, as opposed to what happens in stories.
b If you're having the _____ , you are enjoying yourself more than ever before.
c Your _____ is the part of your life concerned with going out and seeing friends.
d A _____ is a long term in prison, possibly until the prisoner dies.
e A _____ statue or model looks exactly like the living person.
f '_____ !' is what people say when they have to accept a situation they don't like.
g If you make _____ for someone, you do your best to create problems for them.
h A _____ is something you wear to help you float in water.
i Your _____ is the part of your life concerned with your home, family, etc.
j A _____ means you live expensively and have anything you want.
k A _____ is someone whose job is to save people from drowning on beaches, etc.
l The _____ is the best opportunity you will ever have.

3 Choose five of the expressions and write sentences which show the meaning. Compare your sentences in small groups.

Examples:
People love reading about film stars' private lives in gossip magazines.
The way the characters move in this computer game is incredibly lifelike.

STUDY...

Word building with a dictionary

1 Use the extracts below to find:

- the past tense, -ing form and third person (*he, she, it*) form of *satisfy*.
- the noun from *satisfy*, and its opposite.
- three adjectives from *satisfy*. Find the difference in meaning, and the opposite of each one.

satisfaction /sætʃsfækʃən/ *n* a feeling of happiness because you have achieved something [opposite = dissatisfaction]

satisfactory /sætʃsfæktəri/ *adj* something that is satisfactory seems good enough for a particular situation [opposite = unsatisfactory]

satisfied /sætʃsfaid/ *adj* pleased because something has happened as you want, or because you have got what you want [opposite = dissatisfied]

satisfy /sætʃsfai/ *v* satisfied, satisfying, satisfies to make someone pleased by doing what they want

satisfying /sætʃsfai-ɪŋ/ *adj* making you feel pleased and happy, because you have got what you wanted [opposite = unsatisfying]

2 Use the extracts above to help you with exercise 3 below. Before you write in the words, read the sentences carefully and check if:

- you need a verb, noun, adjective, etc.
- there is more than one adjective, noun, etc. Make sure you choose the word which makes sense in the gap.
- you need to add any prefixes, suffixes, etc. (There may be more than one.)

3 Complete the sentences with the correct word from *satisfy*.

a It was very _____ to beat our rivals United in the final.
b Although we could still do better, our overall progress has been _____ .
c There is much _____ with the government over recent failures.
d This work is _____ . You will need to do it again.
e Many people are _____ with the investigation, and want a new one.

PRACTISE...

1 Nouns ☐

Complete the nouns with the suffixes.

-ee	-ence	-iety	-ion	-iour
-ism	-ment	-ness	-ship	

a behav___
b critic___
c depress___
d evid___
e friend___
f happi___
g move___
h employ___
i soc___

▶ **Need to check?** Language summary A, page 145.

2 Gerunds ☐

Underline the words which should be in the *-ing* form.

a Many people who wish to improve their fitness find that go to the gym is easier and more sociable than do exercise at home.

b Join an Internet chatroom has become a popular way of meet new people.

c Don't you think that go out and take exercise in the fresh air is better for you than spend half your life sit in front of a computer screen?

▶ **Need to check?** Language summary B, page 145.

3 Suffixes ☐

Cross out the word in each group which does not belong with the suffix on the right.

a success- / power- / talent-   -ful
b confid- / persist- / pleas-   -ent
c disappoint- / enthusiast- / pessimist-   -ic
d health- / import- / wealth-   -y
e hope- / imagine- / penni-   -less

▶ **Need to check?** Language summary C, page 146.

4 Prefixes to form opposites ☐

Add prefixes to form the opposite of the adjectives.

a ___experienced   b ___legal   c ___loyal
d ___popular   e ___possible

▶ **Need to check?** Language summary D, page 146.

5 Other prefixes which change meaning ☐

Choose the correct definition.

a anti-war   against / in favour of war
b non-violent   against / without violence
c over-confident too confident / not confident enough
d pre-paid   paid for before / after

▶ **Need to check?** Language summary E, page 146.

6 Responding sympathetically ☐

Choose the correct alternative.

a Never / Don't / It doesn't mind.

b How / That sounds / What a shame!

c There's no point in / of / on getting upset about it.

d Don't make / put / take any notice of her.

e Calm / Pull yourself / Quiet down!

▶ **Need to check?** Real life, page 23.

7 Phrases with *life* ☐

Complete the expressions with *life*.

a life_____ (adj) = looking exactly like a real person or thing

b to have the _____ of your life = to enjoy yourself more than ever before

c the _____ of a lifetime = the biggest opportunity you will ever have

d _____ life = for famous people, the part of their life connected with their friends and family, and which is not normally shown to the public

e a life_____ = someone who is responsible for rescuing people from the water at a swimming pool or beach

▶ **Need to check?** Wordspot, page 26.

Pronunciation spot

Stress within word families

a **T2.7** The stress is shown in dictionaries like this: ˈrecord (n) and reˈcord (v). Use a dictionary to mark the stress in the following word families. Then listen and check.

1 imagine (vb)   imagination (n)   imaginary (adj)
2 organise (vb)   organised (adj)   organisation (n)
3 politics (n)   politician (n)   political (adj)
4 psychology (n) psychologist (n) psychological (adj)
5 satisfy (vb)   satisfaction (n)   satisfactory (adj)

b Practise saying the words, paying attention to the different stress patterns.

REMEMBER!

Look back at the areas you have practised. Tick the ones you feel confident about. Now try the MINI-CHECK on page 158 to check what you know!

Adventures and mishaps

▶ **Verb forms in the narrative**
▶ **Continuous aspect in other tenses**
▶ **Speaking and reading:** How adventurous are you?
▶ **Vocabulary and listening:** Mishaps
▶ **Reading and speaking:** *The gentle touch*
▶ **Task:** Tell a story from two points of view
▶ **Pronunciation:** Sentence stress, Intonation
▶ **Writing:** A narrative
▶ **Real life:** Dealing with unexpected problems

Speaking and reading

1 Work through the quiz with a partner. Keep a note of his/her answers.

2 Re-read your partner's answers and decide how adventurous he/she is. Tell the class what you decided and why.

How adventurous are you?

Are you a wild child or do you prefer to play it safe?
Find out from our quiz.

1 Which of these activities appeal to you? Why? Which have you tried?
- hill-walking • karate • motor-racing
- mountaineering • sailing • skiing
- sky-diving • surfing • tennis

2 What is your dream holiday? Why?
a   a golden beach and a good book
b   a self-drive tour of American/European cities
c   a yoga retreat in India
d   two months backpacking in the Himalayas

3 The government has just produced new guidelines about safety in the home. What is your attitude?
a   I'll follow them carefully.
b   I'll decide for myself if they make sense.
c   Nobody takes any notice of that kind of thing, do they?

4 Which of these things have you done? Which would you never do?
a   driven at 150 kilometres per hour
b   hitchhiked either alone or with a friend
c   ridden on the back of a motorbike
d   walked home alone at two o'clock in the morning

5 Which of these things do you dream of doing? Why?
a   buying an old house in the country and renovating it
b   starting a pension plan
c   starting your own business
d   taking a year off from your job/studies and travelling round the world

6 How would you describe your attitude towards rules and authority?
a   I'm a completely law-abiding citizen.
b   I break the rules, but only when I have to.
c   Rules? What rules?

Vocabulary and listening
Mishaps

1 Match words in A to B to make phrases describing mishaps. Which mishaps are shown in the pictures?

A		**B**	
a	you spill	1	and fall over
b	you stumble	2	on some ice
c	you bang your	3	at home
d	you run out of	4	breaks down
e	you lock yourself	5	head / knee / elbow
f	you get	6	in bad traffic
g	you over-	7	for school / work / an appointment
h	you get on the	8	lost
i	you're late	9	your ticket / bag / ID card
j	you miss	10	out
k	you leave something	11	petrol
l	you lose	12	sleep
m	you slip	13	wrong train
n	you get stuck	14	your plane
o	your car	15	your drink over someone

2 **T3.1** Listen to four people talking about one of the mishaps in exercise 1. Which of the following questions can you answer about each anecdote?

a Where was the speaker and what were the circumstances?
b Which other people were involved?
c What went wrong?
d How did the speaker feel?

3 Have any of these mishaps ever happened to you? Choose two or three events to tell your partner about. Use the questions in exercise 2 to help you tell the story.

Reading and speaking

1 a Read and complete the list of crimes / anti-social behaviour below. Cross out the things that are not a problem in your country.

1   dropping litter in the street
2   vandalism and graffiti
3   drinking and driving
4   truancy from school
5   noisy/anti-social neighbours
6   football hooliganism
7   speeding
8   parking where you shouldn't
9   begging
10 drug abuse

b Mark the others as follows:

*   this should not be a matter for the police
**   sometimes the police are needed to deal with this
*** the police should be really tough on this

c Compare and explain your opinions with other students, giving any examples you know of.

2 a Look at the picture at the bottom of page 31. What can you see? Think of three possible interpretations of the situation.

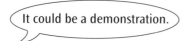

It could be a demonstration.

b Skim the text. What was the correct interpretation?

3 Read the text again and answer the questions.

a   Which city was the writer in?
b   What attracted his attention?
c   What had the boy done?
d   How did the police officers behave?
e   What will happen to the boy?

4 Find the words/phrases in the text that tell you:

a   the police officers were speaking kindly to the boy.
b   the boy was in a confused state.
c   the boy had fallen and hurt himself.
d   the police officers looked capable and efficient.
e   there is very little crime in Denmark.
f   the author was treated harshly by the American police.
g   the writer had a positive opinion of the way the police officers dealt with the situation.

5 Can you guess what the words in bold mean? Discuss with a partner, then check in your mini-dictionary.

a   as **gorgeous** as everyone else in this city (lines 2–3)
b   a **trickle** of blood ran from above his hairline to his cheek (lines 8–9)
c   the most **virulent** crime in the country is bicycle theft (lines 17–18)
d   I found myself following them almost **involuntarily** (lines 30–31)
e   I was stopped by police ... and **frisked** (lines 38–40)
f   taken to the police station and **booked** (lines 40–41)

6 Discuss the following questions in small groups.

•   Do you agree with the approach of the Danish police officers?
•   Do you believe a lenient or a tough approach to crime is more effective?
•   Are there any crimes in your country that you think are treated too harshly, or too leniently?

The gentle touch

The author is walking across a square in Copenhagen, the capital of Denmark, when he sees a small crowd by the town hall. He stops to have a look.

Two police officers, a man and a woman, both young and blond and as gorgeous as everyone else in this city, were talking softly and with sympathy to a boy of about seventeen who had clearly taken the
5 kind of substance that turns one's brain into an express elevator to Pluto. Disorientated by this sudden journey through the cosmos, he had apparently stumbled and cracked his head; a trickle of blood ran from above his hairline to his cheek.
10 The police officers were wearing the smartest commando-style uniforms I have ever seen. They looked as if between them they could handle any emergency, from outbreaks of Lassa fever to disarming a nuclear submarine.
15 And the thing is, this was probably the biggest thing they would have to deal with all evening. The Danes are almost absurdly law-abiding. The most virulent crime in the country is bicycle theft. In the year for which I happen to have the facts, there were
20 six murders in Copenhagen, compared with 205 in Amsterdam, a city of similar size, and 1,688 in New York. The city is so safe that Queen Margarethe used to walk from Amalienborg Palace to the shops every morning to buy flowers and vegetables just like a
25 normal citizen. I once asked a Dane who guarded her in such circumstances, and he looked at me with surprise and replied, 'Why, we all do,' which I thought was rather sweet.

The police officers helped the boy to his feet and
30 led him to their patrol car. I found myself following them almost involuntarily. I don't know why I was so fascinated, except that I had never seen such gentle police. I said in English to the female officer, 'Excuse me, what will you do with the boy?'
35 'We'll take him home,' she said simply, 'I think he needs his bed.'

I was impressed. I couldn't help thinking of the time I was stopped by police in my home town and made to stand with my arms and legs spread against
40 a wall and frisked, then taken to the police station and booked because of an unpaid parking ticket. I was about seventeen at the time. God knows what they would have done with me if they had found me like they found the young man. I suppose I'd be
45 getting out of jail about now.

'Will he be in trouble for this?' I asked.
'With his father, I think so, yes. But not with us. We are all a little young and crazy sometimes, you know? Goodnight. Enjoy your stay in Copenhagen.'
50 'Goodnight,' I said and with the deepest admiration watched them go.

Adapted from *Neither Here Nor There* by Bill Bryson.

Task: Tell a story from two points of view

Preparation: listening

1 The pictures show an unfortunate incident that happened to Bill, a young Englishman, while visiting a friend in another country. The words and phrases in the box all relate to the story.

a Check the meaning of the words in your mini-dictionary, if necessary.

laughing your head off	thick ice
a police car drawing up	a police cell
breaking into a car	shouting
a slippery road	swaying all over the place
a steep hill	swearing

b Which words are illustrated in the pictures?

2 In groups, discuss briefly what you think happened to Bill.

3 You are going to listen to two different accounts of what happened. Work in two groups.
T3.2 Group A: Listen to Bill's version of what happened.
T3.3 Group B: Listen to the old lady's side of the story.
Listen as many times as necessary in order to be sure of the details.

Task: speaking

1 Work with students from the same group. Check that you understood the recording. Then practise re-telling the story.

▶ Useful language a

2 Work in pairs, one person from Group A and one from Group B. Each re-tell the story you heard. Find differences between the two stories and any information that one person mentioned, but the other didn't.

3 With the rest of the class, make a list of the differences you found.

▶ Useful language b

4 Whose side of the story do you believe? Were the police right to arrest Bill and his friend? What do you think happened next?

One winter, several years ago, Bill was visiting his friend, Frank. One night, as they were walking home from a party through a smart area of the city …

Useful language

a For telling the story

He was just *-ing* when …

All of a sudden / Suddenly / At that moment …

She saw/heard them *-ing*

So then he/she/they …

In the end / Eventually …

b For comparing the two stories

According to …

He/She claimed/insisted that …

He/She said …, whereas he/she said …

He/She was absolutely certain that …

He/She mentioned / didn't mention the fact that …

He/She didn't mention anything about …

Language focus 1
Verb forms in the narrative

Look at the sentences below from the story on pages 32 and 33, and choose the best verb form.

1 I came / was coming home from a Christmas party with my friend Frank … it had been / was very, very cold.
2 There had been / was thick ice everywhere and it had been snowing / was snowing for several hours.
3 We laughed / were laughing our heads off and calling to each other for help.
4 Suddenly, this police car drew / was drawing up and two police officers got / were getting out.
5 I had gone / was going to bed at ten, as usual, but I had to / had had to get up to go to the bathroom.
6 As I had been getting / was getting back into bed, I heard / was hearing this dreadful noise.
7 They had obviously been drinking / were obviously drinking … you could see they had been / were drunk.
8 As soon as I realised / was realising what had gone / was going on, I called / had called the police straightaway.

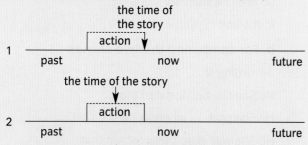

Analysis

1 Complete the table with an example of each verb form from exercise 1.

Past simple	Past continuous
A police car <u>drew</u> up	
Past perfect simple	**Past perfect continuous**

  a Which form describes the main events in the story?
  b Which form describes background events at the time of the story?
  c Which forms describe events which happened **before** the main events of the story?

2 Match the sentences to the timelines.
  a *It had been snowing for many hours.*
  b *We were coming home from a Christmas party.*

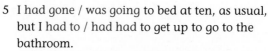

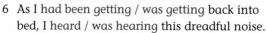

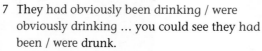

In continuous tenses the action has duration, or is repeated. Why is this important in the two examples above?

▶ Read Language summary A on page 146.

Practice

1 **T3.4** Read some more stories about mishaps that happened while people were travelling. Complete the gaps with the best verb forms. (There may be more than one possibility). Then listen and check.

a

It's not uncommon for people to fall asleep on trains, but snoring loudly in public is another matter. One day recently I (1) _____ (read) my newspaper on the train when I (2) _____ (become) aware of a loud snoring sound coming from the man opposite me. As the train (3) _____ (come) into the last station on the line, I (4) _____ (give) the man a sharp poke with my umbrella to wake him up. Instead of being grateful, he (5) _____ (look) at me furiously: he (6) _____ (not be) asleep at all! The snoring (7) _____ (come) from the enormous dog who (8) _____ (lie) at his feet!

b

My friend (9) _____ (travel) on a domestic flight in South America a few years ago. They (10) _____ (go) for about forty minutes, when the pilot (11) _____ (suddenly start) speaking excitedly in Spanish. Most of the passengers (12) _____ (run) forward, shouting, and in panic, my friend (13) _____ (get) into the crash position, leaning forward with his head between his knees. He (14) _____ (sit) like that for some minutes when the stewardess kindly (15) _____ (explain) to him that they (16) _____ (fly) over the Angel Falls, and would he like to look out of the window like the other passengers?

c

An Australian woman travelling home from Melbourne (17) _____ (drive) down a narrow road one dark evening when she (18) _____ (enter) a tunnel. Although a little surprised at this, as she (19) _____ (not notice) a tunnel on that route before, she (20) _____ (carry on). But after half an hour of twisting and turning, she (21) _____ (run out) of petrol. It (22) _____ (be) completely dark in the tunnel, so she (23) _____ (decide) to wait for help. She (24) _____ (only wait) for a few minutes when she (25) _____ (see) three men coming towards her. Rather surprisingly, the three men (26) _____ (wear) helmets with lamps on the front. The three men (27) _____ (seem) even more surprised to see her. It was then that the woman (28) _____ (realise) that she (29) _____ (drive) into a coal mine.

2 a You are going to tell the story of a mishap or adventure. Spend a few minutes planning what to say, and thinking about the best verb forms to use.

Either Re-tell any of the stories in the module, but from the point of view of another character (for example, one of the police officers). Use these ideas to help you.

We were walking through … when we saw …
He was … because he had …
We decided to … because …

We were having a quiet evening when …
The woman was worried because she thought …
The two young men had …

Or Tell a true story that happened to you or a friend. For example:

– an encounter with the police/authorities
– a journey when something went wrong
– another incident or mishap

Start the story at the most interesting point, giving background information where necessary. Use these ideas to help you.

This happened to me when I was …
I was *-ing* when …
I … because I had/hadn't …

b Tell your story to other students. They listen and ask any questions that they have.

Writing
A narrative

1 Look at the photo and read the story of what happened when the Brown family visited the Grand Canyon. Which way of seeing the Grand Canyon does Mrs Brown think is best?

2 Read the description of how the narrative is structured, and complete the gaps with the words and phrases from the box.

the setting	the narrator
the climax	dialogue
an unexpected problem	an amusing conclusion
the main characters	the beginning
an interesting new character	

- Paragraph A introduces <u>*the main characters*</u> and provides _____ for the story.
- Paragraph B describes the first part of the story and how _____ felt.
- Paragraph C brings in _____ .
- Paragraph D continues the story introducing _____ .
- Paragraph E describes _____ of the story, and uses _____ to make the events more vivid.
- Paragraph F provides _____ which links back to _____ of the story.

3 a You are going to write a story about a frightening experience. You can choose something that happened to you or to someone you know, or an incident from a book or film that you like.

b Spend about ten minutes planning how to tell the story. Use the ideas in exercise 2 to help you.

4 Write a first draft of your story. Read it through to check that you have used the correct narrative tenses. Show your first draft to your teacher or another student. Does he/she have any suggestions?

5 Write the final draft of your story. Display the stories around the class so that you can read each other's. Which story did you like best?

The Grand Canyon is a popular tourist destination in north-west Arizona, USA, known for its amazing rock formations.

A They say there are three ways to experience the Grand Canyon: on foot, on mules or by air. We chose the first. Up early, my husband Dave and I and our three kids – teenagers Matt and Liam and little Laura, aged six – couldn't wait to get started. We decided to walk along a lovely path named Bright Angel Trail. My husband had spoken to a park ranger who told him that walking to the first water station would be no problem.

B As the five of us set out, I was shocked at how narrow the path was – there seemed to be no more than thirty centimetres between us and falling hundreds of metres to our deaths. And I couldn't help noticing that the other hikers weren't dressed like us. They had heavy backpacks and water bottles, strong leather boots and hats. In our shorts, T-shirts and trainers we felt very under-dressed.

C We walked and walked … but unfortunately the beauty of the Canyon was lost on us. As the sun rose higher, Arizona's famous heat seemed to roast us. There was no shade and our legs were aching. We decided to go back, with Laura on my back and the boys far behind. By the time we finally got back, our legs were like jelly.

D The next day, after we'd had a long rest and a good breakfast, we were ready for another view of the Canyon … by air. After our walk the previous day, this would be the easiest thing in the world. For $200, we rented a small plane. The pilot, Joe, was handsome and funny. He joked with the kids and put us all at our ease.

E We called to each other excitedly as the plane took off and circled around the Canyon. But the smiles on our faces vanished as Joe tossed the plane around, pretending he was going to crash and shouting, 'This is the exact spot where another plane … just like this one … crashed!' I was so terrified I could barely croak, 'STOP, TAKE US BACK'! But we had paid for fifteen minutes of airtime, and that's what we got. When we finally arrived back on land, once again our legs were like jelly … but this time, it was from fear, not tiredness. We hardly spoke as we drove back.

F As I said, there are three ways to view the Grand Canyon: on foot, on mule or by air. We never tried the mules, but personally I'd recommend a fourth: buy yourself a good magazine like *National Geographic*. That way, you can see the Canyon and you don't end up an exhausted nervous wreck.

Language focus 2
Continuous aspect in other tenses

Choose the best alternative for each cartoon.

They've waited / 've been waiting to see the doctor for ages.

He's brought / 's been bringing her flowers for weeks.

Analysis

1 Complete the table with forms from the cartoons.

Present perfect simple	Present perfect continuous
Future simple	Future continuous

2 Which form, simple or continuous, is used to show duration or repetition?

▶ Read Language summaries B and C on page 147.

Practice

1 Which is the best ending to the sentences below? Why?

a Careful of the wet grass;
   – it's rained.
   – it's been raining.
b Hurry up
   – or you'll miss the train.
   – or you'll be missing the train.
c I feel exhausted;
   – I've run up and downstairs all morning.
   – I've been running up and downstairs all morning.
d I can't pick you up this evening
   – I'll work.
   – I'll be working.
e Don't come in here;
   – I've dropped a glass on the floor.
   – I've been dropping a glass on the floor.
f My car's broken down,
   – so I'll go to work on the bus next week.
   – so I'll be going to work on the bus next week.
g Can you call me a bit later?
   – I'll have my dinner at that time.
   – I'll be having my dinner at that time.

2 a **T3.6** Listen to two people answering the same six questions. Can you guess what the questions are?

b **T3.7** Listen to the questions and answers together. Did you guess correctly? Listen again and write down the six questions.

c If necessary, change the questions to make them more suitable for your partner. Then ask and answer in pairs.

Example:
How long have you been learning to drive? English?

Real life
Dealing with unexpected problems

1 **T3.8** Listen to four short conversations in which there is an unexpected problem and answer the following questions.

a Where does the conversation take place?
b Who are the people (e.g. waiter/customer)?
c What is the unexpected problem?

2 Do the sentences in the box express acceptance, annoyance or regret?

That's fine.	Oh, that's a pity.	I don't believe it!
Oh, what a nuisance.	I don't see why not.	Oh, what a shame!
Oh, dear!	Right, I see.	Oh, for goodness' sake!
This is ridiculous!	Oh, no! You're joking!	

Pronunciation

T3.9 Listen and practise the sentences in exercise 2. Pay attention to the stress and intonation.

3 a What unexpected problems might occur in these situations?

1 You want to pay your restaurant bill by credit card.
2 You phone up to buy two tickets for a concert.
3 You phone a computer repair company to get your computer fixed.
4 You want to buy a copy of an Italian newspaper at a station newsstand.
5 You phone the hospital to find out how your sick friend is.
6 You want to buy a pair of black trainers in a shoe shop.
7 You arrive at a hotel where you have made a reservation for two nights.
8 You want to park your car in a public car park.

b With a partner, prepare short conversations about two of these problems. Act out one of the conversations to the class.

STUDY...

Noticing and remembering useful collocations

1 A collocation is a combination of two or more words that frequently occur together. These could be:

- adjective + noun: *a domestic flight, a steep hill*
- verb + noun: *miss + a bus, a plane, a train*
- verb + preposition (including phrasal verbs): *break down, run out of (petrol)*
- other common phrases or idioms: *put someone at their ease, laugh your head off*

2 Even if you 'know all the words' in a text, you can still learn a lot by noticing which words occur together. Look back at the text on page 36 and find:

- which adjectives go with *path, backpacks* and *day*
- which verb goes with *a long rest* and *breakfast*
- two phrasal verbs which mean *begin a journey* and *leave the ground*
- two idiomatic phrases meaning *really wanted to do something* and *something very easy*

3 Look at three students' vocabulary notes. Which give the most/least useful information about the phrases?

a run out of: to use all of something
   We ran out of money so we had to go home

b Phrasal verb = run out
   run out of, petrol, money, time
   Time is running out

c Phrasal verbs: run away, run out, run over

4 Make a note of useful collocations from *The Gentle Touch* text on page 31, using the techniques above which you think are useful.

PRACTISE...

1 Narrative tenses ☐

Which of the verbs in the sentences describe:
- **a main event in the story?**
- **a background event?**
- **an event which happened before the other events?**

a Two police officers were talking softly to a boy.

b He had apparently stumbled and cracked his head.

c They were wearing commando-style uniforms.

d They helped the boy up and led him to the car.

e I had never seen such gentle police.

f 'Goodnight,' I said and watched them go.

▶ **Need to check? Language summary A, page 146.**

2 Narrative phrases ☐

Match A and B to make narrative phrases.

A		B	
a	all of a	1	end
b	the car drew	2	up
c	he insists that they	3	anything about the weather
d	in the	4	to each other
e	she didn't mention	5	hadn't been drinking
f	we were calling	6	sudden

▶ **Need to check? Useful language, page 33 and Recordings 3.2 and 3.3, pages 163–164.**

3 Past perfect simple and continuous ☐

Which of the highlighted verbs should be in the Past perfect simple or continuous?

a It was obvious that they play football in the park.

b As soon I saw her, I realised we met before.

c The frustrated passengers waited for several hours before someone finally made an announcement.

d Everyone was amazed at his appearance: they never see anyone with dyed blue hair before.

▶ **Need to check? Language summary A2, page 146.**

4 Continuous aspect ☐

Choose the correct alternative. In some cases, both or neither are correct.

a 'What's wrong?' 'I've been hurting / I've hurt my arm.'

b I've been coming / I've come to this beach for years.

c You seem out of breath. Have you been running / Have you run?

d I've been bought / I've been buying this new scooter. Do you like it?

e We've finished / We've been finishing our homework. Can we go out now?

f We'll be watching / We'll watch the game at home. Would you like to join us?

g I've been trying / I've tried to phone you all morning.

h The Australian swimmer has been winning / has won the gold medal twice before.

▶ **Need to check? Language summaries B and C, page 147.**

5 Collocations with mishaps ☐

Underline the things that you can:

a	bang	your drink / your elbow / your head
b	leave at home	your bag / the bus / your ID card
c	lose	a bus / your keys / your ticket / a train
d	miss	a bus / your keys / your ID / a ticket
e	slip on	your drink / some ice / the traffic
f	spill	your clothes / a drink / the pavement

▶ **Need to check? Vocabulary, page 29.**

6 Unexpected problems ☐

Complete the phrases with the words in the box.

for it oh see shame this what you're

a _____ dear!

b _____ goodness' sake!

c I don't believe _____ !

d _____ is ridiculous!

e _____ joking!

f _____ a nuisance.

g Right, I _____ .

h What a _____ .

▶ **Need to check? Real life, page 38.**

Pronunciation spot

Voiced and unvoiced sounds (1):
/tʃ/, /dʒ/, /θ/ and /ð/

a (T3.10) **Listen to the pronunciation of the words. Notice the different sounds of the letters in bold.**

chat /tʃ/   joke /dʒ/   bath /θ/   bathe /ð/

The /dʒ/ and /ð/ sounds are **voiced**: our throat vibrates when we say them (feel!).
The /tʃ/ and /θ/ sounds are **unvoiced**: our throat does not vibrate when we say them.

b (T3.11) **Put the words in the correct category, according to the pronunciation of the letters in bold. Then listen and check.**

sympathy approach thick cheek gentle theft leather gorgeous jelly check thought father

c **Practise saying the words, paying attention to the voiced and unvoiced sounds.**

REMEMBER!

Look back at the areas you have practised. Tick the ones you feel confident about. Now try the MINI-CHECK on page 158 to check what you know!

The mind

- ▶ The passive
- ▶ *have/get something done*
- ▶ Reading and speaking: *Gender gaps on the brain*
- ▶ Vocabulary: Qualities of mind
- ▶ Task: Analyse the results of a quiz
- ▶ Writing: A formal letter
- ▶ Wordspot: *mind*
- ▶ Song: *You were always on my mind*

Gender gaps on the brain

Did you know that women's brains are smaller than men's? The average male brain weighs about 1.3 kilograms, while the average female brain weighs ten percent less. Since research has consistently shown
5 that the bigger the brain, the cleverer the animal, men must be more intelligent than women. Right? Wrong. Men and women consistently score similarly on intelligence tests, despite the difference in brain size. Scientists have wondered why for years, but now
10 a team of researchers may have come up with the answer. It's not just the size of the brain, they say, it's what's inside that counts. The brain consists of 'grey matter' (the part of the brain that helps us think) and 'white matter' (the part that helps us transfer
15 information). And while men have more of the latter, the amount of 'thinking' brain is almost exactly the same in both sexes.

It has been suggested that, in the case of human brains, smaller may also mean 'more efficient',
20 perhaps because the two sides of the brain appear to be better connected in women. This means that little girls tend to learn to speak earlier, and that adult women can absorb all sorts of information from different sources at the same time, making them more

Reading and speaking

1 Do you believe that men and women are naturally better at certain things? Which sex, if either, tends to be better at the following?

- communicating with people
- languages
- map-reading
- maths
- parking a car
- cooking

2 You are going to read about the differences between men and women's brains. Which statements do you think are true? Discuss with other students, then read and check.

a Men and women's brains are about the same size.
b Men generally do better in intelligence tests.
c Women are better at doing a lot of things at once.
d Men and women are born with exactly the same type of brain.

3 Explain the difference between the following.

a the male and female brain in terms of weight
b 'grey matter' and 'white matter'
c how good men and women are at doing a lot of different things at the same time
d spatial abilities in men and women
e the way male and female toddlers reacted when separated from their mothers
f the different skills needed by men and women in prehistoric times

4 Use the context to guess the meaning of the following words and phrases.

a come up with (line 10)
b the latter (line 15)
c sources (line 24)
d more adept at (line 25)
e multi-tasking (line 25)
f come out on top (line 27)
g tackling (line 28)
h ancestors (line 51)

5 Discuss the following questions in small groups.

- Do you think you have a typical 'male' or 'female' brain? In what way?
- Do you know anyone who is an exception to these stereotypes? Why?
- Which do you think is more important to the way your mind develops: the way you are born or the experiences you have?

₂₅ adept at multi-tasking. When it comes to talking to the boss on the phone, cooking dinner and keeping an eye on the baby all at the same time, it's women who come out on top every time. Men seem to do better tackling one job at a time.

There are other important differences that distinguish male and ₃₀ female brains. White matter is the key to spatial tasks – knowing where things are in relation to other things – and men consistently do better on this kind of exercise. 'Spatial abilities are a big part of sport,' says one researcher. 'A great soccer player, for instance, always knows where he is in relation to the other players. It's not just ₃₅ a question of muscles and speed, it's knowing where to go.' And perhaps knowing where to go – or at least thinking they know – also explains one of life's great mysteries: why men refuse to ask for directions ... and women often need to!

The differences, according to researchers, begin in the womb. At ₄₀ about nine weeks old, differences in testosterone levels mean that male foetuses begin to develop a male brain, and females a female brain. The results can be seen in the behaviour of children as young as one. In one experiment, when a barrier was put between the toddlers and their mothers, the typical boy tried to climb the barrier or push it ₄₅ down. And the girl's strategy? To show distress, and attract help from another person.

In adult life, these brain differences are clearly reflected in the career choices men and women make. 85 percent of the architects in the USA and 90 percent of the mechanics are men: both jobs which ₅₀ require good spatial skills. Meanwhile, 94 percent of speech therapists are women. It may all go back to our ancestors, according to Dr Helen Fisher, an expert in gender differences. 'In prehistoric times, women needed verbal and emotional skills to control and educate their babies, while men needed spatial skills to hunt. We've ₅₅ got a very old brain in a very modern culture.'

If all this depresses you, it shouldn't. As biologist Anne Fausto-Sterling, points out, 'Just because we say we are born a certain way, we shouldn't close down possibilities. For every male or female who is 'stereotypical', I can think of another who isn't. The brain is not static. ₆₀ It changes throughout our lives according to what we do with it.'

Vocabulary
Qualities of mind

1 Work in pairs. How many adjectives in the box can you match to their definitions? Use your mini-dictionary to match the others.

aggressive	articulate	bossy
co-operative	emotional	intuitive
practical	self-confident	stubborn
sympathetic		

a A(n) _____ person is always telling others what to do.
b A(n) _____ person is quick to show their feelings, by laughing or by crying.
c A(n) _____ person can express him/herself very accurately with words.
d A(n) _____ person tries to understand other people's problems.
e A(n) _____ person refuses to change his/her mind.
f A(n) _____ person is very good at repairing or making things.
g A(n) _____ person is happy to work with or help other people.
h A(n) _____ person is not shy or nervous in social situations.
i A(n) _____ person relies on their feelings rather than facts when deciding things.
j A(n) _____ person behaves in an angry or threatening way.

2 Which of these sentences do you agree with? Change any, if necessary, to reflect your opinions.

a Little boys tend to be more aggressive than little girls.
b Generally, women are more emotional than men.
c At school, boys are more self-confident than girls.
d The women in my family are bossier than the men.
e I am the most practical person in my family.

3 Write five sentences of your own, using the words in exercise 1. Compare your sentences with other students.

Task: Analyse the results of a quiz

Preparation: listening

1 Read the 'Brain Facts' below. Is there anything you find surprising?

BRAIN FACTS

Did you know ...?

- Our brain consists of two halves, known as the left and right hemisphere.

- The two halves of the brain are not exactly the same: the left side of the brain is normally larger.

- The two halves of the brain process information in different ways.

- Although one side (usually the left) is dominant in most people, nobody is totally right- or left-brained – just as no one is totally right- or left-handed.

2 **a** You are going to answer a quiz to find out if you are mostly right- or left-brained. Work in pairs.
Student A: Look at Quiz A on this page.
Student B: Look at Quiz B on page 138.

b Read through the quiz, checking any unknown words.

Are you right- or left-brained?

Quiz A

1 Are you often late for class or other appointments?
  a no   **b** yes

2 When you phone a friend to tell them something, do you get to the main point as quickly as possible or give lots of other details first?
  a give lots of other details first
  b get to the main point as quickly as possible

3 Do you find it easier to remember people's names, or people's faces?
  a names   **b** faces

4 Do you think best sitting at your desk, or walking around?
  a sitting   **b** walking around

5 Are you good at judging time even if you don't have a watch?
  a yes   **b** no

6 If you have a lot of things to do, do you try to complete one task at a time, or do several things at once?
  a one task at a time   **b** several things at once

7 Do you prefer reading:
  a non-fiction?   **b** fantasy or science fiction?

8 When you are studying, which of these is most important to you?
  a bright light   **b** background music

9 Someone complains to you about something. What do you respond to first?
  a the points they are making
  b the tone of voice they use

10 When asked for your opinion, do you:
  a think carefully before you speak?
  b say what you think immediately?

Number of a answers _____

Number of b answers _____

Task: speaking

1 Use your quiz to interview your partner. Keep a note of your partner's answers and add up the number of 'a's and the number of 'b's. Do not tell your partner the result yet.

2 a **T4.1** Listen to an analysis of the results. Mark the characteristics in the box L if they are typical of left-brained people and R if they are typical of right-brained people.

linear-thinking	intuition	the ability to visualise
logical thinking	interest in the 'big picture'	learning by explanation
verbal skills	artistic creativity	learning by doing

b Listen again, if necessary, and answer the following questions.

1 What is a typical score?
2 Is there any difference between men and women in this respect?
3 Can you do anything to change the kind of brain you have?

3 Explain your partner's results and what they mean.

▶ Useful language a

4 Discuss the following questions in small groups.

- Were you surprised by your results or not?
- What were the main differences between you and your partner?
- Is this kind of test useful?
- Which questions did you find most revealing?
- Did your education/upbringing encourage one side more than the other?
- Would you like to develop either area more?

▶ Useful language b

Useful language

a Presenting your partner's results

You got mainly 'a's / 'b's.

Your answers were a mixture of 'a's and 'b's.

According to the experts, that means that ...

b Discussing the results

One thing that surprised me was ...

I (don't) think this kind of test is very useful because ...

I found the question about ... very interesting.

At school, we were expected to ...

I was always encouraged to ...

I would like to be more ...

Language focus 1
The passive

1 Answer these questions from an IQ test. Which did you find the easiest / most difficult?

a Joe, Ben and Tony have to be at work at nine o'clock. Ben is never late. On Monday, Tony was late. Only one of the statements below must be true. Which one?
1 Joe is sometimes late.
2 Tony sometimes arrives after Ben.
3 Joe sometimes arrives after Ben.
4 Tony always arrives after Ben.

b Which is the missing shape in this sequence?

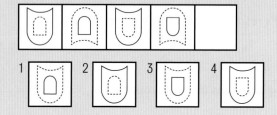

c Which are the next two numbers in this sequence?
34 41 49 43 50 58 52 59 (?) (?)

d Scientists received three messages in a strange language from a distant planet. They studied the messages and found that 'KENDAL DEXTOR BROK' means 'Danger Rocket Explosion' and 'JUBB MINOR KENDAL' means 'Danger Spaceship Fire' and 'DEXTOR GIMILZOR GONDOR' means 'Bad Gas Explosion'. What does 'BROK' mean?
1 Danger   4 Gas
2 Explosion   5 Nothing
3 Rocket

(Answers on page 142.)

2 Read the information sheet about Mensa. Would you like to join an organisation like this?

What is Mensa?

Mensa is a non-profit-making organisation with over 100,000 members in more than 100 countries: The only qualification you need in order to be accepted as a member is to have an IQ in the top two percent of the population.

How did Mensa start?

The society was founded in 1946 by Roland Berrill, an Australian lawyer, and Lancelot Ware, a graduate of Oxford University. It was originally known as the High IQ Society, but later changed its name to Mensa.

What are the principles behind Mensa?

The organisation has always operated on the principle that intelligence 'should be used for the benefit of humanity.' Members are drawn from all professions, from truck drivers to university professors.

What are the benefits of being a member?

Members meet other people like themselves. Regular social events are organised so that members enjoy the company of their intellectual equals. It is not known how many marriages have been made at Mensa meetings!

Analysis 1

1 Which sentence below is passive? How is the passive formed? Underline six more examples in the text on the left.
*The society **was founded** in 1946 by Roland Berrill and Lancelot Ware.*
*Roland Berrill and Lancelot Ware **founded** the society in 1946.*

2 Tick the statements that are true about the passive.
a The person doing the action (the agent) is not the main focus of the sentence.
b The agent is often unimportant or unknown.
c We use it most in informal contexts.
d It is used a lot in newspaper articles and academic writing.

3 In formal contexts, passive phrases are often introduced with *It ...*
It is not known how many marriages have been made at Mensa meetings.

There are many other phrases like this.
It is (not) believed that ...   It is (not) thought that ...
It is (not) expected that ...

▶ Read Language summaries A and B on page 147.

Practice

1 T4.2 Read about Marilyn vos Savant and choose the correct alternative. Then listen and check.

The real significance of IQ tests will probably never (a) establish / **be established**, but nowadays, it (b) says / **is said** that the average score is around 100. Intelligence tests had not (c) invented / **been invented** in the days of composer Wolfgang Amadeus Mozart or naturalist Charles Darwin, but it (d) thinks / **is thought** that the IQs of these well-known geniuses was around 160–170.

Is this the smartest person in the world?

So where does that leave Marilyn vos Savant, who at the age of ten (e) claimed / **was claimed** to have an IQ of 228? That's eighty points above genius level: the highest IQ that has ever (f) recorded / **been recorded**.

Born in 1946, vos Savant (g) educated / **was educated** at Washington State University, but she (h) **soon became** / was soon become tired of college life. She had always (i) **wanted** / been wanted to be a writer, so she (j) **dropped** / was dropped out after only two years to start a career in finance and investment. Within five years she (k) **had made** / had been made enough money to begin her career as a full-time writer.

Since her first book *Brain Building: Exercising Yourself Smarter* (l) published / **was published** in 1990, she has (m) **produced** / been produced over twenty books, which have (n) translated / **been translated** into many different languages. In her latest book, *Growing Up: a Classic*

American Childhood she (o) **claims** / is claimed that if children (p) give / **are given** clear goals from an early age, the chances that they will (q) **succeed** / be succeeded in later life greatly increase. According to vos Savant '(r) **Defeating** / Being defeated is a temporary condition. Giving up is what makes it permanent.'

As one reviewer (s) **remarked** / was remarked, 'I guess we shouldn't (t) surprise / **be surprised** by the excellent information and advice in this book; after all, it (u) wrote / **was written** by the smartest person in the world!'

Analysis 2

Alternatives to the passive

1 In less formal contexts, we often avoid the passive, using *we, you, they, people, someone*, etc. as the subject of the sentence:
It is thought that their IQs were around 160. → *We think their IQs were around 160.*

2 Find the passive versions of these sentences in the Mensa text on page 44 and the vos Savant text on page 45.
a *Nobody* knows how many people from Mensa meetings have got married. (page 44).
b *You* should use your intelligence for the benefit of humanity. (page 44).
c *People* say that the average IQ score is around 100. (page 45).
d *They* have translated her books into many languages. (page 45).

▶ Read Language summary C on page 147.

2 Re-write these sentences in a more conversational style, using the pronoun in brackets.

a It is said that there are about 100 million cells in the human brain. (They)
  They say that there are about 100 million cells in the human brain.
b Brain cells can only be seen with a microscope. (You)
c It is still not known exactly how many aspects of the human brain work. (We)
d It is often thought that the right side of the brain is the 'artistic' side. (People)
e In fact, both sides of the brain are used when we listen to music. (We)
f Pain cannot be felt in the brain, because it has no nerves. (You)
g It has been calculated that messages in the brain travel at over 250 kilometres per hour! (Someone)
h In ancient times, it was believed that the purpose of the brain was to cool the blood. (People)
i It has been suggested that our brains haven't changed much since prehistoric times. (Someone)
j Research is being done into how the brain works. (They)

Writing
A formal letter

1 [T4.3] Listen to the advertisement for the BrainBoost course. What does the course promise to do? What does the 'special package' include and how much does it cost?

2 Phillip buys the BrainBoost course, but is unhappy with it, and telephones the company to complain. Read some of the things he says to Mr Martin, the manager of BrainBoost. Why is he unhappy with what he has received?

> You told me I'd get it in forty-eight hours, but actually it took nearly three weeks.

> Your ad said that the exercises only take ten minutes a day, but I've worked out that they take more like two hours a day.

> And another thing – I just cannot understand how you can say these boring exercises are enjoyable!

3 a Phillip is asked to put his complaint in writing. Read his letter and underline the words he uses to make his complaints from exercise 2.

Mr David Martin
BrainBoost
PO Box 327861

12 Priory Terrace
Bristol, BS12 0RJ

8 January

Dear Mr Martin,

Following our telephone conversation yesterday, I am writing to complain about the 'BrainBoost special package' which I purchased from your company over the Internet six weeks ago.

I am dissatisfied with the product and service that I have received for a number of reasons. Firstly, having paid €5.95 postage and packing I was told that I would receive the course within forty-eight hours whereas in fact it took almost three weeks to arrive.

Your advertisement promised that the necessary exercises would be enjoyable and take only ten minutes a day to complete. However, I have calculated that in order to complete the exercises suggested, it would take closer to two hours a day. Furthermore, I totally fail to comprehend how you can describe these tedious exercises as enjoyable, or suggest that they will 'open up your imagination'.

Finally, I have discovered that the vitamins and CDs which you describe as 'unique' can be purchased in my local supermarket for half the price that you charge.

I am of the opinion that your course has been a total waste of both my time and money, and demand a complete refund of everything that I have paid, including postage and packing.

Yours sincerely,

Phillip Mortimer

Phillip Mortimer

b In what ways are the grammar and vocabulary Phillip uses in the letter different from what he says?

c Find more formal words and phrases in Phillip's letter that mean the following.

1 After (paragraph 1)
2 buy (1)
3 unhappy (2)
4 but actually (2)
5 to do (3)
6 I have worked out (3)
7 I just cannot understand (3)
8 I think (5)
9 I want all my money back (5)

4 Underline any other phrases in the letter that might be useful in a letter of complaint.

5 Look at page 139. Imagine you bought one of the language courses. Think of at least four things that went wrong. Write a letter complaining to the company and asking for your money back.

Language focus 2
have/get something done

Read about how to keep your brain healthy. Can you think of any other ideas?

Five ways to keep your brain healthy

1 Eat well
We all know the saying healthy body, healthy mind. Oily fish like salmon and tuna, along with fruit and vegetables, provide essential vitamins to keep your brain young and fit.

2 Exercise
Regular exercise increases the circulation of blood to your brain, making it more efficient. If you haven't exercised regularly before, get your blood pressure checked to make sure your heart is healthy.

3 Exercise your brain too
Just like your body your brain needs to keep fit. Do crosswords, read books. Test and develop your memory with special exercises.

4 Avoid stress
We all know that when we have too much to do we start to forget things. Take breaks and make time to relax.

5 Get your hearing checked
Hearing loss can seriously interfere with memory, so if you think you might have a problem, have your ears tested right now.

Analysis

1   Compare these sentences from the text above. Who does the testing in each one? What is the difference in the verb form?
    ***Test** your memory with special exercises.*
    ***Have** your ears **tested** right now.*

    Find another example of the second type of sentence in the text above.

2   We also use *get* in this construction. It is more informal than *have*, but the meaning is the same.
    ***Get** your hearing **checked**.*

▶ Read Language summary D on page 147.

Practice

1 Write sentences to describe these pictures.

He's cutting his hair.

2 Look at the business cards below. What can you have done at each of the places? Write three sentences for each.

Harringtons Optician's
Immediate eye tests
Contact lens fitting
Glasses cleaned and repaired
Tel: 01283 445055

FINOLA'S BEAUTY SALON
Facial massages
Hair care
Highlighting
Manicure & Pedicure
Hotel Intercontinental, Dubai   Tel: 971 4 2211349   P.O.Box :11123

Flair Dry Cleaning & Ironing Service
Professional Ironing service
24-hour dry cleaning service
Alterations
Free delivery and collection in Southampton area
Tel: 01924 495209
e-mail: indo@flaironing-service.com

3 T4.4 Listen to someone phoning one of the businesses above. Which business is the customer phoning? Which service is he asking about? With a partner, invent four similar dialogues using the cards above.

47

Wordspot
mind

1 Replace the words and phrases in *italics* with a phrase from the diagram below.

keep your mind off

a A trip to the cinema will help to ~~stop you thinking about~~ the exam tomorrow.

b No, I won't tell you his name! *It doesn't concern you!*

c Try to be *unprejudiced* about Trudi's new boyfriend – don't *decide* about him before you've even met him.

d Although it was an easy question, suddenly *I couldn't remember*, and I was unable to answer.

e Many people are afraid to *give their opinion* because of what others may think.

f Is there *something worrying you*? Can I do anything to help?

g *It's OK for me* if you're late as long as you phone me.

h 'I'm sorry, I dropped a glass on the floor.' *'Don't worry about it.* I'll get a pan and brush.'

i I've *changed my opinion* about that. I'll take it after all.

j *Remembering* his age, I thought he did very well to come third.

k *Would it be possible to move* your car? It's blocking the entrance.

l She is over eighty years old, so it's not surprising Anne's a bit *forgetful*.

m *Be careful with your head.* The ceiling's very low in here.

n I don't know what they're so angry about. *In my opinion* it's a very good scheme.

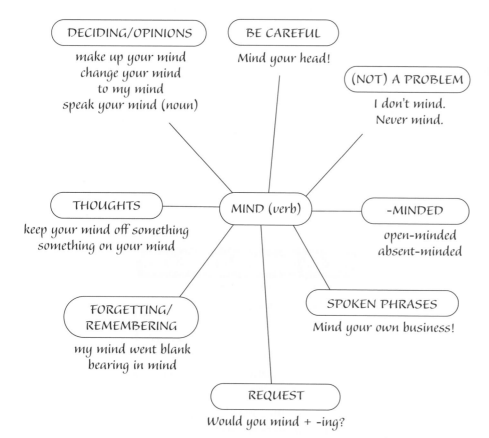

DECIDING/OPINIONS
make up your mind
change your mind
to my mind
speak your mind (noun)

BE CAREFUL
Mind your head!

(NOT) A PROBLEM
I don't mind.
Never mind.

THOUGHTS
keep your mind off something
something on your mind

MIND (verb)

-MINDED
open-minded
absent-minded

FORGETTING/
REMEMBERING
my mind went blank
bearing in mind

SPOKEN PHRASES
Mind your own business!

REQUEST
Would you mind + -ing?

2 a Which phrase with *mind* could complete the last line of each dialogue?

 1

A: And on line two, it's Vince.

B: Hello?

A: Hello, Vince, you're through to Opinion on 96.5 Talk FM. What do you want to say?

B: Well, I'm not sure if I should say this, but …

A: You can say what you like on this show, Vince … go on _____ .

 2

C: Oh, I can't be bothered to cook. Shall we order a takeaway?

D: Yeah, all right. There's nothing much in the fridge anyway.

C: So what'll it be then? Do you fancy a pizza? Or a curry?

D: Either of those would be fine.

_____ .

3

E: Can I borrow your phone?

F: Why? Where's yours?

E: I must've left it at home. I'm not sure …

F: No, you didn't. Look it's over there. You left it on the table. Honestly, what's the matter with you? You're so _____ these days!

b **T4.5** Listen and check.

3 Work with a partner. Write at least three similar conversations of about four to five lines. Include a phrase with *mind* in each one.

Listening
Song: *You were always on my mind*

1 **a** All the verbs in the song are grammatically correct. Which do you think fit the song best?

Maybe I didn't ¹listen to / treat / understand you
Quite as good as I should have
Maybe I didn't ²listen to / love / respect you
Quite as often as I could have
Little things I should have ³said and done / given you / made
I just never ⁴had / knew / took the time

You were always on my mind
You were always on my mind

⁵Say to / Tell / Promise me that your sweet love hasn't
⁶died / ended / gone away
⁷Allow me / Give me / Let me have one more chance
To ⁸keep / leave / make you satisfied, satisfied

Maybe I didn't ⁹hold / look after / phone you
All those lonely, lonely times
And I guess I never ¹⁰let you know / said to you / told you
¹¹I feel / I'm / I've been so happy that you're mine
If I ¹²help / let / make you ¹³feel / look / seem second best,
Girl, I'm sorry, I was blind

You were always on my mind
You were always on my mind

b 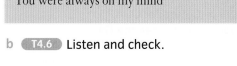 Listen and check.

2 Choose the best explanation for the phrases in bold.

a You were always **on my mind**.
   I was always thinking about you. / I forgot about you. / You used to annoy me.
b as often as I **could have**
   wanted to / needed to / was able to
c **one more chance**
   good luck / a last opportunity / more time
d **I guess**
   I don't know / I suppose / I wonder
e **second best**
   important / not needed / unimportant
f **I was blind**.
   I didn't know what was happening. / I ignored you. / I was angry at you.

3 Complete the list of things the man in the song is sorry he did, and a list of things he'd like her to do.

Things he's sorry he did
He didn't treat her well.

Things he'd like her to do
Tell him that she still loves him.

A Vocabulary: Word hunt

Work in pairs. Complete the gaps in the word hunt.

1 Module 1, pages 8–9, Reading

Find words in the paragragh about The Corrs that mean:
a very impressive (adj) _____
b international / global (adj) _____
c a mixture (n) _____
d brothers or sisters (npl) _____

2 Module 1, page 13, Writing

Find adjectives in the Rowan Atkinson text that mean:
a unable to do things well (paragraph 1) _____
b nervous and embarrassed when meeting new people (paragraph 2) _____
c strange and unpleasant to look at (paragraph 2) _____
d boring and uninteresting (paragraph 4) _____

3 Module 2, page 19, Reading

Complete the gaps in the hyphenated words.
a a _____-fat diet
b low _____-esteem
c _____-tempered
d better co-_____

4 Module 2, page 22, Language focus 2

Find adjectives that are opposite in meaning to:
a poor _____
b pessimistic _____
c rich _____
d worthless _____

5 Module 2, page 26, Wordspot

Find a phrase with *life* that means:
a something that can save your life _____
b someone who can save your life _____
c connected with friends and going out _____
d connected with home and staying in _____

6 Module 3, page 36, Writing

Read the text and find:
a a phrasal verb meaning 'to begin a journey' _____
b an adjective meaning 'wearing too few clothes' _____
c a phrasal verb meaning 'left the ground' _____
d a colloquial phrase for someone who is very frightened _____

7 Module 4, page 41, Vocabulary

a Find three adjectives which are generally **negative**
_____ _____ _____
b Find three adjectives which are generally **positive**
_____ _____ _____

8 Module 4, page 48, Wordspot

Find a phrase with *mind* that means:
a to decide _____
b it doesn't concern you _____
c Don't worry about it _____
d you keep thinking about something and worrying _____

B Active and passive verb forms

Look at the newspaper article heading. Check the meaning of any new words in your mini-dictionary. Then complete the gaps in the correct form of the verbs (active or passive) in brackets.

Fortune-teller offers to remove curse on money

A fortune-teller in Colorado, USA, (1) _____ (arrest) a few years ago after she (2) _____ (trick) a pensioner into giving her $30,000. As she (3) _____ (tell) her fortune one day, Sonya Adamson, 24, (4) _____ (persuade) a sixty-four-year-old widow that a curse (5) _____ (place) on all her money by evil spirits, and that she would have to take it to her home for the curse (6) _____ (remove). When the woman (7) _____ (return) in order to pick up her money, she (8) _____ (find) that Adams (9) _____ (disappear) and all the furniture (10) _____ (take) from her apartment. Police (11) _____ (arrest) Adamson as she (12) _____ (board) a plane to Miami – her ticket (13) _____ (paid for) in cash a few minutes earlier with the old woman's money. 'I (14) _____ (not usually deceive) so easily,' (15) _____ (say) the old lady. Her money (16) _____ (return) to her a few months later.

C Speaking: Forming nouns and adjectives

1 Look at the nouns describing personal qualities. Write the adjective of the word in bold.

a   being able to accept **criticism**   *critical*
b   **creativity**   _____
c   **determination**   _____
d   **enthusiasm**   _____
e   physical **fitness**   _____
f   **good looks**   _____
g   **honesty**   _____
h   **optimism**   _____
i   **persistence**   _____
j   **self-confidence**   _____
k   natural **talent**   _____
l   personal **wealth**   _____

2 a Choose the **four** most important qualities to be a successful:

* businessman _____
* politician _____
* pop star _____

b Compare your opinions in groups. Add any other words or phrases you think are needed.

D Listening: Passive forms with *have* and *get*

a   **C1** You will hear some people talking about things they once had or got done. Listen and complete the table below.

Name	What they had done	Where / When	How they felt at the time	How they feel about it now
Karen				
Nigel				
Penny				

b Have you ever had or got any of these things done? Do you know anyone who has? Would you ever have or got any of them done? Discuss in groups.

E Speaking: Real life

1 Work in pairs. What would you say in the following situations? If you cannot think of any suitable phrases, look at the appropriate page.

a   You are chatting to a friend. He is keen to continue the conversation, but you have something urgent to do. How do you end the conversation politely?
(Module 1, page 16)

b   You've just started a new job, and need some help with the photocopier. The only person around is a colleague you don't know, who is busy reading something. What do you say?
(Module 1, page 16)

c   You are walking down the street with a friend. She is angry because a shop assistant has been rude to her. What do you say to calm her down?
(Module 2, page 23)

d   Your friend tells you he/she is too scared to go out shopping with you, because he/she is worried people will laugh at his/her new hairstyle. What do you say?
(Module 2, page 23)

e   Your central heating / air conditioning system is broken. You phone the company to get it fixed, but no one can come for at least another five days. What do you say?
(Module 3, page 38)

f   You are in restaurant which is famous for its pizza. The waiter tells you there is no pizza available today because the oven isn't working.
(Module 3, page 38)

2 Choose one situation and expand it into a dialogue of six to eight lines. Act out your dialogue to the class, or write it out.

Unusual achievements

▶ Perfect tenses in the past, present and future
▶ More about the Present perfect simple and continuous
▶ Reading and vocabulary: Remarkable *achievements*
▶ Vocabulary: Verb–noun combinations
▶ Task: Talk about an achievement
▶ Pronunciation: Question tags
▶ Wordspot: *first*

Reading and vocabulary
Remarkable achievements

1 Look at the photos and the headings. Can you guess what the people have achieved?

2 Read the articles and check. Then summarise each person's achievement.

3 **a** If necessary, check the meaning of the words in **bold**. Which person/people in the articles do you think …

1 has **made a fortune**?
2 is **exceptionally talented**?
3 has **raised** a large sum of money for charity?
4 has **provided** an important **role model** for other people?
5 has taken huge **risks**?
6 has shown a lot of **dedication** and **stamina**?
7 **overcame** a difficult early life?
8 has had to **cope with** unexpected problems?
9 seems to have no **sense of danger**?

b Compare and explain your opinions with a partner.

> Who do you think has made a fortune?

> I suppose Halle Berry has, because …

4 **a** Put the five achievements in order: 1 = the most impressive to 5 = the least worthwhile. Compare your ideas with other students.

b Would you like to do any of these things yourself? What and why?

Prestigious business award for Fabiola

Born in Spain, educated in the USA and married to a South African, Fabiola Arredondo was unknown just a few years ago. But she has recently won an award offered by the USA's leading financial newspaper, as Europe's Most Influential Businesswoman.

As managing director of Yahoo!, now Europe's leading Internet network, she took the organisation from a tiny operation employing just thirteen people, to a giant worldwide company with a turnover of more than $100 million. Her good looks and eloquence have made her something of a celebrity in European business circles.

Prodigies graduate

A teenage brother and sister, who were the youngest siblings ever to go to university, have graduated with Maths degrees. Iskander Yusof, fifteen, and his sister Noraisha, nineteen, have been given their degrees by Warwick University. Neither went to school before university, but had been taught at home by their father who is a mathematician. Iskander, who began his university studies at the age of twelve, achieved a first class honours degree. Asked if he had any regrets about going to university so young, Iskander said, 'I do not feel I have sacrificed anything at all, we would not have benefited from going to school.' Their elder sister Sufiah was accepted at Oxford University at the age of thirteen, and the family's youngest daughter, Zuleihka, aged eight, is currently preparing to take her A levels.

Juggler breaks world record

On 15–16th July, Ricardinho Neves (Brazil) juggled a regulation football non-stop for 19 hours 15 minutes and 31 seconds with feet, legs and head, without the ball ever touching the ground at the Los Angeles Convention Centre, California, USA. The record time for ball control by a woman is 7 hours 5 minutes 25 seconds by Claudio Martini (Brazil) at Caxias do Sol.

Supergran safely home

She had to make an emergency landing in Jordan, battled 160 kilometres-per-hour Arctic storms, and faced a terrifying moment when her engine nearly failed over the Mediterranean. But now Jennifer Murray is safely back in the UK and celebrating becoming the first woman to circle the globe solo by helicopter. The sixty-year-old grandmother, from Frome in Somerset, completed the 35,000 kilometre journey in ninety-nine days. 'My motive was to create a world record and have a fantastic adventure,' she said, 'However, I didn't want to do this without raising money for charity as well.'

Her journey raised over one million euros for Operation Smile, a charity which provides facial surgery for children in developing countries.

Another first for Halle

Actress Halle Berry has made history by becoming the first African American to win an Oscar for Best Actress, following her performance last year in *Monster's Ball*. In a moving acceptance speech, the actress paid tribute to all the African American actresses whose achievements had inspired her.

Born in Ohio in 1968, Berry had a tough inner city upbringing, but success as a beauty queen at the age of seventeen gave her the opportunity to escape. She was the first African American to represent the USA in the Miss World competition, and has been named no less than seven times in *People Magazine*'s list of the fifty Most Beautiful People in the World. However, she has also received warm praise for her acting skills, and has the distinction of being the only 'Bond Girl' ever to win the Best Actress award.

Language focus 1
Perfect tenses in the past, present and future

1 **T5.1** Listen to the information about Elsie Gamble, Git Kaur Rhandawa and James Hughes and complete the notes about each of them.

Elsie Gamble
Occupation: *Teacher*
Date she began at Coteswood School:
School fees then:
School fees now:

Git Kaur Rhandawa
Number of driving tests taken before she passed:
Amount of money spent on driving lessons:

James Hughes
Saw first film:
Number of films seen up to now:
Number of films sees a year:

2 a Choose the best way to complete the sentences.

1 Elsie Gamble …
   a is a teacher for more than seventy-five years.
   b has been a teacher for more than seventy-five years.
   c was a teacher for more than seventy-five years.

2 Git Kaur Rhandawa felt really happy because …
   a she's finally passed her driving test.
   b she finally passed her driving test.
   c she had finally passed her driving test.

3 By the time he's forty, James Hughes hopes he …
   a has seen 20,000 films.
   b will have seen 20,000 films.
   c will see 20,000 films.

b In your answers, find examples of the Present perfect, Past perfect and Future perfect.

Analysis

All perfect verb forms link together two times. Answer the questions. Then complete rules a, b and c.

1 Present perfect
She's been a teacher for more than seventy-five years.
Is she a teacher now? When did she become a teacher?

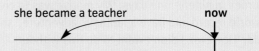

she became a teacher   now

   a The Present perfect links the present and the time before / after now.

2 Past perfect
She felt really happy because she had finally passed her driving test.
Underline the two verbs. Which action happened first?

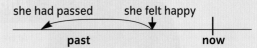

she had passed   she felt happy
        past   now

   b The Past perfect links a time in the past with the time before / after that.

3 Future perfect
By the time he's forty, James Hughes will have seen 20,000 films.
Will he see his 20,000th before / after / when he's forty?

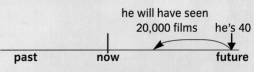

he will have seen
                20,000 films   he's 40
   past   now   future

   c The Future perfect links a time in the future with the time before / after that.

▶ Read Language summary A on page 148.

Practice

1 Complete gaps 1–10 in the texts on the right with the correct perfect verb form of the verbs in brackets and gaps a–g with the time words in the box. (There is one extra time word.)

> ago before by (x2) the time
> over the last since then

2 Complete ten of the following sentences to make them true for you.

a I *'ve been* at this school for *three years* .

b I _____ interested in _____ since _____ .

c When I woke up this morning, my _____ had already _____ .

d I hope I'll have learnt to _____ by the time I'm _____ .

e I'd never _____ until this year.

f I haven't _____ recently.

g I'd already _____ when this lesson began.

h I hope I'll have _____ by this time next year.

i When I was _____ years old, I had never _____ .

j I'll probably have _____ , by midnight tonight.

k I've _____ so far today.

l I've never _____ .

m My father/mother has _____ since _____ .

n By the end of today, I'll have _____ .

3 Compare your sentences with a partner. Choose the most interesting to read to the class.

Written by a fifteen-year-old Dutch girl during World War II, *The diary of Anne Frank* (1) _____ (sell) 25 million copies (a) _____ its publication in 1947.

By (b) _____ she was eighteen, 1980s tennis star Tracey Austin (2) _____ (win) the US Open and was ranked Number One in the world. But just four years later, she (3) _____ (already retire), the victim of injury and the intensity of the professional tennis circuit. Since (c) _____ however, she (4) _____ (become) a successful TV commentator and coach.

In the hundred-year history of the modern Olympics, thousands of men and women (5) _____ (win) Olympic medals. The youngest was a French boy, aged between seven and ten, who was in the Dutch rowing team at the Paris Olympics of 1900 – but even to this day, no one (6) _____ (discover) his name!

Two years ago, ninety-two-year-old Fauja Singh ran the London Marathon in 6 hours 11 minutes. Not bad for someone who (7) _____ (only take up) running three years (d) _____ ! If all goes to plan, (e) _____ his ninety-fifth birthday, he (8) _____ (take part) in further Marathons in Toronto and New York!

Although the surviving members, Paul McCartney and Ringo Starr, are now well into their sixties, The Beatles (9) _____ (be) among the world's best-selling groups (f) _____ thirty-five years. If sales continue at the current rate, they (10) _____ (sell) more than 1.5 billion albums (g) _____ the year 2010.

Vocabulary
Verb–noun combinations

1 **a** Which verbs in the box can combine with the nouns below?

> beat   cope with   make   raise
> set   show   win

1 _____ an award / the final / a competition

2 _____ the previous record / the other team / your rivals

3 _____ an important issue / money / standards

4 _____ a good example / someone a challenge / a world record

5 _____ great courage / an interest in something / support for someone

6 _____ a difficult boss / financial problems / university life

7 _____ a fortune / progress / something possible

b Use your mini-dictionary to check your answers.

2 Work in pairs. Think of examples of the following.

a a famous businessperson who has made a fortune

b an actor or actress who has recently won an award

c a famous person who raises a lot of money for charity

d a world leader who has shown great courage

e a sportsman/woman who has set a world record

f someone you know who has won a competition

g a sports team who have beaten one of their biggest rivals this year

h a famous person who has had to cope with financial difficulties

i an older person who has always shown an interest in you

j a classmate who sets a good example to the rest of the class

Task: Talk about an achievement you find amazing
Preparation: listening

1 Work in groups. Read the list of achievements below. Can you think of an example for each?

- The invention of an important piece of technology *the invention of the aeroplane*
- A 'basic' scientific advance that we couldn't live without
- The discovery of an important cure or medicine
- Outstanding leadership in a period of crisis
- A great step forward in human rights
- A great social or political advance
- An incredible artistic achievement
- An amazing piece of engineering or architecture
- An outstanding sporting achievement

2 Compare your answers with the class. Which achievements on your list are the work of one person, and which are collective human achievements?

3 **T5.2** Listen to five people talking about achievements that they find amazing and answer the questions.

a What is the achievement and which category above does it fall into?

b What reasons do they give for admiring these achievements?

c Do you agree with what they say? Can you add any more arguments to the ones they give?

d Which of these achievements do you find most/least amazing?

Task: speaking

1 You are going to talk about an achievement you find amazing. *Either* Choose from the ideas you discussed in the preparation stage. *Or* Think of an idea of your own. It could be the achievement of someone you know personally, rather than a great leader/writer, etc.

2 Spend about ten minutes planning what you will talk about. Include the following in your talk. Ask your teacher for any words or phrases you need.

- some factual information about what the achievement is (including any dates, statistics, etc. that you happen to know)
- the influence/impact that it has had
- why you find it so interesting/admirable

▶ Useful language a and b

3 Give your talks either in large groups, or to the class. Listen to each talk, and at the end, ask any questions that you have.

4 **a** Which of the achievements you have just heard about do you find most amazing? Explain to other students why.

b What do you hope that human beings will achieve in the next few years?

Useful language

a Talking about a general achievement

One of the things I always find amazing is …

… has completely changed our lives.

As a result of this …

Just imagine life if …

If we didn't have … our lives would be …

It's incredible to think that …

b Talking about the achievements of a particular person

His/Her achievements have really changed the world because …

I really admire the way he/she …

What I find particularly impressive/amazing is …

He/She (has) achieved so much.

Language focus 2
More about the Present perfect simple and continuous

Which sentence, a or b, describes each picture best?

1

a   … and Alberto has been scoring the winning goal!
b   … and Alberto has scored the winning goal!

2

a   They've played cards for hours.
b   They've been playing cards for hours.

3

a   He's been painting the ceiling.
b   He's painted the ceiling.

4

a   She's made phone calls all morning.
b   She's been making phone calls all morning.

5

a   He's written five reports this morning.
b   He's been writing five reports this morning.

6

a   He's been owning the restaurant for twenty-five years.
b   He's owned the restaurant for twenty-five years.

Analysis

1   Which sentence(s) from the cartoons above …
   a   describe a state?
   b   describe an action that lasts only for a moment?
   c   describe actions which are finished?
   d   describe an action which lasts for a period of time?
   e   describe an action which is repeated?
   f   describe an action which is not finished?
   Which tense is used in each case?

2   Continuous verb forms are often used to emphasise the duration/repetition of an action (see module 3). Sometimes these actions are not complete.
   a   How do the Present perfect continuous verbs from the cartoons show these ideas?
   b   Why isn't the Present perfect continuous used in sentences 1, 5 and 6?

▶ Read Language summary B on page 148.

Practice

1 a You are going to find someone in the class who has done / been doing the things below. First choose the best verb form. Which sentences could have both forms?

Find someone who …

1 has lost / has been losing some money recently.
2 has changed / has been changing their hairstyle in the last few months.
3 has gone / has been going out a lot recently.
4 has felt / has been feeling tired this week.
5 has broken / has been breaking an arm or leg.
6 has passed / has been passing an important exam this year.
7 has studied / has been studying a lot recently.
8 has already done / has already been doing all their homework this week.
9 has spent / has been spending a lot of money recently.
10 has been / has been going abroad this year.
11 has forgotten / has been forgetting things recently.
12 has left / has been leaving something important at home today.

b Decide what questions to ask, then ask as many other students as you can. Tell the class what you discovered.

2 a Look at the pictures. What kind of problem do you think the girl has?

b Put the dialogue between Marina and her friend, Jane in the best order.

Jane knew that her flatmate was having boyfriend problems, so it was no surprise when she came home to find Marina looking red-eyed and tearful …

No, I'm fine. I've just been watching a sad film, that's all. ☐
Who? Oh, him. No. I haven't thought about him all day, actually. ☐
Marina. Your phone … it's ringing. Aren't you going to answer it? ☐
No, it's not true. I've been trying to get through to him all day. ☐
Oh, I see. Tell me, have you heard anything from Andrew today? ☐
No. I've left about ten messages on his voice mail. Oh, why doesn't he phone? ☐
Oh, really? So you've forgotten about him already, have you? ☐
Hi, Marina … what's the matter? You've been crying again, haven't you? ☐1☐
Haven't you managed to speak to him, then? ☐

c [T5.3] Listen and check.

3 a Work in pairs. Write the dialogue between Andrew and Marina using some of the phrases below in the Present perfect simple or continuous.

You (try) to phone me ?	Please listen to me …
(Not listen) your messages?	What (do) all day?
Where (be) you all day?	I (feel) … all day.
I never want to …	I (be) really busy, honestly.
I (think) about you …	

b Act out your dialogue to the class. Which did you like best? Were there many differences in what was said?

Pronunciation

1 a [T5.4] Listen to these lines from the dialogue. Does Jane's voice go up or down at the end?

You've been crying again, haven't you?
So you've forgotten about him already, have you?

b Do you think Jane is really asking, or does she already know the answer to her question?

2 a [T5.5] Listen and write down eight more sentences with question tags. Then listen again and mark them ↑ or ↓.

b Practise saying the sentences, copying the voices on the recording.

Wordspot

first

1 Use a word or phrase with *first* from the box to complete the sentences below. Check the meaning of any new phrases with *first*.

first-class	first thing	on first name terms	in first place
in first gear	first aid	at first sight	first-choice
first language	at first	first impressions	first of all

a   So you've never been to Russia before. Tell me, what are your _____ ?

b   _____ I felt a little bit nervous, but once I got started it was OK.

c   Carl is very well-connected with all the important people – he claims to be _____ with the Prime Minister!

d   It's very difficult to attract really _____ teachers on the low salaries we offer.

e   At least one member of staff should be trained in _____ in case there's an accident at work.

f   As soon as I met Andrea, I knew we'd marry one day: it was a case of love _____ .

g   Good evening, everybody. Professor King will be answering your questions in a moment, but _____ let me introduce myself.

h   I'll e-mail the details through before I leave work tonight, so we can discuss them _____ in the morning.

i   And as the runners come to the finishing line, it's still Kamouchi who is _____ .

j   It's a good idea to choose an alternative holiday, in case your _____ resort is not available.

k   We spent hours stuck in the traffic jam driving _____ .

l   Of the island's population, about twenty percent have Spanish as their _____ .

2 Put the phrases with *first* from exercise 1 in the correct place on the diagram.

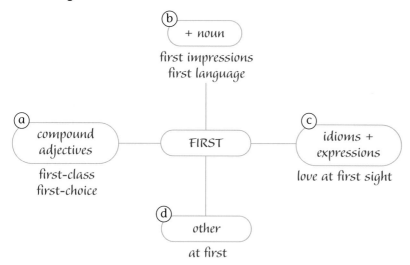

(b) + noun

first impressions
first language

(a) compound adjectives

first-class
first-choice

FIRST

(c) idioms + expressions

love at first sight

(d) other

at first

3 Study the words and phrases for a few minutes, remembering as many of them as you can. Then look at the questions on page 142. Answer them using a phrase with *first*.

STUDY...

Improving your accuracy when speaking

1 Everyone can improve their accuracy when speaking. This list of tips may help you.

- Ask your teacher to correct important mistakes while you are speaking.

- Ask your teacher to note important mistakes, and correct them after you've spoken.

- Record your voice. Then listen and try to identify your mistakes.

- Say a phrase in English as well as you can and ask your teacher for the correct version; or ask your teacher to help translate a phrase from your own language.

- Use phrases like 'Is it correct to say …?' or 'Can I say …?' before (or after) phrases you are not sure about to get feedback from your teacher.

- Listen to as much spoken English as you can, either talking to English speakers or listening to the radio, CDs, TV, etc. Make a note of any new or unfamiliar phrases you hear.

- Try to 'think in English' as much as you can and not always translate things from your own language when you're speaking.

- Spend a few moments thinking about how you are going to say things before you say them.

2 Which of these tips do you already do? Which do you think are most helpful for improving your speaking? Choose three or four techniques you would like to try. Can you add any extra ideas of your own?

PRACTISE...

1 Perfect tenses ☐

Look at the sentences below. Are the statements True (T), False (F) or Not Sure (NS)?

a *My grandparents lived in this house for fifty years.*
- They live in the house now. ___
- They don't live in the house now. ___
- They used to live in the house. ___

b *They've lived in France for nearly two years.*
- They live in France now. ___
- They used to live in France. ___
- They moved to France two years ago. ___

c *Dave had had his dinner when Sally and I arrived home.*
- Dave finished eating before we arrived home. ___
- Dave was eating when we arrived home. ___
- We arrived after Dave's dinner. ___

d *We'll have raised more than €100,000 by the end of January.*
- We haven't raised €100,000 yet. ___
- We'll have €100,000 before February. ___
- We've already raised €100,000. ___

▶ **Need to check? Language summary A, page 148.**

2 Present perfect simple and continuous ☐

Which of the sentences below describes:

a an action which lasts only for a moment? ___
b a state? ___
c a longer action? ___
d the number of times something has happened? ___
e an action which is repeated? ___
f an action which is not necessarily finished? ___
g a question about the results of an activity? ___
h a question about an activity? ___

1 Kate has been doing her homework.
2 I've seen this movie hundreds of times.
3 They've been waiting outside for several hours.
4 You've broken the window!
5 I've been trying to contact you all morning.
6 What have you been doing up there?
7 Have you fixed the printer?
8 I've always liked water polo.

▶ **Need to check? Language summary B, page 148.**

3 Time words ☐

Choose the correct alternative.

a We've interviewed ten people since / over the last week.
b They left about half an hour ago / before we arrived.
c By / Since then, he will have finished the report.
d By the time / Then she was eighteen she had won a major tournament.

▶ **Need to check? Language focus 1, page 55.**

4 Verb–noun combinations ☐

Write two things you can:

a win _____
b raise _____
c set _____
d make _____
e cope with _____

▶ **Need to check? Vocabulary, page 56.**

5 Phrases with *first* ☐

Cross out the words and phrases that do not go with *first*.

aid assistance ceiling choice choose class expressions floor gear impressions language of all speed thing in the morning tongue type

▶ **Need to check? Wordspot, page 60.**

Pronunciation spot

Diphthongs (1): /eɪ/, /əʊ/, /aɪ/ and /aʊ/

a **T5.6** Listen to the pronunciation of the words. Notice the different sounds of the letters in bold.
bay /eɪ/   boat /əʊ/   bite /aɪ/   bow (v) /aʊ/

b Circle the words where the:

1 'a' is pronounced as in *bay*: actress / danger / face / made / talented
2 'o' is pronounced as in *boat*: cope / host / model / moving / won
3 'i' is pronounced as in *bite*: fingers / life / rivals / tribute / while
4 'ow' is pronounced as in *bow*: below / however / known / now / show

c **T5.7** Listen and check. Then practise saying all the words, paying attention to the diphthongs.

REMEMBER!

Look back at the areas you have practised. Tick the ones you feel confident about. Now try the MINI-CHECK on page 159 to check what you know!

Getting it right

- ▶ Use and non-use of articles
- ▶ Different ways of giving emphasis
- ▶ Reading and vocabulary: *Worst case scenarios*
- ▶ Task: Make a list of tips on *How to …*
- ▶ Pronunciation: Stress for emphasis, Intonation for giving advice
- ▶ Listening and writing: Taking notes
- ▶ Real life: Giving advice and making suggestions

Reading and vocabulary

1 Look at the titles of the four texts and answer the questions.

a Which text do you think the items in the box relate to?
b Do you think they are useful or dangerous in that situation?

chimneys and fireplaces	a bandage	open fields
a piece of rope or string	a desk or table	isolated trees
stiff pieces of cardboard	a piece of clothing	a metal fence
the sound of thunder		

2 Do you know what to do in these circumstances? In groups, make a list of ideas, but do not read the articles yet.

3 Read and check. Which ideas on your list were correct? Were you surprised by any of the advice?

4 Use the context to guess the meaning of these words.

a a wound (line 2)   d to antagonise (line 41)   f to distract (line 48)
b a splint (line 8)   e to outrun (line 46)   g a threat (line 69)
c debris (line 32)

5 Discuss the following questions in pairs.

a Why shouldn't the splint on a broken leg be too tight?
b Why do you think the kitchen is a dangerous place in an earthquake?
c Why are hallways and inside walls safer, do you think?
d Why is it helpful to count the time between lightning and thunder?
e Why do you think you should kneel rather than lie flat on the ground to avoid lightning?

6 Discuss the following questions with the rest of the class.

- Have you, or anyone you know, ever experienced these or similar dangers? What happened?
- Do you ever worry about 'worst case scenarios' like this? Which of the situations would you find most frightening?
- What kind of disasters most frighten you? Why?

Worst case scenarios

How good are you at coping in an emergency? Would you know what to do if the worst happened? Read what the experts have to say, and never be caught out again!

How to treat a broken leg

If the skin is broken, do not touch or put anything on the wound. You must avoid infection. If the wound is bleeding severely, try to stop the flow of blood by
5 applying steady pressure to the area with sterile bandages or clean clothes.
Do not move the injured leg. You need to put a splint around the wound to stabilise the injured area.
10 **Find two stiff objects of the same length, wood, plastic or folded cardboard, for the splints.** Put the splints above and below the injured area (or on the side if moving the leg is too painful).
15 Tie the splints with string, rope or belts, whatever is available. Do not tie the splints too tightly: this may cut off circulation. You should be able to slip a finger under the rope or fabric.
20 **Get the injured person to lie flat on their back.** Do not move the injured person unless absolutely necessary. Treat the leg, then go and get help.

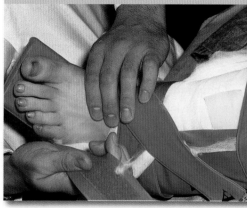

Adapted from the *Worst case scenario handbook.*

How to survive an earthquake

If you are indoors, stay there! Get under a desk or
table and hang onto it, or move into a doorway. The
next best place is in a hallway or against an inside
wall. Stay clear of windows, fireplaces and heavy
furniture or appliances. Get out of the kitchen, which is
a dangerous place. Do not run downstairs or rush
outside while the building is shaking, or while there is
any danger of falling and hurting yourself or being hit
by falling glass or debris.

If you are outside, get into the open away from
buildings, power lines, chimneys and anything else
that might fall on you.

If you are driving, stop, but carefully. Move your
car as far out of the traffic as possible. Do not stop on
or under a bridge, or under trees, light posts, power
lines or road signs. Stay inside your car until the
shaking stops.

How to deal with a charging bull

Do not antagonise the bull and do not move. Bulls will
generally leave humans alone unless they become angry.
**Look around for a safe haven – an escape route,
cover or high ground.** Running away is not likely to help
you unless you find an open door or fence to jump as
bulls can easily outrun humans.

**If a safe haven is not available, remove your shirt, hat
or another item of clothing.** Use this to distract the bull. It
does not matter what colour the clothing is. Despite the
colours bullfighters traditionally use, bulls do not naturally
head for red – they react to and move towards
movement, not colour.

**If the bull charges, remain still and throw your shirt or
hat away from you.** The bull should head towards the
object you've thrown.

How to avoid being struck by lightning

**Loud or frequent thunder indicates that lightning is
approaching.** When you see lightning, count the number of
seconds until the thunder is heard. If the time delay between
seeing the flash (lightning) and hearing the boom (thunder) is less
than thirty seconds, seek a safe location immediately.

**No place is completely safe from lightning. However, some
places are more dangerous than others.** Avoid high places
and open fields. If in an open area, do not lie flat – kneel with your
hands on the ground and your head low. Avoid isolated trees,
picnic shelters, or any metal objects, such as metal fences. Avoid
bodies of water: oceans, lakes, swimming pools and rivers.

Wait for the storm to pass. The lightning threat generally reduces
with time after the last sound of thunder, but may persist for more
than thirty minutes. There can still be a threat even when it is sunny
or clear sky is visible.

Task: Make a list of tips on *How to ...*
Preparation: reading and listening

- How to learn a foreign language
- How to be successful in exams
- How to stay fit
- How to dress well
- How to manage your personal finances
- How to give up smoking
- How to travel on a low budget
- How to find the perfect partner
- How to learn to play a musical instrument

a Read what some experts said. Can you guess which words or phrases go in the gaps? Match the advice below to the topics above.

1
'Take every (a) _____ to use the language ... speaking to foreigners in chat rooms, whatever and try to (b) _____ the temptation to translate everything word for word. Sometimes it just isn't possible!'
Silvia, language teacher

2
'(c) _____ never wear something just because everyone else is wearing it. (d) _____ , wear what you feel comfortable wearing and what looks good on you. Fashion is about expressing your own identity.'
Amanda, fashion journalist

3
'Be (e) _____ not to overdo it. You (f) _____ easily injure yourself (g) _____ not used to taking exercise.'
Brian, personal trainer

4
'Of course you should make an (h) _____ be friendly, but at the same time (i) _____ you don't appear too keen or over-friendly as this can put people off.'
Liza, relationships expert

5
'(j) _____ by finding the right teacher. It must be someone you like and trust, and who will give you good advice and encouragement ... and above all, allow plenty (k) _____ for practice. Playing well requires time and dedication. There are no short cuts.'
Vladimir, piano teacher

b T6.1 Listen and check. Do you think the advice given is good or not?

Task: speaking

1 a Work in pairs or groups. Agree on a topic from the list in the preparation section, or choose your own topic.

b Make a list of at least five dos and don'ts for the topic you have chosen. Ask your teacher for any words or phrases you need.

▶ Useful language

2 Form new groups with students who have worked on other topics. Tell them about your list of tips, and find out if the others can add any ideas to your list. Do they disagree with any of your suggestions?

3 Which were the best pieces of advice on each topic? Then compare answers with the rest of the class.

Useful language

Dos

Always remember …

Start by -*ing*

Take every opportunity to …

Don'ts

Resist the temptation to …

Avoid …

Both

Make sure you (don't) …

It's important (not) to …

You should (never) …

You might … if you don't …

Be careful (not) to …

Language focus 1
Use and non-use of articles

1 Do you ever chew gum? Does it help you in any way? Why do you think that some people object to people chewing gum?

2 Read the text below and choose the best title.

1 Concentrate better – chew gum
2 Chewing gum can aid memory
3 Three good reasons for chewing gum

A Teachers have always tried to ban it, but a new study has revealed that people can actually benefit from chewing gum: the author of the study, Dr Andrew Scholey, claims that there is a link between chewing and memory. The link may be connected with the production of oxygen in the brain.

B For (a) a / the / – study, (b) a / the / – volunteers at (c) a / the / – Northumbria University performed (d) a / the / – number of tests designed to test their memory and (e) a / the / – concentration. (f) A / The / – first group were allowed to chew (g) a / the / – gum: (h) a / the / – second only pretended to chew, while (i) a / the / – third did not chew at all. There was no difference between (j) a / the / – three groups in terms of (k) a / the / – concentration part of (l) a / the / – test, but in (m) a / the / – memory tests, there was (n) a / the / – big difference: (o) a / the / – group who had been allowed to chew performed thirty-five percent better than (p) a / the / – other groups.

3 Read Part A again and underline the following.

– all the indefinite articles *(a, an)* like this _____
– all the definite articles *(the)* like this ....
– all the nouns which do not have an article like this 〰〰

Analysis 1

1 Find an example in Part A of the following.
 a the indefinite article for something that is 'one of many'
 b the definite article for something or someone that has been mentioned before
 c the definite article for something or someone that is unique
 d the 'zero' article for talking about things 'in general'

2 Notice some common phrases that take the definite or indefinite article. Add two more examples to each group.
 a Phrases that express quantity: *a lot of, a few*
 b Ordinals: *the first, the second*
 c Superlatives: *the biggest, the worst*
 d Before certain common adjectives: *the last, the same*

▶ Read Language summary A on page 149.

Practice

1 Read Part B of the text again and circle the correct alternative. (– means no word.)

2 Look at the general knowledge quiz on page 67 and complete the gaps with *a, an, the* or –. Then answer as many of the questions as you can.

3 `T6.2` Listen to the questions and the answers. How many questions and answers did you get right?

Analysis 2

Use of definite article with places and times
Which of the following need a definite article? Find examples in the quiz. Are there any exceptions to these rules in the quiz?

Places: cities, countries, continents, rivers, lakes, points of the compass, seas and oceans, mountain ranges, world, institutions (e.g. prison, school)

Times: dates, days, parts of days, months, years, decades

▶ Read Language summary A3 on page 149.

4 a Work in two teams. Team A: Look at page 139. Team B: Look at page 141. Complete the questions with the correct articles. Then write three more similar questions of your own.

b Take turns to ask and answer the questions. Your teacher will give you two marks for the correct use of articles in the question and two marks for each correct answer. Which team won?

General knowledge quiz

1 When do ____ Chinese people celebrate New Year?

  a around ____ end of ____ January

  b in ____ summer

  c on ____ 1st of ____ January

2 When is it common for people in some countries to have ____ siesta?

  a in ____ morning   **b** in ____ afternoon

  c around eleven o'clock at ____ night

3 Newcastle is ____ city in which part of ____ UK?

  a in ____ north-east of ____ England

  b in ____ Scotland

  c on ____ south coast of ____ England

Greetings from Newcastle

4 Which is ____ largest sea or ocean in ____ world?

  a ____ Atlantic Ocean   **b** ____ Pacific Ocean

  c ____ Red Sea

5 Jeanne Louise Calment, who died on ____ 4th of ____ August 1997, is famous for being:

  a ____ world's oldest woman

  b ____ tallest woman in ____ world

  c ____ President of ____ France

6 If you went for a boat trip on ____ River Vltava, and went climbing in ____ Sumava Mountains and went sightseeing in ____ Prague which country would you be in?

  a ____ Czech Republic   **b** ____ Russia

  c ____ Slovakia

7 Where will ____ next Summer Olympic Games be held?

  a in ____ China   **b** in ____ USA

  c in ____ Sydney

8 ____ Lake Titicaca is:

  a ____ largest lake in ____ Africa

  b ____ largest lake in ____ South America

  c ____ largest lake in ____ world

9 Austrian Reinhold Messner is famous as:

  a ____ pop singer

  b ____ first man to climb ____ Mount Everest without ____ oxygen

  c ____ youngest-ever Prime Minister of ____ European country

10 When was ____ former President of ____ South Africa, Nelson Mandela, released from ____ prison?

  a in ____ 1980s   **b** at ____ end of 1995

  c in ____ 1990

Language focus 2
Different ways of giving emphasis

1 Do you often lose things? What? What about the people you live with? Read the conversation between Hannah and Dan. What has Hannah lost?

HANNAH: Oh, this is ∧annoying. Where ∧did I put my car keys?

DAN: Not again! Have you looked on the kitchen table?

HANNAH: I've looked everywhere.

DAN: Hannah, you∧'re hopeless.

HANNAH: Thank you. I suppose it's too much trouble for you to help look for them. Oh, look, here they are under this magazine.

DAN: Well, that just goes to show! ∧you need ∧some kind of system for where you put things. You're always losing things, it'∧s ridiculous.

HANNAH: You've got∧a nerve! ∧You ∧lost all your credit cards the other day, and∧I found them for you!

DAN: Yes, I know, and I'm∧grateful to you, but you ∧need to get yourself organised with keys.

2 **T6.3** Listen and write in the missing words in the conversation. Does the conversation make sense without these words? What effect do these words have?

Analysis

The extra words give special emphasis to what the speaker is saying. Answer these questions.
a Which three words go before an adjective to make it stronger? Do you know any other words like this?
b What is the difference between *so* and *such*?
c Find an example of an 'extra' auxiliary verb to add emphasis. What happens to the sentence stress with auxiliaries like this?
d Find two more examples similar to this.
   It was you who lost all your credit cards the other day.
e Which words can be added to a question word to make it more emphatic?

▶ Read Language summary B on pages 149 and 150.

Practice

1 Match the sentences in A with a reply in B. Then think of a way to make the phrases in bold more emphatic.

A
a **I'm exhausted.** Let's stay in and rent a video.
b **I like living here** because **it's near** the centre of town.
c Thanks for everything, we've had **a nice evening**.
d I suppose you want to see Liz.
e **Why are we** inside on such a beautiful day?
f Ouch! This tooth is **painful**.
g What's all this broken glass! **What have you been doing?**
h Your friend **was lovely. I hope** you'll invite him again.
i Come on, let's go to that new club.
j **I think** you ought to apologise to her.

B
1 Yes, I will. I think **he enjoyed** the evening as well.
2 Well, **you wanted to** spend the day at a museum.
3 **Why** should I apologise? **I didn't start** the trouble.
4 You're welcome. Come again soon!
5 You know **you need** to go to the dentist's.
6 Look, **I think** it's time we went home. It's nearly three.
7 Oh, **you're boring** these days. I want to go out.
8 That's true, but it gets **noisy** at night.
9 No, actually **I wanted to see you**.
10 Don't blame me! **I didn't break** it!

2 **T6.4** Listen and compare your answers with the recording.

Pronunciation

1 Sentence stress is also important for giving emphasis.

   I'm *absolutely* exhausted. Let's stay in and rent a video.

   You're *so* boring. I want to go out.

2 Listen again and mark the words that are specially stressed on the tapescript on page 167.

Listening and writing
Taking notes

1 Discuss the following questions in small groups.

- In what situations do you have to take notes?
- Do you write a lot of notes or just a few key points?
- What do you do with your notes afterwards?

2 Have you heard of Maria Montessori? Read about her below.

Maria Montessori was a famous Italian educator of the early 20th century, who pioneered the Montessori method of teaching children.

3 **a** Read the notes a student made during a lecture about Montessori. Find examples of these things and mark them with the appropriate letter.

B = bullet point X = asterisk
H = highlighting Ab = abbreviation
MH = Main heading SH = sub-heading
U = underlining Q = Quotation mark
Br = Brackets S = symbol

> # MARIA MONTESSORI:
> ## BIOGRAPHICAL NOTES
>
> 'Among greatest educators of C20th'
> • pioneer of education for < 12s
> • founder of Montessori schools
> * 'Follow the child'
>
> ### Early Life
> b. Ancona (Italy) 1870. Middle-class family.
> Studied medicine @ Rome Uni.
> First woman graduate of medicine (1896).
> contact w/ children of poor families when working as physician
>
> ### Development of Montessori schools
> Founded first school (at request of govt.) 1907.
> From 1910, worked only in children's education
> First Montessori schools opened in USA 1911
> Wrote > 20 books on educ. theory & practice.
> Developed Montessori method

b Why are these techniques used? Do you know any other useful techniques for making notes?

4 **T6.5** Listen to the next part of the lecture and make notes of your own. You may need to listen more than once.

b Check that your notes are clear, then swap with a partner. Can you follow each other's notes? Did either of you miss anything?

5 Discuss the following questions in small groups.

- Why do you think Maria Montessori is considered such an important figure in education?
- Have her ideas influenced the way children are educated in your country, do you think?

Real life
Giving advice and making suggestions

1 This posting appeared in a discussion forum called
englishadventure.com, which gives advice to people who want to
work or study in English-speaking countries.

a What does Stefan want advice about?
b Which countries are suggested in the five replies?
c What reasons are given for recommending each country?

Q

I'm thinking of spending some time abroad to improve my English ... but
how can I choose the best country to study in! There are so many! USA?
Britain? Australia? New Zealand? Other? Suggestions anyone?
Stefan

A

Take my advice – go to Australia. Australia is a great place to study – Sydney
is a truly international city and there are plenty of foreign students there.
Or you could always try New Zealand – the countryside is really beautiful.
Huan

Have you thought of coming here to Malta? It's quiet, the weather is good,
the people are friendly and everyone speaks English! Check out our
website at www.englishinmalta.com.
Luigi

I have just returned from a three-week English course in England. It was a
very good experience – the people were friendly, and the food was good
when you got used to it! The most important thing is to pick the right
school – there's a list of recommended schools at uklangschools.com. I'd
check there if I were you.
Joan, Barcelona

If you ask me, you can't beat the USA for an ESL programme. Try logging
on to the *Study in the USA* website at studyusa.com ... I promise you
won't regret it!
Murray

How about coming to Ireland? The people are the friendliest in the world.
Ciaran

Pronunciation

T6.6 Listen to the pronunciation of the phrases for giving advice.
Practise saying them, copying the voices on the recording.

---

2 Imagine someone wrote a similar posting asking for advice about
work and study in your country. Write some advice and
suggestions about the best places to go, etc.

STUDY ...

Guessing from context

**1 Read the sentences giving
advice about worst case
scenarios. Are the words in
bold a noun, a verb, an adverb
or an adjective? Here are some
things that might help you.**

- Typical endings for verbs (*-ed,
  -ing,*) nouns (*-ion, -ness*),
  adjectives (*-ous*) or adverbs (*-ly*)

- Words which come before nouns
  (*a, the, adjectives*) or verbs
  (auxiliary or modal verbs, e.g.
  be, have, may, should, etc.)

- Plural nouns ending in 's'

a You can never be sure what'll
  happen in life: something
  horrible could be **lurking** just
  around the corner.

b If a female bear fears that her
  cubs are in danger, she may
  attack.

c In order to move a car out of
  your way, you should **clip** the
  back of it ...

d Immediately wrap a bandage
  tightly around the snake bite ...

e If you found yourself in the
  wilderness without any
  matches or shelter, would you
  know how to protect yourself?

f Although it can be difficult to
  build a shelter in such **harsh**
  conditions.

**2 Try to decide what the words
in bold mean. Think of a word
that could replace it in that
sentence. Then check in your
mini-dictionary. Remember to
look for the infinitive form of
verbs ending in *-ing* or *-ed*, etc.**

PRACTISE...

1 Articles ☐

Add _a_ or _the_ to the sentences, where necessary.

a My brother works as travel representative in Canada.

b President of USA has resigned!

c Sahara is largest desert in Africa.

d He was last person to see victim alive.

e I'll see you next week.

f Weather is better in south of country.

g I live near hospital.

h He'll be here in morning.

▶ **Need to check? Language summary A, page 149.**

2 Ways of giving emphasis ☐

Choose the correct alternative.

a That TV programme was absolutely / completely / so funny. What a pity you missed it.

b I know you don't believe me, but I really / did / have try to phone you.

c That / What / Which I really enjoyed about the film was the acting.

d He / It / That 's my son who's the expert on computers in our house.

e What at / in / on earth do you mean by asking me that?

f It was so / such / very an uncomfortable journey we couldn't sleep at all.

▶ **Need to check? Language summary B, page 149.**

3 Verb forms ☐

Write the correct form of the verbs in brackets.

a Resist the temptation _____ (translate) everything.

b You should never _____ (wear) something because everyone else is wearing it.

c Be careful _____ (overdo) it.

d Start by _____ (find) the right teacher.

e Make sure you _____ (appear) too keen or over-friendly.

f You might easily _____ (injure) yourself if you're not used _____ (take) exercise.

▶ **Need to check? Task, page 64.**

4 Phrases for _How to ..._ ☐

Match A and B to make phrases.

A	B
a lie	1 anything on the wound
b do not move	2 downstairs
c go and get	3 flat on the ground
d do not run	4 help
e stay clear of	5 the injured person
f do not touch or put	6 areas of water such as swimming pools

▶ **Need to check? Reading, pages 62–63.**

5 Giving advice and making suggestions ☐

A word or phrase in the sentences is incorrect. Correct the mistake.

a Take my advise – go to Australia.

b Or you should always try 'Marina's' restaurant.

c Have you thought of do a course in Philosophy?

d The more important thing is to choose the right hotel.

e I'd book it online if I would be you.

f When you ask me, the library is the best place to study.

g Try contact the tourist office for information.

h How about to come to Croatia for your holidays?

▶ **Need to check? Real life, page 70.**

Pronunciation spot

Voiced and unvoiced sounds (2): /s/, /z/ and /ʃ/

a [T6.7] Listen to the pronunciation of the words. Notice the different sounds of the letters in bold.

advi**c**e /s/   advi**s**e /z/   ca**sh** /ʃ/

The /z/ sound is **voiced**. The /s/ and /ʃ/ are **unvoiced**.

b [T6.8] Put the words in the correct category, according to the pronunciation of the letters in bold. Then listen and check.

choose   **c**itizen   di**sc**ipline   discu**ss**ion   down**s**tairs   experien**c**e   international   o**c**ean   ru**sh**   **s**tring   vi**s**ible   web**s**ite

c Practise saying the words, paying attention to the voiced and unvoiced sounds.

d How do you pronounce the letters in bold below? Now practise reading the text aloud.

Children should learn **th**rough purpo**s**eful activity – not ju**s**t play, but activitie**s** wi**th** a purpo**s**e ... given a **ch**oice, children will **ch**oose work rather **th**an play. Toys whi**ch** do not **s**erve a **s**pecific purpo**s**e are **th**erefore di**sc**ouraged.

REMEMBER!

Look back at the areas you have practised. Tick the ones you feel confident about. Now try the MINI-CHECK on page 159 to check what you know!

Big events

- ▶ Relative clauses
- ▶ Quantifiers
- ▶ **Vocabulary and speaking:** Events and celebrations, Extreme adjectives
- ▶ **Task:** Describe a memorable event
- ▶ **Pronunciation:** Reading aloud, sounding polite
- ▶ **Reading and vocabulary:** *Food festivals around the world*
- ▶ **Real life:** Awkward social situations
- ▶ **Wordspot:** *take*

Vocabulary and speaking
Events and celebrations

1 a What different events and celebrations can you see in the photos? Which would you most/least like to attend? Why?

b In which photos can you see the following things?

an audience clapping	a bride and groom
a carnival	people carrying placards
a huge crowd	people in fancy dress
people going wild	people in traditional dress
outdoor concert	people singing and chanting
spectators cheering	people waving flags and banners
a procession	a demonstration

2 Spend a few minutes studying the photos. Now ask and answer the questions on page 139 with your partner, but without looking at the photos. What can you remember?

3 Discuss the following questions in small groups.

- Do you have any carnivals in your country? What happens?
- Do you enjoy being in huge crowds or not? Why / Why not?
- If you are in a crowd with a lot of people singing or chanting, do you join in?

Vocabulary 2
Extreme adjectives

1 The word *huge* (as in 'huge crowd') means 'very large'. Match the extreme adjectives in A with their equivalents in B.

A		B	
a	huge	1	very angry
b	tiny	2	very large
c	terrifying	3	very noisy
d	deafening	4	very wet
e	freezing	5	very hungry
f	gorgeous	6	very funny
g	furious	7	very beautiful
h	soaked	8	very cold
i	terrible	9	very bad
j	hilarious	10	very tired
k	starving	11	very small
l	exhausted	12	very frightening

2 Which intensifiers (*very, quite, really, absolutely,* etc.) can you use before extreme adjectives?

3 Complete the gaps with an extreme adjective from exercise 1.

a The procession takes place at night in the middle of winter: wear warm clothes or you'll be absolutely _____ .

b The group were so far away, all we could see were some _____ figures in the far distance.

c It was a _____ moment when violence broke out between the police and the demonstrators.

d The crowd had been standing in the rain for hours and were absolutely _____ , but everyone remained good-humoured.

e The crowd were really _____ when the referee sent off the home team's captain.

f We were sitting right in the front row, so at times the noise of the group was absolutely _____ .

g The film was so _____ that many members of the audience walked out before the end.

h Pictures of the concert were projected onto a _____ video screen, so everyone could see perfectly.

i The march lasted for hours and after they'd been walking for such a long time everyone was _____ .

j The evening got off to a great start with a _____ speech by the principal: the whole audience was laughing.

k There were huge queues at the food stalls, so by the time we got to the front we were absolutely _____ .

l All her fans agreed that Lucinda looked absolutely _____ in her designer dress.

Task: Describe a memorable event

Preparation: listening

1 Work with a partner. Which of the following events have you both been to?

> a big football match
> a big concert
> a carnival or procession
> a demonstration
> a peace march
> a festival or national celebration
> an important religious celebration
> a performance by a famous singer or actor
> a special party
> a visit by an important leader or member of royalty
> a wedding
> another big sporting occasion
> another important event

2 **T7.1** Listen to four people describing a memorable event they attended and answer as many of these questions as you can for each person.

a   What was the event?
b   Where and when did it take place?
c   Which other people are mentioned?
d   What was the atmosphere like?

3 **a** Look at the sentences from the recordings in exercise 2. Which event is each sentence about?

1   The bodies were being passed along by the other people in the audience. *concert*
2   We had to … throw rose petals into the sea.
3   I must have been one of about a million people.
4   There were loads and loads of people all over the place.
5   I had to wear only white and gold clothes.
6   They had this choir with five hundred voices.
7   I found myself crying at some points and laughing at other points.
8   It was utterly spectacular.
9   In some way it was really, really magical.
10 It was one of the most moving events I've ever been to.
11 People from the audience were … just diving off the stage.
12 They just closed off streets and they had street fairs and parties.
13 The atmosphere was so positive.
14 The city just completely came alive.

b Look at the tapescript on page 167 and check.

Task: speaking

1 a You are going to interview each other about a memorable event you have attended. Choose one or more from the list on page 74.

b Spend a few minutes deciding what to say. Ask your teacher for any words or phrases you need.

▶ Useful language a

2 Work in pairs. Take turns to interview each other, using the questions in exercise 2 on page 74 to help you think of questions.

▶ Useful language b

3 Summarise briefly to the class the event your partner told you about.

4 Which events described would you like to have attended yourself? Why?

Useful language

a Describing the event

What I liked most about it was …

It was the most … I've ever …

On the whole, it was extremely impressive / good fun.

It was rather disappointing.

It went on a bit too long.

It was absolutely huge/ fascinating/exhausting, etc!

Looking back, what I remember best was …

b Asking about the event

Who/How many people were there with you?

How did you feel when …?

What impression did you get of …?

What was the highlight of the day for you?

Was it how you'd expected?

Language focus 1
Relative clauses

1 Have you heard of the celebrations in the texts? What do you know about them?

2 a Complete the texts with the phrases in the box.

> when children
> when Japanese families
> where the day
> which their children have lovingly prepared
> which became known
> who have died
> which used to be
> which are made into
> who lived away from
> that has special meaning

b **T7.2** Listen and check.

Children's Day

A national holiday in Japan since 1948, Children's Day on May 5th, (1) _____ known as 'Boys' Day', is the day (2) _____ wish their children happiness, good health and success. In Korea, (3) _____ has only been a holiday since 1975, there are parades, special excursions and visits to movies and museums.

Mother's Day

In seventeenth-century England, young servants (4) _____ their families were allowed to visit their mothers on a day (5) _____ as 'Mothering Sunday'. Nowadays it's the day (6) _____ of all ages treat their mum to something special: it's one of the busiest days of the year for florists and restaurants, and millions of mums enjoy a special breakfast in bed, (7) _____ .

Day of the Dead

One day (8) _____ in Mexico is November 2nd, which, according to legend, is the 'Day of the Dead'. Families gather to remember relatives (9) _____ and have a special picnic by their gravesides, with unusual foods including chocolate and sweets, (10)_____ a variety of animal or skull shapes.

Analysis

Revision

1 The information in the gaps in the texts on page 76 is given by using relative clauses. Underline the relative pronoun in each phrase. Which relative pronoun(s) are used to refer to people, places, things, times and dates?

2 In which of the two sentences below can the relative pronoun be omitted? Why?
This is the outfit that I'm going to wear.
That's the man who took the photographs.

Defining and non-defining relative clauses
a In which sentence below is the relative clause necessary to understand the sentence? (This is a defining relative clause.)
*Tanya Robson is the actress **who** won the Oscar for best actress.*
*Tanya Robson **who** won an Oscar for best actress is coming to the première.*

b Which sentence gives 'extra' information in the sentence? (This is a non-defining relative clause.)

c Which one needs commas in it? Write them in the correct position.

▶ Read Language summaries A and B on page 150.

Practice

1 a Complete the sentences with a relative pronoun, only if necessary. Then write your answers in random order on a piece of paper.

1 The name of a country _____ you'd really like to visit.
2 The name of someone _____ you haven't seen for several years.
3 The month _____ you usually go on holiday.
4 The name of someone _____ looked after you when you were young.
5 Something _____ you never leave home without.
6 The name of someone _____ music you particularly enjoy.
7 The name of someone _____ music you can't stand.
8 The name of a place _____ you always feel relaxed.
9 A month _____ you celebrate something important (for example, a birthday).
10 Something _____ you often forget.

b Show your answers to a partner. Take turns to ask questions about the answers on the piece of paper. Answer using a relative clause.

> Why did you write 'Thailand'?

> It's a country (that) I'd really like to visit.

> Who is Jean Rochefort?

> He's an actor who is famous in my country.

2 Combine the sentences using a non-defining relative clause. Start with the words in bold.

a **The Cannes film festival** takes place in May every year. It attracts the biggest names in the film industry.
The Cannes film festival, which takes place in May every year, attracts the biggest names in the film industry.

b **Steve Redgrave** has won medals at five Olympic Games. He is one of Britain's best-known sportsmen.

c **The Winter Olympics** are held every four years. They normally take place in January or February.

d **Madonna** has been an international star for over twenty years. She had her first hit single in 1984.

e Pamplona is a city in northern Spain. **The annual bull-running festival** takes place there.

f **Cuban singer Compay Segundo** made his first recording in the 1930s and found fame in the 1990s with Latin group *The Buena Vista Social Club*.

g During the festival of Ramadan **eating and drinking are forbidden during the day**. It takes place in the ninth month of the Muslim calendar.

h **The Maracaña Stadium** is in Rio de Janeiro. It has a capacity of 205,000 people.

Pronunciation

1 **T7.3** Commas tell us when to pause when we are reading aloud. The intonation ⤴ tells the listener that the sentence has not yet finished.

The Cannes film festival, // which takes place in May every year, // attracts the biggest names in the film industry.

It's the day when Japanese families wish their children happiness, // good health and success.

2 **T7.4** Listen to the first five sentences in exercise 2. Practise saying the sentences, paying attention to the pauses and intonation.

Reading and vocabulary

1 a You are going to read about four unusual festivals involving food. Look at the photos and the titles. Use your mini-dictionary, if necessary.

1 Which food does each festival centre around?
2 Can you guess what happens?

b Scan the texts quickly. Where and when does each festival take place?

2 a Check the words in bold in your mini-dictionary. Discuss in pairs which festival you think these customs are associated with.

1 There is a fifty metre **course**, strictly divided into **lanes**.
2 There are official 'fight-starters'.
3 They use **wooden replicas** of the food rather than the real thing.
4 People eat vegetables covered in chocolate.
5 You can find **intricate carvings**.
6 10,000 people attend, from all over the world.
7 People jump in the river at the end of it.
8 You can find religious and **mythical images**.

b Read and check. What other customs and facts did you learn about each festival?

3 Can you guess the meaning of these words and phrases from the context? Choose the correct definition.

a **humble** (line 5) rare and expensive / simple
b **inaugurated** (line 17) banned / started
c **pungent** (line 21) strong-tasting or smelling / sweet
d **bizarre** (line 24) beautiful and elegant / strange and funny
e **make your head spin** (line 37) make you dizzy / make you tired
f **sample** (line 40) taste / smell
g **isn't for you** (line 46) doesn't belong to you / isn't suitable for you
h **squishy** (line 51) full of liquid / hard
i **get things going** (line 52) start things off / try to stop trouble
j **hurled** (line 54) given away / thrown

4 Discuss the following questions in small groups.

*   Which of these festivals would you like to go to? Which would you avoid? Why?
*   Which festivals and celebrations in your country traditionally involve food? Are any special dishes cooked?
*   Which foods/dishes from your country would you most recommend to a foreign visitor?

Oaxaca Radish Festival

Religious scenes, historical events, mythical tales … all are common subjects for art in many countries around the world. But carved from radishes? Only in Oaxaca, Mexico, and only on the night of December 23rd. For
5 the city's annual Night of the Radishes, the humble plants are transformed into saints, animals and even revolutionary heroes and any resemblance to the vegetable you might see on your dinner table has completely vanished. While the origins of this unique
10 festival are unclear, it is known that in the 19th century, Christmas Eve markets sold salt-dried fish and vegetables after midnight mass. To distinguish one stall from another, vendors carved tiny radish figures, decorating them with turnips, onions, lettuce and
15 flowers. Housewives sought out the most interesting for their Christmas tables. In 1897, the mayor of Oaxaca inaugurated the first exhibition of radish art and the rest is history.

Food festivals around the world

Stilton Cheese Rolling

May Day is a traditional day for celebrations, but the 2,000 residents of the English village of Stilton – famous for its pungent blue cheese – must be the only people in the world who include cheese rolling in their annual plans. Teams of four, dressed in a variety of bizarre costumes, roll a complete cheese along a 50-metre course. On the way, they must not kick or throw their cheese, or go into their opponents' lane. Competition is intense and the chief prize is a complete Stilton cheese weighing about four kilos (disappointingly, but understandably the cheeses used in the race are wooden replicas). All the competitors are served with beer or port wine, the traditional accompaniment for Stilton cheese.

Fiery Foods Festival – The Hottest Festival on Earth

Every year more than 10,000 people head for the city of Albuquerque, New Mexico. They come from as far away as Australia, 35 the Caribbean and China, but they all share a common addiction – food that is not just spicy, but hot enough to make your mouth burn, your head spin and your eyes water. Their destination is the Fiery Food and BBQ Festival (official slogan 'Proud Sponsor of Global Warming') which is held over a period of three days every March, 40 and is a chance to sample the world's hottest sauces, mustards and dips, and also to watch cookery demonstrations dedicated to all things hot and spicy. You might like to try a chocolate-covered habanero chilli pepper – officially the hottest chilli pepper in the world – or wasabi and apple sauce, or any one of the thousands of 45 products that are on display. But one thing's for sure – if you don't like the sensation of a burning tongue, this festival isn't for you!

La Tomatina – The World's Biggest Food Fight

On the last Wednesday of every August, the Spanish town of Buñol hosts La Tomatina – the world's largest food fight. A week-long celebration leads up to a monstrous tomato battle as the climax of 50 the week's events. Early in the morning sees the arrival of large trucks with their precious cargo of squishy tomatoes – official fight-starters get things going by pelting the crowd – who can be sure to retaliate.

The battle lasts little more than half an hour, in which time around 50,000 kilograms of tomatoes have been hurled at anyone or 55 anything that moves, runs, or fights back. Then everyone heads down to the river to make friends again – and for a much-needed wash!

Language focus 2
Quantifiers

T7.5 Read the 'Food facts' below. Which words and phrases from the box do you think go in the gaps? Listen to an expert's advice and complete the sentences.

any	a few	a great deal of
a lot of	a number of	plenty of
some	too many	too much
very little		

Food facts

- There is (1) _____ evidence that people who eat (2) _____ burgers can become ill.
- Although humans can't actually survive without (3) _____ salt, we actually need (4) _____ of it. (5) _____ salt can be extremely bad for you.
- Apples contain (6) _____ sugar so if you eat (7) _____ apples, it's a good idea to clean your teeth afterwards.
- There are (8) _____ varieties of mushroom which are poisonous, and (9) _____ which can actually kill you. There are (10) _____ deaths through eating poisonous mushrooms every year.

Analysis

1 **a** Underline the foods above. Which are countable nouns and which are uncountable?

   b Are the quantifiers in the box above used with countable nouns (C), uncountable nouns (U), or both (B)?

2 What is the difference in meaning between the pairs of sentences below?
   a He's bought **a lot of** vegetables.
      He's bought **too many** vegetables.
   b We've got **enough** milk.
      We've got **plenty of** milk.
   c We've only got **a few** left.
      We've got **quite a few** left.
   d I like **some** pasta dishes.
      I like **any** pasta dish.

▶ Read Language summary C on page 151.

Practice

1 Make twelve sentences that are true for you.

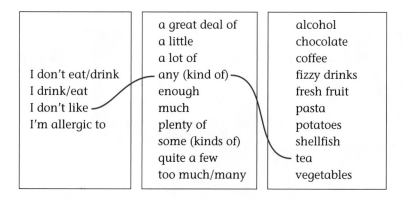

	a great deal of	alcohol
	a little	chocolate
	a lot of	coffee
I don't eat/drink	any (kind of)	fizzy drinks
I drink/eat	enough	fresh fruit
I don't like	much	pasta
I'm allergic to	plenty of	potatoes
	some (kinds of)	shellfish
	quite a few	tea
	too much/many	vegetables

2 Choose the best quantifier to complete the text. If both make sense, what is the difference in meaning?

The Lazy Cook's Survival Guide

- Always keep a supply of these things in your store cupboard: (a) some / any olive oil, (b) a few / plenty of anchovies, some olives, (c) too much / plenty of rice and pasta, lots of black pepper, (d) a few / too many tins of tomatoes, and a good-sized piece of cheese. This way you always have something for dinner.

- (e) Some / Any kinds of dishes (casseroles, soups, curries) improve with keeping, so it's a good idea to make enough for more than one meal.

- If you cook pasta, make sure you don't cook (f) too much / enough: there is nothing you can do with it the next day. On the other hand, cook more potatoes and rice than you need. There are (g) lots of / quite a few ways to use yesterday's potatoes and rice.

- Always check that you have (h) enough / plenty of coffee, tea, milk (or whatever your morning drink happens to be) before you go to bed – and while the shops are still open. That way you'll have (i) anything / something nice to wake up to.

- (j) Very few / Quite a few people can be bothered to cook a big meal every day. Remember you can live on just soup and bread, though this does get rather boring after a while.

3 Write a similar advice sheet about one of the topics below, using the quantifiers in exercise 1.

- What you need for the perfect picnic.
- What you need for the perfect party.
- What to put in a small suitcase for a perfect week's beach holiday.
- What you need in your rucksack for a perfect weekend's hiking.

Real life
Awkward social situations

1 In the pictures, Bella finds herself in some difficult social situations. Discuss what the problem is in each case. What would be a good way to respond?

Go on, have a bit more. I insist! Have the last piece, Bella!

Oh, no! I can't possibly eat any more!

Oh dear, how clumsy of me. I'm terribly sorry! Let me get a cloth.

Oh, no! My lovely new blouse! I don't believe it!

You know Vera, don't you, Bella?

Vera? Vera who? Oh, where do I know her from?

You must try some of this spinach salad, Bella. It's their speciality.

Yuck. I hate spinach. It makes me feel sick just thinking about it.

2 **T7.6** Listen to find out what Bella actually said. What do you think of the way she responded?

Pronunciation

T7.7 If you want to sound polite, your intonation is more important than the phrases you use. Listen to the polite phrases Bella uses again and copy Bella's intonation.

3 a Here are some similar situations. Work in pairs. Make dialogues of about five to six lines, using some of the phrases in the tapescript on page 168.

- two people meet, but one of them doesn't remember the other person's name or where they met
- someone spills something because they are nervous
- someone keeps on offering food to someone who isn't hungry
- someone recommends a dish which the other doesn't like
- someone refuses an invitation to a social event

b Act out some of your dialogues.

It's been lovely to see you again, Bella. You must come and spend a day with us some time, mustn't she, Mary? How about next weekend, for Sunday lunch?

A whole day with Uncle Geoff and Aunt Mary? Help!!

Wordspot
take

1 Complete the sentences with a phrase from the box. Use the correct form of *take*.

it takes	take after	take care of
take notes	take off	take part
take a photo of	take place	take a seat
take it seriously	take your time	take up

a   Excuse me, could you _____ us all with this camera?

b   Halloween _____ on 31st of October.

c   Fortunately, Carmen's father can _____ the baby while she's at work.

d   Would you mind _____ for a moment? I'll tell Mr Evans you're here.

e   Philip spends loads of money on tennis lessons. He really does _____ .

f   I wish I'd _____ during the lecture, because I can't remember anything now.

g   _____ roughly an hour to get from the airport, depending on traffic.

h   Everyone says Michael _____ his father, but I think he's more like his mother.

i   Thousands of people _____ in yesterday's demonstration.

j   It's getting hot in here – I think I'll _____ my jacket.

k   Jo was getting overweight, so she decided _____ jogging.

l   Don't worry, we're not in a hurry. You can _____ getting ready.

2 **a** **T7.8** Listen to twelve questions with *take* and write brief answers for yourself.

b How many of the questions can you remember from your answers? Check the tapescript on page 168.

c Work in pairs. Ask and answer the questions with your partner.

> Have you ever taken part in a concert?

> Yes, when I was at school. I sang in the junior choir at the end-of-year concert.

STUDY ...

Improving your reading speed

1 **If you want to study in English or read documents connected with your work, it's important to read quickly and efficiently. A good reading speed is about 150–200 words a minute. Here are some tips to help you read more efficiently.**

Do ...

- Read the first and last sentences of the paragraph carefully. They usually contain the most important information.

- Skip over words and phrases you don't know, or can't guess immediately. You can come back to them later.

- Try to summarise the three or four main points of what you have read after you have finished the text.

- Read as much as you can in English – newspapers, graded readers, websites ... anything! You won't improve your reading speed without practice!

Don't ...

- Say the words to yourself as you read – you should read much faster than you speak.

- Stop every time you find a word you don't know. You can do this later.

- Keep re-reading phrases you didn't understand completely. Try to get a general understanding of the whole text.

- Get distracted! Set yourself a time to read a text and don't stop until you've finished.

2 **Read the text on page 159 in 60 seconds. Try to use some of the techniques above.**

PRACTISE...

1 Relative pronouns ☐

Which phrases are incorrect? Correct them.

a a shop what sells second-hand computer games

b someone who looks after animals

c the woman we saw yesterday

d the couple who house is for sale

e someone who is good at languages

f the place which I was born

g the hotel which we're staying at

h the beach where he works at

▶ **Need to check? Language summary A, page 150.**

2 Relative clauses ☐

Put a word or phrase from the box in the correct place.

> , in which , which to whom , who on

a The fishing trade, which the whole town depends, has been badly affected by pollution.

b This house Dickens lived as a child, is now a museum.

c Our new computer system cost several thousand euros, is still not in operation.

d The receptionist was clearly in a bad mood, told us to wait outside.

e He is a man the whole nation will always be deeply grateful.

▶ **Need to check? Language summary B, page 150.**

3 Quantifiers ☐

Choose the phrase which is closest in meaning to the one in bold.

a **Several** people have applied for the job.

   hundreds / loads / more than a few

b There are **too many** people in the recording studio.

   dozens of / hundreds of / more than we need

c We have **very little** time before the bus leaves.

   enough / not much / plenty of

d This project has already cost us **a great deal of** money.

   a bit of / a lot of / not enough

e You can get a free map at **any** Tourist Office.

   all of them / none of them / some of them

▶ **Need to check? Language summary C, page 151.**

4 Awkward social situations ☐

Choose the correct alternative.

a I couldn't certainly / definitely / possibly / probably manage any more!

b It doesn't matter in the lightest / slightest / smallest / tiniest.

c How lovely see / seen / to be seen / to see you again!

d I'm afraid / frightened / scared / terrified I can't eat any more.

e I 'd / 'll / 'm / 've love to come to your party.

▶ **Need to check? Real life, page 81.**

5 Extreme adjectives ☐

Choose the correct definition.

a huge = very big / very small

b starving = extremely angry / extremely hungry

c terrible = very bad / very frightening

d hilarious = very frightening / very funny

e soaked = very tired / very wet

f gorgeous = very beautiful / very small

▶ **Need to check? Vocabulary 2, page 73.**

6 Phrases with *take* ☐

What phrase with *take* means the following:

a to happen

b to begin (a hobby)

c to look after

d to sit down

e to leave the ground

f to resemble

g not to hurry

h to participate

▶ **Need to check? Wordspot, page 82.**

Pronunciation spot

Different pronunciations of the letter 'e'

T7.9 Put the words in the box in the correct category, according to the pronunciation of the letters in bold. Then listen and check.

> cheese cookery demonstration enough
> festival flower vanished precious sensation
> three eccentric vegetable

- In stressed syllables, the letter 'e' is often pronounced /e/ as in Wednesday.
  Other examples: _____ _____

- In unstressed syllables, the letter can be:
1 pronounced as /e/ as in revolutionary.
   Other examples: _____ _____
2 pronounced /ə/ (schwa) as in celebration.
   Other examples: _____ _____
3 pronounced /ɪ/ as in event.
   Other examples: _____ _____
4 silent as in every.
   Other examples: _____ _____
5 double 'ee' is usually pronounced as a long /iː/ as in week.
   Other examples: _____ _____

REMEMBER!

Look back at the areas you have practised. Tick the ones you feel confident about. Now try the MINI-CHECK on page 159 to check what you know!

83

Fame and fortune

▶ Gerund or infinitive?
▶ Different infinitive and gerund forms
▶ **Reading and vocabulary:** *How to be a celebrity*
▶ **Vocabulary and speaking:** The road to fame
▶ **Song and writing:** *Do you know the way to San José?*
▶ **Task:** Summarise an article
▶ **Writing:** Linking ideas and arguments
▶ **Wordspot:** *big* and *great*

Reading and vocabulary

1 Discuss the following questions in small groups.

• Which famous people are in the news most in your country at the moment? What are they famous for?
• In which ways do people become famous? Make a list of ideas.

2 a Read the titles in the *How to be a celebrity* text. Are any of your ideas mentioned? Which other ways does the author mention?

b Can you guess how the people in the pictures are trying to become famous? Which pictures do the phrases below relate to?

| a daring stunt | someone drowning |
| an outrageous dress | a species of beetle |

3 Now read the text. How did these people become famous? Have you heard of any of them?

a Charles Blondin   d Ivana Trump
b Eric Moussambani   e Bill Gates
c John Kennedy Junior

4 According to the text, which of the ways of becoming famous ...
a cost the people involved a lot of money? 3
b makes ordinary people into stars?
c risked the person's life?
d led to TV appearances in lots of different countries?
e has not produced the result promised?
f may only make you famous for a short time?
g might make you unpopular?
h requires imagination and originality?
i requires very little talent or ability?
j was repeated several times?

Discuss and compare your answers in pairs.

1 Do something unusual

Celebrity is all about standing out from the crowd, so do something out of the ordinary and you'll grab your piece of fame. A daring stunt is a guaranteed crowd puller – the more dangerous the better. The legendary Charles Blondin started it all off 150 years ago when he strung a tightrope across the Niagara Falls, and in front of a crowd of 10,000 breathless spectators made his way across the waters from the Canadian to the American side. After his success, Blondin crossed the Falls many more times in a variety of ways: blindfolded, in chains, on a bicycle, and once, pushing a man in a wheelbarrow.

5 Find phrases in the text that mean the following.

a being different from everyone else (section 1) *standing out from the crowd*
b sure to attract a large audience (section 1)
c an unsuccessful person that everyone is fond of (section 2)
d attracted (section 2)
e an instant success (section 2)
f extremely quickly (section 5)
g increases by itself (section 6)
h become really famous (section 7)
i do something that others have already done (section 7)

6 Which of the methods of becoming famous most/least appeal to you? Why?

84

How to be a celebrity

There are many routes to fame - some are more challenging than others.

2 Be the worst

If a thing's worth doing, it's worth doing badly. People love a loser. Think of the ultimate lovable loser, Homer Simpson. The Olympics is the perfect place for failure and every games catapults one brave loser to stardom.

The winning loser of the Sydney Games was 'swimmer' Eric Moussambani (also known as Eric the Eel). Moussambani, representing Equatorial Guinea, finished his heat of the 100 metres freestyle in the slowest time ever recorded, and almost drowned in the attempt. But Moussambani captured the imagination of a global television audience and he became an overnight sensation, making guest appearances on TV shows around the world.

3 Buy your way to fame

Money can't buy you love, but it can buy you fame. In 2000, an Internet auction site gave ordinary people the chance to bid for a part in a movie. The winning bids ranged from $12,000 to $72,000 and included bids from a fire fighter, a florist, a psychic and an international model. They were given acting classes from top Hollywood teachers, and a script was written but no release date for the movie was ever set!

4 Discover something

The bad news is: there are no countries left to discover. The good news is: in the tropical rainforests of Brazil, there are an estimated three million unnamed species of beetle. One of them could be yours. Discover a deadly disease and give it your name. Though no one will enjoy hearing your name, you will be famous — at least until someone comes along and discovers a cure.

5 Appear on reality TV

There have never been more opportunities for 'regular' people to become celebrities. The growth of 'reality TV' shows like *Big Brother* and *Pop Idol* which star ordinary members of the public, mean that potentially anyone can become a star.

The good news about reality shows is that they bring you fame at the speed of light. The bad news is that they bring you obscurity just as fast. While the show is being aired, you're the biggest star in the galaxy, but once the publicity goes, real life is waiting round the corner.

6 Be famous for being famous

Becoming famous for being famous is relatively easy to achieve, but extremely difficult to sustain. First something is needed to bring you into the public eye. You could be the child of someone famous (John Kennedy Junior, Jade Jagger), marry somebody famous (Princess Diana, Ivana Trump) or just wear the most outrageous dress you can find (Liz Hurley). Once you have attention, you can get more. Your fame takes on a momentum of its own. The original reason for your celebrity is forgotten.

7 Create your own formula for success

If you want to make it really big, don't take any established, familiar path to celebrity and don't follow in anyone else's footprints. Create your own unique route.

Someone said that genius is the ability to invent one's own occupation. People like Oprah Winfrey, the Queen of Talk Shows, or Bill Gates, the Chairman of Microsoft have reshaped and redefined an occupation and even an industry in their own image. Their fame is assured.

Vocabulary and speaking
The road to fame

1 Discuss the following questions in small groups.

- Have you ever wanted to be famous? Why / Why not?
- Why do you think fame is so important for some people?

2 a The sentences below describe the rise and fall of a famous person. Put the sentences into a logical order, starting with sentence 1 as shown.

The movie was a huge **hit**, and he became **an overnight sensation**. ☐

Slowly but surely, his career **went into decline** and he rarely left his **huge mansion**. ☐

After several years of struggling to **make ends meet**, he finally got his first **big break** in a popular TV soap opera. ☐

As a child, he had **a burning ambition** to be rich and famous. ☐1

Some years later, he attempted to **make a comeback**, but he was unable to recapture the success of his early years. ☐

Soon he was the **idol** of millions of people, and was the centre of constant **media attention**. ☐

The soap **got him noticed**, and soon afterwards he was offered the **starring role** in a Hollywood movie. ☐

As well as doing casual jobs, he took any acting parts he could get in order **to gain experience**. ☐

But **hounded by the paparazzi**, he became tired of constantly being **in the public eye** and began to be seen less and less in public. ☐

Whilst still a teenager, he **ran away from home** and went to live in the big city. ☐

b **T8.1** Listen and check. Was your order the same?

3 a Work in pairs. Spend a few minutes preparing the roleplay below.

Student A: You are a journalist interviewing a celebrity like the one in the story. Write five or six questions to ask about his/her 'road to fame', using phrases from exercise 2.

> How did you get your first big break in show business?

> How does it feel to be always in the public eye?

Student B: You are a celebrity (either real or imaginary). You are going to answer questions about how you became famous and what it feels like. If necessary, invent details of your life. Use phrases from exercise 2.

b Act out the interview between the journalist and the celebrity.

Listening and writing
Song: *Do you know the way to San José?*

1 a What is Hollywood famous for? Why do you think hopeful young actors, models, etc. go there?

b The pictures on page 87 represent the story in the song that you will hear. Make five predictions about the story.

2 **T8.2** Listen to the song and complete the gaps.

3 Work in pairs. Answer the questions.

a Where does the girl come from?
b Where has she been living?
c Why did she go there?
d Did her plans work out?
e What kind of city do you think San José is?
f Which of your predictions in exercise 1 were correct?

Do you know the way to San José?

Do you know the way to San José?
I've been away so (a) _____ I may go wrong and
lose my (b) _____ .
Do you know the way to San José?
I'm going back to (c) _____ some peace of
(d) _____ in San José.

LA is a great big freeway.
Put a hundred down and buy a (e) _____ .
In a week, maybe two, they'll make you a (f) _____ .
Weeks turn into years. How quick they (g) _____ .
And all the stars that never (h) _____
Are (i) _____ cars and pumping gas.

Do you know the way to San José?
They've got a lot of (j) _____ . There'll be a place
where I can (k) _____ .
I was (l) _____ and raised in San José.
I'm going back to (m) _____ some peace of mind in
San José.

(n) _____ and fortune is a magnet.
It can pull you far away from (o) _____
With a dream in your heart you're never (p) _____ .
Dreams turn into dust and (q) _____ away
And there you are without a (r) _____ .
You pack your car and (s) _____ away.

I've got lots of friends in San José.
Do you know the way to San José?
Can't (t) _____ to get back to San José.

4 Explain the meaning of these lines from the song.

a 'I'm going back to find some peace of mind in
    San José.'
b 'In a week, maybe two, they'll make you a star.'
c 'Weeks turn into years. How quick they pass.'
d 'All the stars that never were . . . are parking cars
    and pumping gas.'
e 'Fame and fortune is a magnet.'
f 'Dreams turn into dust and blow away.'

5 Discuss the following questions in small groups.

• Do you think the woman will be happy back in
  San José?
• Do you feel sorry for her or not?

6 *Either* Write an imaginary account of the woman's
time in Hollywood, from her point of view. Include
some of the following.

• why she went there
• what happened to her while she was there
• why she decided to go home
• how things worked out for her when she went back
  to San José

Or Choose a famous person whose life you know
something about. Write an imaginary account of
his/her early life before becoming famous, and what it
feels like now to be famous.

Include phrases from the vocabulary on page 86
where appropriate.

Language focus 1
Gerund or infinitive?

1 Read the quotations below about wealth and fame. Which do you like best?

> It is not necessary to be rich and famous to be happy. It is only necessary to be rich.
> **ALAN ALDA, actor**

> Being a star was never as much fun as dreaming of being one.
> **MARILYN MONROE, film star**

> A celebrity is a person who works hard all his life to become well-known, then wears dark glasses to prevent people recognising him.
> **FRED ALLEN, comedian**

> Money doesn't make you feel any happier. I've got $50 million. But I was just as happy when I had $48 million.
> **ARNOLD SCHWARZENEGGER, actor and Governor of California**

> I don't want to achieve immortality through my work. I want to achieve it through not dying.
> **WOODY ALLEN, comedian and film director**

2 Underline all the infinitive forms in the quotations, and circle all the gerunds (-*ing* forms).

Analysis

1 Find an example in the quotations for each of the following.
Gerunds
  a a verb + gerund
  b a gerund as subject of the sentence
  c a preposition + gerund
Infinitives
  a a verb + infinitive
  b a verb + infinitive without 'to'
  c an adjective + infinitive
  d an infinitive that describes why someone does something

2 Which of these verbs and phrases are followed by an infinitive or a gerund? Use your mini-dictionary to check.

  avoid deny don't mind expect have trouble
  pretend refuse threaten

▶ Read Language summaries A and B on page 152.

Practice

1 a Complete the text with the gerund or infinitive form of the verbs in brackets (with or without *to*). Use your mini-dictionary, if necessary.

Have you got what it takes to be a celebrity?

- I would refuse (1) _____ (go) to a club or restaurant that looked cheap or unfashionable.
- I loathe people (2) _____ (take) my photograph.
- When I meet new people I expect them (3) _____ (remember) who I am.
- I regularly spend more than an hour (4) _____ (get) ready to go out.
- I would make a special effort (5) _____ (be) nice to someone if I thought they could help me in my career.
- I sometimes make people (6) _____ (wait) (7) _____ (see) me in order (8) _____ (make) them (9) _____ (appreciate) me more.
- I sometimes ignore people if I think they are not worth (10) _____ (know).
- I can't stand (11) _____ (go) to big parties with lots of people I don't know very well.
- I avoid (12) _____ (be) the centre of attention in big groups if I can.
- I sometimes tell lies about myself (13) _____ (make) myself sound more interesting.
- If I'm buying an outfit for an important occasion, I try (14) _____ (find) something that will make people (15) _____ (notice) me.
- If I saw someone embarrassing at a party I would pretend (16) _____ (not know) them.
- I don't really mind (17) _____ (not have) much money.
- I would rather (18) _____ (arrive) at a party a bit late, in order (19) _____ (make) a big entrance.
- I want everyone I meet (20) _____ (like) me.

b Discuss in pairs. Which statements do you associate with a potential celebrity?

2 Now ask and answer questions with your partner to find out if he/she has got what it takes to be a celebrity.

> Would you refuse to go to a club or restaurant that looked cheap or unfashionable?

Language focus 2
Different infinitive and gerund forms

Choose the correct form below. Can you explain why?

1 Celebrities love publicity – they …
   a want to see all the most fashionable parties.
   b want to be seen at all the most fashionable parties.
2 However, when people become very famous they often go to great lengths to avoid …
   a photographing in public.
   b being photographed in public.
3 Mariella, the eighteen-year-old supermodel, has been taken to hospital suffering from exhaustion. She …
   a seems to find the pressure of work too much.
   b seems to be finding the pressure of work too much.
4 For me, Marilyn Monroe was the most glamorous film star of all time. I …
   a would love to meet her.
   b would love to have met her.

Analysis

Find examples above of the following:
a a continuous infinitive   c a passive infinitive
b a perfect infinitive   d a passive gerund

How are these formed?

▶ Read Language summary C on page 152.

Practice

1 Choose the correct form in the sentences below.

a Although it's probably annoying for celebrities (1) to ask / to be asked for their autograph in the street, the time (2) to worry / to have worried is when people stop (3) asking / being asked them!
b Harrison Ford is thought (4) to be / to have been one of the few movie stars (5) to be working / to have worked as a carpenter.
c I'd like (6) being seen / to have seen the last episode of *Secret Life* last night. Let's hope it's going (7) to be released / to have released on DVD some time.
d Although the food isn't particularly good at San Pedro's, apparently it's _the_ place (8) to see / to be seen.

2 Read the texts on the right. Complete the gaps with the correct form of the verbs in brackets.

3 Work in groups. Make a list of five things to worry about if …

– you're a teenager.   – you're married.   – you haven't got a job.

Ten things to worry about if you're rich and famous

1 Whether or not people really like you, or just like _____ (see) with someone famous.
2 _____ (follow) by the paparazzi whenever you go to a fashionable party.
3 _____ (not get) any peace because fans are always trying _____ (take) photographs of you.
4 Whether or not your dress sense is going _____ (criticise) by the fashion journalists.
5 Ex-lovers who threaten _____ (sell) their story to the newspapers.
6 Whether or not it's going to be possible for your children _____ (have) a normal childhood.
7 Having trouble _____ (find) a reliable chauffeur, cleaner and cook.
8 Worrying about your family _____ (kidnap).
9 Wondering whether or not it's worth _____ (sell) your third home.
10 _____ (not know) if your accountant is cheating you.

Ten things to worry about if you're _not_ rich and famous

1 Wondering why all your friends seem _____ (be) more successful than you.
2 Never _____ (invite) to any fashionable parties.
3 _____ (not have) enough money _____ (be) able to go on holiday.
4 Not having anything _____ (spend) on new clothes.
5 Ex-lovers who refuse _____ (see) you because they've found someone richer and better-looking.
6 Whether or not you can afford _____ (have) children in your current financial position.
7 The fact that you are expected _____ (drive) to the shops, clean the house and prepare something _____ (eat) without any help.
8 Worrying about not having enough money _____ (buy) birthday presents for relatives.
9 Your debts, the fact that your scooter won't last much longer, and whether or not it's time _____ (sell) it.
10 Worrying about _____ (give) the wrong change in the supermarket.

Task: Summarise an article

Preparation: reading and listening

1 What do you know about the celebrities in the photos? Can you guess what the article is about from the photos and the title?

2 Read the article, using your mini-dictionary, if necessary. Then make notes about these questions.

a What, very generally, is the article about?

b What are the main points of the article (including examples, key words, etc.)?

c What events/research, etc. does it describe (including important facts and figures)?

d What issues does the article raise and what are your opinions about them?

3 **T8.3** Listen to someone discussing the notes she took. Did she mention the same things that you did?

Are you a celeb worshipper?

By James Chapman, Science Correspondent, *Daily Mail*

Do you wake up thinking of David Beckham? Or wonder what Brad Pitt is eating for breakfast? If so you could be one of a startling number of Britons suffering from a newly identified psychological condition: Celebrity Worship Syndrome (CWS). One in three people is so obsessed with someone in the public eye that he or she is a sufferer, say psychologists. And one in four is so taken with their idol that the obsession affects their daily life. Psychologists at the University of Leicester, who used a celebrity worship scale to rate the problems, found that thirty-six percent suffered from some form of CWS, and that the number was going up.

While many are obsessed with glamorous film and pop stars, such as George Clooney and Jennifer Lopez, others had unlikely objects of affection, including British Prime Minister, Tony Blair.

One theory is that in a society dominated by TV and with a decline in extended familes and communities, celebrities have taken the place of relatives, neighbours and friends for many people. Respect for family members has been replaced by the worship of the famous.

The study of around 700 people aged eighteen to sixty discovered there were three types of Celebrity Worship Syndrome. Those with a mild form — twenty-two percent of the sample — were likely to be extroverts, with a lot of friends. Their worst symptom — at least for their friends — was a passion for talking about their chosen celebrity. Twelve percent of the sample showed signs of the moderate form which meant they had an intense personal identification with their idol. The third group, the hardcore CWS sufferers, are solitary, impulsive, anti-social and troublesome, with insensitive traits. They feel they have a special bond with their celebrity, believe their celebrity knows them and are prepared to lie, or even die, for their hero. Around two percent of people had the most serious form of the syndrome, meaning their celebrity worship was borderline pathological.

Task: speaking

1 Work in pairs or individually.
Either Read the headlines and opening sentences of the articles on the right. Guess what each story is about. Then choose one article you would like to read.

Or Choose an interesting article from a current newspaper (either in English or your own language) that you would like to discuss with the class.

2 a Read the article carefully and make notes about the questions in exercise 2 on page 90.

b Decide how to summarise the article. Try not to use the exact words of the article unless you are quoting facts or statistics. Ask your teacher for any words or phrases you need.

▶ Useful language a

3 Work in groups with students who have read different articles. Listen to the summary of each article and then give your own opinions.

▶ Useful language b

Useful language

a Phrases for summarising the article

This article is all about … / describes how / …

Basically, what happened is …

The main point the article is making is that …

According to the article …

The article claims that …

Apparently, what happens is / happened was …

b Questions arising from the article

What I wondered was whether …

It raises the question of whether …

What interests me is whether or not …

I'd be interested to know what other people think about …

Entertainment: Stalking the stars

Stardom has always guaranteed wealth and abundant media attention, but now, it seems, it attracts something more sinister: stalkers.

See page 140 for the complete article.

A NATION OF SHOPAHOLICS

It's the sort of thing men joke about in the pub. 'My wife's addicted to shopping,' they'll say while their mates grin and nod sympathetically.

See page 140 for the complete article.

Woman banker stole €150,000 for clothes

A bank executive stole more than €150,000 from her employers and blew it on clothes and make-up to 'escape the stresses of being a working mother'.

See page 140 for the complete article.

The show must go on for pop diva

Serbian pop star Goca Trzan got the shock of her life when she walked onstage for her sell-out show at the Sava Concert Hall in the capital city of her country, Belgrade.

See page 141 for the complete article.

Writing
Linking ideas and arguments

1 a The sentences below describe some of the advantages and disadvantages of being rich. Underline the linkers (phrases that link the ideas together).

1   Rich people may not have to worry about paying the bills. <u>However</u>, wealth brings other worries of its own.
2   Whereas most of us worry about not having enough money, rich people worry about what to do with all the money they have.
3   Although being famous has its own rewards, it can mean a loss of privacy.
4   Rich and famous people find it hard to trust people; what is more, other people find it hard to behave naturally when they meet. For this reason, many famous people find it hard to make true friends.
5   Despite having achieved a great deal in life, many rich people still feel very insecure.

b Write the linkers in the correct section of the table.

1	to link arguments for and against *However*
2	to give more reasons for your argument
3	to explain the consequences of something
4	to compare two different situations

2 Add these linkers to the correct group in exercise 1b.

besides	even though
furthermore	in spite of
nevertheless	on the other hand
therefore	while

▶ Read Language summary D on page 153.

3 Choose the best linkers in the composition about mobile phones.

Mobile phones: should they be banned in public places?

Many people have mixed feelings about the use of mobile phones in public places like restaurants and cinemas. (a) Whereas / However they were almost unknown twenty years ago, these days they are part of everyone's life, and the world would now feel a strange place without them.

One of the strongest arguments in favour of banning mobile phones is the annoyance they cause other people.(b) Although / Despite people are always asked to turn off their mobiles when they go to the cinema, you can be sure that the film you are watching will be interrupted by the sound of at least five ringing tones! (c) Therefore / What is more many people insist on continuing their conversation, (d) in spite of / even though hundreds of people can hear them! (e) For this reason / Besides many people would welcome a ban on mobile phones in places where they might irritate other people.

(f) On the other hand / Although there are a number of arguments against such a ban. It is really difficult to stop people bringing their mobile phones into public places, and (g) however / therefore it would be virtually impossible to enforce any ban. Some people would see this as an infringement of their rights, (h) even though / while other people would say they need them in case of an emergency. And (i) despite / besides being asked to turn their mobile phones off, some people insist on leaving them on, or simply forget to silence them. Perhaps the most important point is that, (j) although / in spite of all the disadvantages, many people these days simply feel that they can't live without their mobile.

It seems to me that a ban on mobile phones would be pointless. People will always find a way round any ban. (k) Nevertheless / Although, people should be discouraged from using them in places like restaurants, unless it is absolutely necessary. People should be made aware that it's very bad manners to use them at certain times. (l) However / Furthermore, there will always be someone who thinks their call is much more important than other people's peace and quiet!

Wordspot
big and *great*

1 The diagrams below show the basic differences in meaning between *big* and *great*. Notice that the meanings overlap.

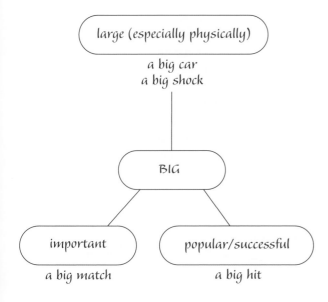

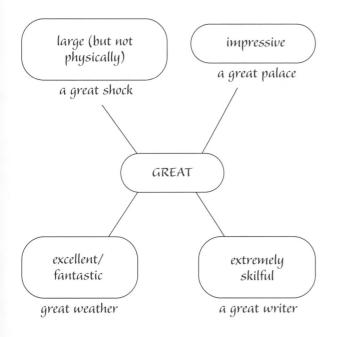

2 Complete the gaps with *big* or *great*. Are there any sentences where you could use both?

a   It was time for her to make the _____ decision: should she agree to marry him?

b   Although the group never enjoyed much success in the USA, they were really _____ in Europe at one time.

c   Internet crime is becoming a _____ problem.

d   Although an unknown in his lifetime, Van Gogh is now seen as a _____ artist of his period.

e   Losing weight has really been good for Louise. She looks _____ now, doesn't she?

f   Ferdinand is certainly a _____ man, but he's not in any way fat.

g   Apparently there's been another bomb explosion – it's really _____ news.

h   If you look to your left now, you will see the _____ fifteenth-century tower.

i   Nelson Mandela will go down in history as a _____ man.

3 There are a number of other phrases with *big* and *great*. Circle the correct alternative. Use your mini-dictionary, if necessary.

a   It seems that everyone had a really big / great time on the trip to the mountains.

b   If you want to earn really big / great money, I suggest that you try to expand your business abroad.

c   My big- / great-grandmother emigrated from Ireland in the nineteenth century.

d   He may be the best player in the team, but that's no reason for Carl to be so big- / great-headed.

e   The government has spent a big / great deal of money attempting to help the region.

f   Exciting news! My big / great sister's going to get married!

g   I don't really care about failing the exam. It's no big / great deal, really.

h   'I've passed my driving test!' 'That's big / great!'

4 Ask and answer these questions with a partner.

a   What's the biggest decision you've ever had to make?

b   If someone is looking great, are they looking fat or looking fantastic?

c   Is it a good or a bad thing to be big-headed?

d   Talk about a day when you had a really great time with some friends.

e   Do you know the names of any great English writers?

f   In your opinion, who is the biggest movie star in the world right now?

g   Name a profession in which it's possible to earn big money.

CONSOLIDATION

A Use of articles

Complete the gaps with *a/an*, *the* or – (= no word).

1 Britain's hardest-working man?

(a) _____ hardest-working man in
(b) _____ Britain has decided to take life
(c) _____ little easier. James McSporran has
retired as (d) _____ only police officer on
(e) _____ tiny island of Gigha in (f) _____
north-west Scotland. However, he will continue
to serve Gigha's 200 inhabitants in (g) _____
number of other roles, for he is also (h) _____
postman, (i) _____ ambulance man,
(j) _____ shopkeeper and (k) _____ taxi
driver for (l) _____ island. (m) _____ police
job wasn't that demanding, he told (n) _____
Times newspaper. (o) _____ people on the island
are all either (p) _____ relatives or (q) _____
friends, so (r) _____ crime is unknown!

2 Teenager on the road to millions

As (a) _____ teenager, Chris Mole dreamed of
studying (b) _____ marine engineering. But
disastrous exam results ended any hopes of going
to (c) _____ university. However, (d) _____
eighteen year old didn't allow this failure to make
him depressed: instead, he borrowed €75,000 and
used (e) _____ money to start (f) _____
company selling (g) _____ second-hand
computers to (h) _____ students. The company
was (i) _____ immediate success, and in
(j) _____ first year it made (k) _____ profit
of €12 million.

Chris still lives with his parents in Morpeth,
(l) _____ small town in north-east England and
he still works in (m) _____ garden centre at
weekends. 'It helps keep me in touch with
(n) _____ reality,' he says.

B Word combinations

1 The words and phrases in the box all come from
Modules 5–8. Write BE (for Big events), FF (for Fame
and fortune), I (for Injuries) and UA (for Unusual
achievements). Some may fit in more than one
category. Then compare your answers with a partner.

bandage	beat the record	be in the public eye
cheering	a huge crowd	media attention
infection	a huge mansion	hurt yourself
painful	a procession	get your big break
a wound	raise money	waving flags
spectators	make a fortune	win an award

2 Now test your partner. Give a definition of one of
the words or phrases and see if your partner can
guess what it is. Use your mini-dictionary if necessary.

This is a piece of
cloth that you tie
around a wound.

A bandage.

C Perfect tenses: Record breakers

Choose the correct alternative to complete the
fascinating facts.

1 The world's oldest president

No politician (a) has held / has been holding
the office of President for longer than Joaquín
Balaguer of the Dominican Republic – when
he finally retired in 1996, he (b) has been / had
been President of his country for a total of
twenty-two years in four different decades –
the 60s, 70s, 80s and 90s.

2 The slowest marathon

When Lloyd Scott finally completed the
Edinburgh Marathon in June 2003, it
(c) had taken / had been taking him six days,
four hours, thirty minutes and fifty-six seconds
to complete the forty-two kilometre course.
He
(d) had been walking / has been walking for
an average of nine hours, at a speed of one
kilometre an hour – mainly because he was
wearing a sixty kilogram diving suit!

3 The world's longest marriage

When Liu-Yang-Wan died peacefully at her home in Taiwan at the age of 103, it brought an end to the world's longest marriage – she and her husband (e) had been married / have been married for no fewer than eighty-five years – but they (f) had been living / have been living in the same house even longer. According to the tradition of that time, Liu went to live in her husband's house at the age of five.

4 The world's biggest Pepsi cola fan

Dr Christian Cavaletti, from Corropoli, Italy, (g) has been collecting / had been collecting Pepsi cola cans since 1989. In this time, he (h) has been collecting / has collected more than 3,000 cans from over seventy countries.

5 The world's biggest breakfast

Five cooks in Croatia, (i) have been using / have used 1,111 eggs to create the world's largest serving of scrambled eggs. The local director of tourism said, 'We called the *Guinness Book of Records* two months ago and they told us no one (j) had ever tried / had ever been trying to make such a big breakfast!'

6 The world's most patient fiancé

When Octavio Guillan from Mexico finally named the wedding day in June 1969, his bride Adriana Martínez, eighty-two, (k) had been waiting / has been waiting sixty-seven years. Guillan, also eighty-two, (l) has first proposed / had first proposed marriage in 1902!

7 The world's exploding population?

The world's population (m) has been increasing / had been increasing by around 1.5 percent per year for the last thirty years. It is estimated that the population (n) has reached / will have reached nine billion by the year 2050.

8 The world's richest teenager

Athina Roussell became the world's richest teenager when she inherited $2.7 billion in 2003. Despite her huge wealth, Athina's life (o) has been touched / had been touched by tragedy, however – her mother, Christina Onassis, (p) had suffered / has suffered four failed marriages before she died in 1988.

D Relative clauses

1 Put the phrases from the boxes into the correct place in the texts and add the correct relative pronoun.

a Toddler Aruw Ibirum (1) , *who lives in Bradford, Yorkshire* , miraculously survived after a thirty-eight-tonne lorry ran her over as she lay in her pushchair. The lorry driver, (2) _____ , pulled up after he heard an unusual scraping noise. Aruw, (3) _____ , was discovered with just a few cuts and bruises. An astonished elderly woman (4) _____ told reporters 'You wouldn't have believed a child could have come out of that alive.'

> ~~lives in Bradford, Yorkshire~~
> pushchair had been dragged along for nearly a kilometre
> saw the whole thing happen
> was unaware of what was happening

b An Australian man (5) _____ finally discovered the cause of his acute backache last week. It was due to a shark's tooth (6) _____ . Leo Ryan, sixty-six, (7) _____ , had been attacked by the shark as a teenager. In the accident, (8) _____ , (9) _____ , he also lost three fingers and part of his arm. 'That shark was determined to hang onto me,' he told reporters.

> happened off the Gold Coast
> had been stuck in his spine for almost forty-eight years
> has been suffering for years
> will be having an operation to remove the tooth
> he had been swimming

2 〔 C1 〕 Listen and check.

E Speaking: Two-minute talk

1 Work in groups. Choose one of the topics and spend about five minutes preparing a short talk about it. Be ready to speak about the topic for two minutes.

- A big sporting event
- A party I'll never forget
- A useful piece of advice
- How to get rich
- My favourite movie star
- Something I'm extremely proud of
- Weddings in my country
- Why I love/hate shopping
- Why I would/wouldn't like to be famous

2 Take turns to speak for two minutes about your topic. Listen to the other students and decide which topic they chose.

Mysteries, problems, oddities

Vocabulary and speaking
Strange events

1 Match the words and phrases below with one of the situations 1–12.

a   a case of mistaken identity
b   a coincidence
c   a ghost story
d   a hoax
e   a miracle
f   a mysterious disappearance
g   a natural phenomenon
h   a premonition
i   supernatural powers
j   telepathy
k   a trick
l   an unsolved murder

2 Check the words and phrases below in your mini-dictionary. Which of the things above do you find …

a   amazing?   e   ridiculous?
b   disgraceful?   f   spooky?
c   disturbing?   g   suspicious?
d   hard to believe? h   weird?

Compare your answers with a partner.

3 Discuss the following questions in small groups.

• Do you know of any cases similar to the ones above?
• Has anything similar ever happened to you, or to anyone you know?

1   An old woman is seriously ill and unable to walk. The doctors say there is no hope for her. Suddenly, she stands and claims she has been cured.

2   At an airport in a strange city, you get into conversation with a man you have never met before. After a few minutes, you discover that you both went to the same school.

3   A man appears on a TV chat show and demonstrates that he can bend spoons and other small metal objects simply by concentrating hard.

4   During winter, in Norway, Alaska and Finland it is possible to observe the 'Northern Lights': a brilliant display of natural lights caused by solar particles which have been thrown out by the sun.

5   A woman dreams of a plane falling from the sky and wakes up in a panic. The next day there is a devastating plane crash near her city.

6   A boat carrying fifteen passengers on a trip along a remote stretch of river disappears. No trace of the boat, or of any survivors, is ever found.

7   A wealthy businessman is found dead in his flat with two bullet holes in his head. There were no obvious clues, and no suspect has ever been arrested.

8   A Mr James Allen is arrested in a foreign country, accused of being involved in smuggling arms. Two days later, he is released without charge. The police admit they had arrested the wrong James Allen.

9   Scientists fused part of a human skull with part of an orang-utan skull and claimed to have found the 'missing link' between apes and humans. They named it the Piltdown Man.

10   A man wakes up in the middle of the night to find the figure of a man dressed in nineteenth-century clothes standing over him. When he turns on the light, the figure disappears.

11   A pair of identical twins claim to know what the other is thinking to the extent that they often say exactly the same thing at the same time.

12   Someone tells you to choose a card from a pack without telling him what it is. You put it back and he says he will show you the card. He finds it first time.

Listening
Mysteries of everyday life

1 Discuss the following questions in groups.

- Are you very ticklish?
- Do you often get hiccups? How do you usually cure them?
- Have you ever sleepwalked? What happened?

2 Do you know the answers to the questions below? Compare your ideas in pairs.

a Why do so many men go bald but almost no women?
b Why do we laugh when people tickle us?
c Why do some people sleepwalk?
d Why do people yawn – and why do people cover their mouth when they do it?
e What causes hiccups and what's the best way to stop them?
f Why do people say 'bless you' when someone sneezes?

3 a **T9.1** Check these words in your mini-dictionary. Then listen to the explanations for the questions in exercise 2. Which questions do these words and phrases relate to?

The Bubonic Plague   the diaphragm   The Middle Ages
oxygen   pre-adolescent boys   the soul   a state of panic
stress   swallowing rapidly   testosterone

b Listen again. Why are these words and phrases important in each explanation?

4 How many answers did you get right in exercise 2? Which information did you find the most surprising or interesting?

Language focus 1
Modals and related verbs

Cross out the modals that are incorrect in the sentences below. Then choose the one(s) that are best in the context.

1 Regular sleepwalkers have to / ought to be careful about safety.
2 In many cultures, people believe that you should / must cover your mouth if you yawn.
3 It must / should be quite frightening if you wake up to find yourself sleepwalking.
4 It mustn't / can't be very comfortable if you have hiccups for a long period of time.
5 In adults, sleepwalking can / may be a sign of severe stress.
6 There can / may / might / could be an effective cure for baldness in the next few years.

Analysis

1 In sentences 1 and 2, which modals mean
  a it is necessary?
  b it is a good idea or 'the right thing to do'?

2 Modals often express how probable we think something is. Which modal(s) in sentences 3–6 mean the following?
  a The speaker is sure this is true.
  b The speaker thinks this is possibly true.
  c The speaker is sure this isn't true.

3 Why is *can* correct in sentence 5, but not in sentence 6?

▶ Read Language summary A on page 153.

Practice

1 Cross out the modal verb that does not fit in each sentence.

Rather than investing in expensive scientific equipment to predict earthquakes, perhaps scientists (a) must / ought to / should spend more time watching their pets.
Many scientists now believe that the behaviour of certain animals (b) could / may / has to help them to predict certain natural disasters. For example, Chinese scientists in the 1970s thought that reports of farm animals running round in circles (c) can / could / might indicate an impending disaster. They decided to evacuate the city of Haichin, which shortly afterwards was hit by a huge earthquake. Thousands of lives were probably saved as a result.
Japanese scientists have also discovered that catfish become livelier several days before moderately strong earthquakes. Many scientists now accept that this (d) can't / mustn't / may not be pure coincidence; they believe that the explanation (e) can / could / may be linked to slight changes in the Earth's magnetic field. Although human beings (f) aren't able to / can't / mustn't perceive such changes, it is thought that the sensitive nervous systems of some animals (g) could / have to / must be affected by them. Now scientists (h) have to / must / shouldn't discover exactly which animals are affected in this way, so that more lives (i) can / may / should be saved in the future.

2 Match the animals to the information below. Then complete the gaps with a modal. (There may be more than one possibility).

bats	camels	cats	elephants	horses	sharks	snakes	tigers

a | camels | They *can* survive for long periods without water.

b | | They _____ become extinct unless action is taken to protect them.

c | | They make high-pitched sounds which _____ be heard by human beings.

d | | You _____ never approach one from behind as it _____ kick or run away.

e | | They _____ grow to a length of up to eight metres.

f | | They _____ keep swimming all their lives or they will die.

g | | Although they are usually kept as pets, most of them _____ survive in the wild if they had to.

h | | They _____ not be hunted for their white tusks, according to international law.

3 **a** Read the commonly held beliefs below. Only three are actually true. Do you know which?

1 A sudden fright or terrible shock can turn your hair white overnight.

2 Women have one more rib than men.

3 New-born babies have more bones in their bodies than adults.

4 One bite from a tarantula is usually deadly.

5 Elephants are afraid of mice.

Fact or Myth?

6 If you are struck by lightning, you will die.

7 Turkeys cannot fly.

8 Water going down a plughole travels in the opposite direction in the northern hemisphere to how it travels in the southern hemisphere.

9 When faced with danger, ostriches bury their heads in the sand.

b Compare your answers in groups. Use modal verbs of possibility to express your opinions.

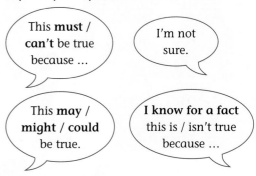

This **must / can't** be true because …

I'm not sure.

This **may / might / could** be true.

I know for a fact this is / isn't true because …

c **T9.2** Listen and check to find out if you were right.

Wordspot
wrong

1 Look at the expressions with *wrong*. Then match them with the definitions below.

a You've got a wrong number.
b Everything's gone wrong.
c There's something wrong with it.
d There's nothing wrong with it.
e What's wrong?
f It's the wrong way up.
g It's the wrong way round.
h It's in the wrong place.
i You were completely wrong about her!

1 … means 'what's the problem?'
2 … means 'it has a problem / doesn't work'.
3 … means that the bottom is where the top should be.
4 … means that the front is at the back and the back is at the front.
5 … means something is working OK.
6 … means something is not where it should be.
7 … is used when you get a phone number you didn't want.
8 … means you judged someone unfairly.
9 … means everything's failed or turned out badly.

2 Spend a few minutes studying the expressions with *wrong*. Then look at the sentences on page 139. Re-write the part of the sentence in bold using an expression with *wrong*.

99

Language focus 2
Past modals

1 a Check the words in your mini-dictionary. Then look at the pictures telling the story of a mysterious disappearance.

a carriage	to conspire / a conspiracy	a hotel register
the Plague	to wreck something	a mental asylum
velvet	to trace someone	insane/insanity

b Work in pairs. Discuss what you think happened.

2 **T9.3** Listen to Part A of the story. (You can read the tapescript on page 170.) Answer the questions.

a   What was happening in Paris in 1889?
b   Where were Eleanor and Clara Redwood going? Why had they left India?
c   What happened when they arrived at the hotel?
d   What happened when Eleanor called the doctor?
e   Where and why was Eleanor sent to get the medicine?
f   How long did the journey take?
g   Why was she surprised when she got back?
h   What did she find when she went back to room 342?
i   What happened when she went to the British Embassy with her story?
j   Did she ever trace her mother?

3 **T9.4** What do you think is the explanation for Clara's disappearance? Compare your answers in pairs. Listen to Part B for a possible explanation.

4 **T9.5** Choose the correct alternative. (There is one sentence where it may be both.) Then listen and check.

a   The ladies could book / managed to book the last two rooms available at one of the most famous hotels in Paris.
b   Almost immediately however, the mother fell ill and they had to call / must have called the hotel's doctor.
c   Eleanor could only speak / managed only to speak a little French and didn't understand what they were saying.
d   The doctor explained that he couldn't leave / can't have left Mrs Redwood because she was too ill.
e   Eleanor could persuade / managed to persuade them to take her back to room 342, but the room was empty.
f   Many experts now believe that Mrs Redwood must have brought / had to bring the Plague back with her from India.
g   The hotel manager might have conspired / could have conspired with the doctor to keep the terrible news a secret.
h   The British Embassy should certainly have / must certainly have investigated her story more fully.
i   But surely they can't have disposed / mustn't have disposed of the body and redecorated room 342 in just four hours?

100

Analysis

1 Which modal or related verb in exercise 4 means:
   a were obliged to?
   b had the ability to?
   c was able to do successfully?
   d wasn't able to?
   Why is *could* wrong in sentences a and e, but correct in sentence c?

2 Which perfect form of the modal verbs above mean:
   a logically it seems certain that this happened?
   b logically it is possible that this happened?
   c logically it seems impossible that this happened?
   d this was a good idea, but it didn't happen?

▶ Read Language summary B on page 154.

Practice

1 Re-write these sentences about the story, replacing the underlined words with a modal.

a <u>Perhaps the hotel manager and the doctor sent</u> Eleanor to the other side of Paris, deliberately, so that they <u>had the ability to</u> dispose of Mrs Redwood.
(The hotel manager ...)
The hotel manager and the doctor might have sent Eleanor to the other side of Paris deliberately, so that they could dispose of Mrs Redwood.

b <u>Surely the doctor sent</u> a letter with Eleanor when she went to his surgery.
(The doctor ...)

c <u>It would have been a good idea for the British Embassy to check</u> this.
(The British Embassy ...)

d <u>Eleanor was probably obliged to wait</u> for a long time at the doctor's surgery.
(Eleanor ...)

e Eleanor <u>was able to</u> get back to the hotel with the medicine successfully eventually.
(Eleanor ...)

f <u>Surely it is impossible that they removed</u> Mrs Redwood's signature from the hotel register.
(They ...)

g <u>Perhaps they didn't take</u> Eleanor back to room 342 when she returned to the hotel. <u>Perhaps it was</u> a different room.
(They ...)

h It is a shame that Eleanor <u>wasn't able to</u> persuade embassy officials to believe her.
(It is a shame ...)

i <u>It wasn't a good idea for the authorities to put</u> a young girl like Eleanor in a Mental Asylum.
(The authorities ...)

j <u>It is possible that Eleanor invented</u> the whole story.
(Eleanor ...)

2 Complete the gaps with an appropriate past modal and the correct form of the verbs in brackets.

a You _____ (leave) your glasses at work – I saw them in the kitchen a few minutes ago.

b You _____ (leave) your glasses at work. I haven't seen them since you got home.

c I _____ (study) medicine, but I decided to go travelling instead.

d I _____ (study) medicine – my parents insisted on it.

e Vera and Jack _____ (get) lost – they said they'd be here by three.

f Vera and Jack _____ (get) lost – they've been here dozens of times.

g Annie _____ (go) home, her car's still in the car park.

h Annie _____ (go) home, her coat's gone.

i Katie _____ (buy) a lot of new clothes to look smart in her new job.

j Katie _____ (buy) a lot of new clothes, she's completely changed her image.

3 ▶T9.6◀ You will hear some people talking about one of the sentences below. Which answer belongs to each sentence?

a Something you had to do yesterday (but didn't want to).

b Something you should've done recently, but forgot about.

c Something people couldn't do twenty years ago.

d Something you didn't have to do ten years ago that you have to now.

e Something you shouldn't have done when you were younger.

f Something you could do when you were twelve years old that you can still do now.

Pronunciation

1 ▶T9.7◀ Listen to the sentences from exercise 3. Notice the stress and weak forms with *should have* and *shouldn't have*.
   /ʃəd hæv/
   I should have **paid** in a **cheque**.
   /ʃʊdnt həv/
   I **should**n't have **start**ed **smok**ing.

2 ▶T9.8◀ Listen and write down the eight sentences you hear. Which words do you think are stressed, and which do you think are weak?

3 Listen again and practise the sentences.

4 Work in pairs. Talk about the sentences in the same way as the people on the recording in exercise 3.

Task: Solve the mysteries
Preparation: reading and vocabulary

1 Do you know of any unsolved real life mysteries? Tell the class.

2 Read the four stories below. Check the words in bold in your mini-dictionary, as you read. Don't worry about the questions at this stage.

3 Work in pairs. Summarise briefly the mystery in each case.

Real Life Unsolved Mysteries

❷ The case of the vanishing children

One warm Sunday afternoon in June 1905, neighbours of the Vaughan family from near Gloucester in England, were asked to join a **search party** for three missing children. The three Vaughan children, a boy aged ten and his two sisters aged three and five, had been playing in a field and had failed to return for their lunch. Their father could find no sign of them, so he raised the alarm, and crowds of neighbours began searching the area for the three youngsters, but without success.

The following morning the newspapers reported that the Vaughan children had been **kidnapped**, and within hours there were newspaper reporters everywhere. Hundreds more volunteers joined the search, **scouring** every centimetre of the surrounding fields for the slightest sign of the children. As one witness at the time said later, 'If there had been a dead dog in those fields, we would have found it.'

And yet, four days later, a farm labourer looked in a **ditch** only a few metres from the children's home and found all three of them fast asleep. The children were completely unaware of the fuss around them, and when asked, could only reply that they had been sleeping. There was no sign that any harm had been done to them.

❶ The case of Isidor Fink

On 9th March, 1929, the body of thirty-one-year-old Isidor Fink, was found in the back room of the laundry that he owned on Fifth Avenue, New York.

Fink was an **immigrant** from modern-day Lithuania, who had few friends and no family. He had no known connections with the gangsters who terrorised much of New York at that time. However, he was certainly frightened of something, for he had made his laundry into a kind of **fortress**: it was equipped with the best locks that money could buy, and the windows were fitted with heavy **iron bars**.

When the police finally found him, his body was lying ten metres from the doorway with two **bullet holes** in his chest, and another in his left wrist. There was no gun in the room, and there was money in both Fink's pocket and in his **cash register**. But what made the case so strange was that the room was locked and **bolted** from the inside.

Questions
a Was it significant that Isidor Fink had no family or friends?
b Why did he have so much security?
c Had he been burgled?
d Did he commit suicide?
e Was he murdered?
f Why was there a bullet hole in his wrist?

Questions
a Could the search parties have missed the children?
b Had they been kidnapped?
c Could they have been asleep for four days?
d Were they lying for any reason?
e What do you think had happened to them?

Supernatural happenings in the temples?

In September, 1995 thousands rushed to Hindu temples throughout India, after reports of a miracle: **marble** statues of the elephant headed god Ganesha had apparently started drinking the traditional spoonfuls of milk offered by **worshippers**. The **miracles** were soon being reported by the news media throughout the world, and tens of thousands of people flocked to Hindu temples everywhere, and found that the miracle was being repeated. One small statue in Hong Kong reportedly consumed over twenty litres of milk.

Questions

a What was the 'miracle' and where did it first occur?

b In what way did the miracle spread?

c Can you think of any explanation?

Is this a photograph of the Loch Ness Monster?

Throughout 1933 rumours had been appearing in newspapers that

there was a huge **prehistoric monster** in Loch Ness in Scotland, but no proof could be found.

Then, in April 1934, Colonel Robert Wilson a distinguished doctor was driving along the banks of Loch Ness with an unnamed friend. The friend apparently saw a **commotion** in the water, and shouted 'It's the monster!' Grabbing a camera, the friend took four photographs, three of which were blank when they were developed. But the fourth, above, soon appeared in the *Daily Mail*, a British newspaper, leading to massive publicity.

For the next sixty years the photograph was used as **proof** that the monster existed, and scientific tests seemed to confirm that it was authentic.

Questions

a What happened to Colonel Wilson and his friend?

b Why do you think Wilson was considered a reliable witness?

c Do you think it is significant that the friend was never named in the newspapers?

d What happened after the photo was developed? Did people believe it was real?

e Do you think it was real or not? Why / Why not?

Task: speaking and listening

1 **a** Work in groups. Your teacher will give each group a different mystery to discuss.

b Read the mystery again and think about the questions below individually. Ask your teacher for any words or phrases you need.

▶ Useful language a

2 Discuss what you think happened in groups. Can you agree on an explanation?

3 **a** When you have finished, read another mystery. Then discuss the questions in groups.

b Present your solutions to the class. Do other groups agree?

▶ Useful language b

4 **T9.9** Listen to the explanations that have been offered by experts. Did you come to the same conclusions or not?

Useful language

a Discussing solutions

... might/must/can't have ... because ...

I think I know what might have happened ...

One possible explanation is that ...

It seems likely/unlikely that ... because ...

On the other hand ...

How do you explain the fact that ...?

b Presenting conclusions

We think ... must/can't have ... because ...

We're pretty certain that ... because ...

The only logical explanation is that ...

We couldn't agree about this, because ...

Real life
Saying what's wrong with things

1 Which sentences in the box could apply to the things in the photos?

It's got a hole in it.	It's got a stain on it.
It doesn't fit.	It doesn't suit you.
It's burnt.	It doesn't work.
It's chipped.	It's scratched.
It's shrunk in the wash.	It isn't what you ordered.
There's a part missing.	It's the wrong colour.
It's the wrong size.	It isn't charging.

2 **T9.10** You are going to hear four conversations in which people are talking about one of the items above. Complete the table below.

What the item is	What the problem is	How the conversation ends
1		
2		
3		
4		

3 Prepare a similar short conversation (about twelve lines), using these ideas to help you.

Where it happens / who the speakers are	What the problem is	How the conversation ends
• shop • restaurant • over the phone • in an office	• problem with the food • problem with goods delivered • problem with an item of clothing	• goods exchanged • refund • customer gives up • huge argument

STUDY...

Improve your listening

Many learners complain that spoken English is 'too fast'. Although listening to English spoken slowly can help you in the early stages, you need to get used to English spoken at normal speed too. Here are some tips:

- As with reading, listening a little every day is better than not listening at all for long periods.

- Don't expect to understand every word. Try to get the general sense of what people are saying. Don't panic if you 'lose' the sense of what you hear – keep listening and try to pick it up again.

- You can usually get the sense by concentrating on the stressed words. Don't worry too much about the unstressed words (articles, prepositions, auxiliary verbs, etc.).

- If you have access to TV programmes or films in the original English, try listening to them without looking at the sub-titles and see how much you can understand. You can also download sound files from the Internet, or listen to the BBC World Service.

- Many Longman graded readers have cassettes or CDs. Try listening without looking at the book!

- Listen to different varieties of English (British, American, Australian, etc.) to help get used to different accents and vocabulary. Also listen to English spoken by people whose first language is not English – they are the vast majority of English speakers!

PRACTISE...

1 Modal verbs ☐

Tick the sentence which is closest in meaning to the first sentence.

a *You shouldn't say anything.*
- It's not a good idea to say anything.
- It's forbidden to say anything.

b *You mustn't say anything.*
- I say you're not allowed to say anything.
- It's not necessary to say anything.

c *This can't be the right way!*
- I'm sure that this isn't the right way.
- Perhaps this isn't the right way.

d *You don't have to tell him.*
- It's not necessary to tell him.
- It's prohibited to tell him.

e *That must be Tim at the door.*
- I'm sure that's Tim at the door.
- Perhaps that's Tim at the door.

f *It can snow in March.*
- It's possible for it to snow in March, it sometimes happens.
- Perhaps it will snow in March.

g *The match could be postponed.*
- Perhaps the match was postponed.
- Perhaps the match will be postponed

▶ **Need to check? Language summary A, page 153.**

2 Past modal verbs ☐

Are the sentences the same or different in meaning?

a We have to wait for a long time. / We've got to wait for a long time.

b We should've got up early. / We had to get up early.

c They couldn't rescue him. / They weren't able to rescue him.

d He could've escaped. / He was able to escape.

e You ought to be more careful. / You ought to have been more careful.

f They can't have understood what I said. / They couldn't understand what I said.

▶ **Need to check? Language summary B, page 156.**

3 Strange events ☐

Complete the strange events words.

a c _ _ n c _ d _ n c _   d s _ p _ r _ _ t _ _ a _
b h _ _ x   e p r _ m _ n t _ _ n
c m _ r _ cl _   f t _ l _ p _ t h y

▶ **Need to check? Vocabulary, page 96.**

4 Saying what's wrong ☐

Match the phrases with the sentence beginnings.

a It doesn't …	1 burnt.
b It's got a …	2 part missing.
c It's …	3 wrong colour.
d It isn't …	4 stain on it.
e It's the …	5 charging.
	6 wrong size.
	7 suit you.
	8 what I ordered.
	9 fit.

▶ **Need to check? Real life, page 104.**

5 Phrases with *wrong* ☐

Add *wrong* in the correct position in the sentences.

a I'm sorry you must have got the number.
b Unfortunately, things went from the start.
c They put it the way up.
d There's absolutely nothing with this.
e You're wearing your pullover the way round.

▶ **Need to check? Wordspot, page 99.**

Pronunciation spot
Diphthongs (2): /ɪə/ and /eə/

a **T9.11** Listen to the pronunciation of the words. Notice the different sounds of the letters in bold.
/ɪə/ here near cheer
/eə/ there wear care

b **T9.12** Put the words in the correct category, according to the pronunciation of the letters in bold. Then listen and check.

everywhere hair hemisphere pair severe unaware volunteer weird

c Practise saying all the words, paying attention to the diphthongs.

REMEMBER!

Look back at the areas you have practised. Tick the ones you feel confident about. Now try the MINI-CHECK on page 160 to check what you know!

MODULE 10

Getting together

- ▶ Review of future forms
- ▶ Future continuous and Future perfect
- ▶ Vocabulary: Getting together
- ▶ Reading: *Getting together 21st-century style*
- ▶ Task: Decide who's coming to dinner
- ▶ Pronunciation: Contractions
- ▶ Writing: Types of message
- ▶ Real life: Dealing with problems on the telephone

Vocabulary
Getting together

1 Which of the people in A take part in the events in B? Discuss in pairs. (There may be several answers.)

A	B
boyfriend and girlfriend	an appointment
business associates	a blind date
clients	a business meeting
colleagues	a celebration meal
delegates	a conference
ex-classmates	a date
friends	a dinner party
guests	a family get-together
neighbours	a housewarming party
political leaders	a school reunion
relatives	a summit meeting
speakers	
strangers looking for a partner	

2 Which of these verbs can you use with the events in B in exercise 1?

have	*an appointment*
make	*an appointment*
go on	
attend	

3 Work in small groups. Choose a memorable 'get-together' that you have been to. Describe it to other students, giving details about the following.

- – why, when and where it was held
- – who was there
- – why it was so memorable

Reading

1 Work in pairs. Make a list of ways people can do the following things. Then compare your lists with other students.

- – get to know new people
- – get in touch with old friends
- – meet a future partner

2 Read the article about four ways of getting together and answer the questions.

a Explain briefly how the people get together in each case.
b What kind of people is each way most suitable for?

3 Check the words in bold in your mini-dictionary. Then discuss the following questions in pairs.

a Why does the author compare **speed dating** to fast food?
b Why is speed dating 'less **anonymous** than online and less risky than **blind dates**'?
c Why might people be surprised that Rajev and Vandana had an **arranged marriage**?
d Why do Rajev and Vandana think they are so **compatible**?
e In what ways does Rajev believe their marriage is the same as any other?
f In what sense is Friends Reunited a **dot com phenomenon**?
g Why does it appeal to people's **nosiness**?
h Why does it seem strange, in the modern world, that reading groups are so popular?
i Why do you think their members 'love the **buzz**'?

4 Discuss the following questions in small groups.

- Which of these ways of meeting people would you try? Which appeals to you least? Why?
- What would you say about yourself in three minutes if you were 'speed dating'?
- Is there anyone that you would particularly like to get in touch with through a website like Friends Reunited?

Getting together 21st-century style

Traditionally, people have found friends and partners through school, work and mutual friends. But these days there are so many other ways people can get together – not just for dating, but for marriage or just to broaden their social life!

Speed dating

Forget about candlelit dinners and flowers. That was so nineties, and so time-consuming. For those ready to embrace a new world of love and marriage, it's all about speed ... speed dating that is. It's fast food for starving singles and just about as romantic.

However, speed dating has other attractions. To start with, it's fun ... for those who can tell their life story in three minutes flat. The dating company hires a bar or restaurant and you have a series of three-minute conversations with up to fifteen people in one evening. You are not allowed to ask for a date, phone number or e-mail address. At the end of the conversation, you fill in a card saying 'date', 'friend' or 'miss'. The company will arrange a meeting for any couple who both ticked 'date' within forty-eight hours.

Practical, pragmatic, less anonymous than online, less risky than blind dates, more serious than the bar scene. Synchronise your watches. Get ready. Get set. Date.

Arranged marriages

Maybe you associate arranged marriages with the past, but they are still very much alive and well in the twenty-first century. Rajev and Vandana are a modern couple with two incomes and two boys aged six and eight, but an arranged marriage suits them perfectly.

Rajev explains, 'At the age of twenty-seven, I called my parents in India and told them I was ready to get married. My parents searched for a young woman who'd been raised in India, spoke good English, and was prepared to live abroad.' They came up with more than fifty candidates and sent pictures and CVs – Vandana was the first one he liked.

Meanwhile, Vandana's parents had been searching for a husband for her too. 'With our similar upbringings, our values were bound to be compatible,' she says, 'A meeting was arranged ... and here we are ... we are getting ready to celebrate our eleventh wedding anniversary.'

They expect that their two boys will want to choose their own partners, and have no problem with that. But if either asks for an arranged marriage, they'll be happy to help.

Friends Reunited

Friends Reunited was the brainchild of Julie and Steve Pankhurst, who set up this dot com phenomenon from their living room in North London. It all started when, pregnant with her first child, Julie's mind turned back to her school days. 'I just started to wonder what my old schoolmates were up to now.' The idea was very simple: using a list of 40,000 schools, colleges and universities, members obtain details of old school friends who have also registered, and can then e-mail them and meet up with them if they wish. Friends Reunited is now the most visited website in the UK, with around 3.6 million visits a day. 'What I didn't expect is the nosiness the site allows,' says Steve, 'Everybody is curious to find out what old friends are doing now.'

There has been a surprising off-shoot. When twenty-seven-year-old Mike Breach set up a spoof version called 'Convicts Reunited' as a joke, he received a massive response from the ex-inmates of Britain's jails. Today it too boasts over 4,000 members, eager apparently to 'share memories, and work together on their latest ventures'.

Reading groups

Nowadays people say that the art of reading is dead, killed off by modern media, the Internet and other leisure pursuits. Try telling that to members of one of Britain's fastest-growing leisure activities – reading groups. The movement has been sweeping through Britain since the 1990s, and is still growing all the time, with an estimated 50,000 people now signed up.

The idea couldn't be simpler – members of the group agree to read a certain book, and then, a few weeks later meet up to exchange opinions over tea, coffee, or a glass of wine. Readers meet mainly in people's homes, but also in prisons, pubs, a zoo ... and, in one case, a dentist's waiting room! In Britain, sixty-nine percent of the groups are all-female, and very few members are under the age of thirty. So why are they so popular? 'I love the buzz and the sharing of opinions and chat,' one reader said. 'I love reading and it gives me a few hours to myself away from the kids.'

Language focus 1
Review of future forms

T10.1 James and Richard are arranging a trip to a football match. Read their telephone conversation below and choose the best future forms in this context. Then listen and check.

JAMES: Richard, how're you doing?

RICHARD: Fine, yes. Yourself?

JAMES: Yeah, good. Busy.

RICHARD: I'm sure. Listen, the reason I'm calling is (a) I'll take / I'm going to take my nephew Sam to his first football match on Saturday. United (b) are playing / will play City, as I'm sure you know. I just wondered if you fancy coming too?

JAMES: I'd love to … ah, but I've just remembered … (c) we're having / we'll have lunch over at my mum's on Saturday, so it depends on the time …

RICHARD: Well, (d) it's going to start / it starts at five … I've just phoned to check.

JAMES: Five o'clock? Hmm … that means I'd have to leave about half three … yeah, I'm sure Mum (e) doesn't mind / won't mind if I (f) leave / will leave then … (g) I'll tell / I'm going to tell her it's something really important. I'm sure (h) she'll understand / she's going to understand.

RICHARD: Well, what could be more important than going to your first football match?

JAMES: Exactly. By the way, have you thought about how to get there? (i) Are you going to take / Do you take the train like we did last time?

RICHARD: No, I've decided (j) I'm going to drive / I'll drive. It's easier with my nephew. My sister (k) drops / 's dropping him at my place around three, so that we've got plenty of time. (l) I'm going to pick you up / I'll pick you up from your mum's if you like.

JAMES: That would be great. About what time?

RICHARD: We'd better leave about four, in case the traffic (m) is / will be bad.

JAMES: Yeah, it's (n) likely to be / unlikely to be pretty busy, I guess. I tell you what, give me a call just before you (o) leave / will leave for Mum's.

RICHARD: Yeah, that's a good idea. Speak to you then.

JAMES: Yeah, see you on Saturday.

Analysis

1 Which two questions below do we usually use to ask people about their plans for Saturday afternoon?

a *What **do you do** next Saturday afternoon?*

b *What **are you doing** next Saturday afternoon?*

c *What **will you do** next Saturday afternoon?*

d *What **are you going to do** next Saturday afternoon?*

What is the difference between these two questions? Which examples in the dialogue express the same idea?

2 Which sentence below expresses a **new idea**? (The speaker has just thought about it.) Which expresses an **old idea**? (The speaker thought about it before.)

a ***I'm going to** take my nephew to his first football match.*

b ***I'll** tell her it's something really important.*

3 Generally we do not use the Present simple to talk about the future. Why is it used in sentences d, f, m and o in the dialogue?

4 *I'm sure she**'ll** understand.*
Here *will* is used to make a prediction. Which other phrases in the dialogue are used to make predictions? Do you know any other phrases like this?

▶ Read Language summaries A, B and C on pages 154 and 155.

Practice

1 Complete the gaps with the correct future form of the verbs in brackets.

a 'Have you decided what colour to paint the bathroom?'
'Yes, we _____ (paint) it yellow. It's such a cheerful colour.'

b 'Where _____ (go) for your holidays?'
'Well, actually we _____ (stay) at home this year. We _____ (buy) a new car this weekend, so can't really afford a holiday.'

c 'Have you got a name for the new baby yet?'
'Well, we _____ (call) her Alice if it _____ (be) a girl, but if it _____ (be) a boy, we don't really know.'

d My train _____ (leave) at 5.55 a.m. tomorrow, so I _____ (have) a really early night.

e Is it four o'clock already? I don't think we've got time to finish this today – we _____ (finish) it tomorrow morning.

f The referee looks furious, I think he _____ (send) Ricardo off!

g 'I'm afraid we've run out of today's special.'
'OK, never mind. I _____ (have) the pasta instead.'

h I think I _____ (make) a few extra copies of these notes in case anyone _____ (forget) theirs.

i We _____ (stay) in a lovely hotel, we had to book it ages ago.

j He's been ill for a while, but I'm sure Charles _____ (be) okay for his 70th birthday party.

2 Work in pairs. Each of you should choose three of the topics in the table below. Then prepare a short talk (about thirty seconds) on each. Think carefully about which future form you should use. Take it in turns to talk about each of the three topics.

A	plans for a party or celebration in the near future
B	journeys you are likely to make in the next few months
C	your career plans
D	your sporting predictions for the next few weeks/months
E	what the weather will be like in the next week
F	your plans for the rest of this week
G	your plans for when you finish this English course
H	how the world will be different when you are sixty
I	your plans for this weekend
J	your hopes for the future
K	your plans for this evening
L	your next birthday
M	how your life will be different in ten years' time
N	what you're planning to do with your money over the next few months
O	sporting fixtures in the next couple of weeks
P	what you're going to do in the next break

109

Task: Decide who's coming to dinner
Preparation: listening

1 Look at the picture below. How many of the people do you recognise? What is strange or unusual about the picture? Can you guess why the people are together at the dinner table?

2 **T10.2** You are going to organise the most amazing dinner party of all time – you can select any famous people from history to attend. Listen to six people making suggestions about guests. Make notes about who each person would invite and why.

3 Which of their suggestions do you like best? Why?

Task: speaking

1 a Work individually. Make a list of possible guests for the dinner party.

b Make notes about who they are/were and why you would like to invite them. Ask your teacher for any words or phrases you need.

▶ Useful language a

2 Work in groups of four. Compare your lists and then choose the best ten guests from the different lists. You should try to include a fair balance of areas of interest, historical periods, men and women, and nationalities.

▶ Useful language b

3 When you have agreed on the final list, draw up a seating plan. Decide whether you will put people together who have something in common, or who might disagree, for a more lively evening.

▶ Useful language c

4 Change groups and explain your guest list and seating plan to another group. Which group devised the most interesting guest list?

Language focus 2
Future continuous and Future perfect

1 How often do you use the following means of communication and what for? Compare your answers in pairs.

– chat rooms – e-mail – phone – text messaging

2 Read the posting that appeared on an Internet site. What kind of person is the writer? What is his attitude towards modern means of communication?

Is the art of conversation dying?

The other day, my wife and two teenage children did something we haven't done for ages. It didn't require access to the Internet, a TV screen, batteries … or anything else for that matter. But we all enjoyed it so much we're thinking of doing it again some time.

We had a conversation. The kind of real, live stimulating conversation that was common when I was growing up, but which seems all too rare these days. Today we have chat rooms, text messaging, e-mailing … but we seem to be losing the art of communicating face-to-face. We all know when young people are out on a date these days, they spend most of that time answering their mobile. And teenagers nowadays seem to prefer catching up with their friends by texting rather than actually speaking to them.

If we carry on like this, by the year 3000 we'll all be living in our own separate little hi-tech bubbles, it seems to me. We'll have lost the use of our voices – apart from singing along tunelessly to karaoke music – and we will be communicating only via our thumbs, which will be the size that our arms are now.

Am I exaggerating? What do you think? E-mail me, and who knows? Maybe we could even have a real conversation about it!

3 Write your own ideas about this. Then compare with another student.

Analysis

Look at the sentences and then tick the correct answer.
1 *By the year 3000 we'll all be living in our own hi-tech bubbles.*
Does this mean we will start living in them:
a in 3000?
b before 3000 and continue after 3000?
c only for the year 3000?

2 *By the year 3000, we'll have lost the use of our voices.*
Does this mean we will lose the use of our voices:
a before 3000? b in 3000? c after 3000?

3 *We will be communicating only via our thumbs.*
Is this something that:
a we plan to do?
b is happening now?
c will happen in the normal course of events?

▶ Read Language summary D on page 155.

111

Practice

1 **a** Read about Jay Fielding. Who is he and why is he going to Brazil?

Actor, singer and fashion icon Jay Fielding is on a promotional tour of Brazil and has a busy schedule of events and gatherings to attend in order to promote his new clothing range.

06:00	Arrive São Paulo airport
06:30–7.30	Drive from airport to hotel
07:30	Check in at hotel
8:00–12:00	Rest
12:00-12:45	Meet representatives of the Brazilian fashion industry
12:45–1:00	Travel to British Consulate
1:00–2:30	Arrive British Consulate – lunch with Consul at British Consulate
2:30–3:00	Photo call with VIPs at British Consulate
3:30–4.00	Drive back to hotel
4:00	'Meet the fans' session at hotel – autographs, photos, etc.
5:00–6.00	Rest
6:00–7:00	Press conference – hotel

b Write answers to these questions using the Future continuous or the Future perfect.

1 What will Jay be doing at 6:40?
He'll be driving from the airport to the hotel.
2 What will he have done by 8:00?
3 What will he be doing at 9:30?
4 Will he have had his rest by 1:00?
5 What will he be doing at 1:15?
6 What will he have done by 2:30?

c Write questions for these answers using the Future continuous or the Future perfect.

1 He'll be meeting representatives of the Brazilian fashion industry.
2 He'll have arrived at the British Consulate.
3 He'll have finished his VIP photo call.
4 No, he won't. He'll still be on his way back to the hotel.
5 He'll be having another rest.
6 He'll be answering questions at the press conference.

Pronunciation

1 **T10.3** Listen to six sentences and count the number of words in each (I'll = two words). Then listen again and write the sentences.

2 Practise saying the sentences, paying attention to the contractions.

---

2 Complete the questions with either the Future continuous or the Future perfect of the verbs in brackets. Use contractions where possible.

a _____ (drive) anywhere this weekend? Where do you think _____ (go)?
b _____ (sit) on a bus or train at any time today? When? What _____ (do) while you're travelling?
c By the end of the year, _____ (travel) abroad anywhere? Where?
d _____ (eat) at home tonight? Who _____ (do) the cooking?
e Do you think you _____ (get) married five years from now?
f Do you think you _____ (study) English this time next year?
g When do you think we _____ (finish) this book?
h Do you think people _____ (speak) English as an international language in 100 years' time?
i Do you think you _____ (retire) by the time you're sixty?

3 *Either* Ask and answer the questions with a partner.
Or Walk around the class asking different questions to different people (including your teacher). Speak to at least five people.

Writing
Types of message

1 a Look at the five messages below. Which is:

- a text message sent to a group of teenagers who are in a drama group together?
- an e-mail giving details of travel arrangements for a business trip?
- a message in a card?
- a note pushed under someone's door?
- a note to a family member or flatmate?

b Complete the gaps in the messages with the phrases in the box.

> We're all delighted for you!!
> Hope you had a good day at work
> I'll be out of the office tomorrow (Fri)
> Please be more considerate in future
> By the way, can you set the video for me
> Can you let me know if these flights suit ASAP?
> Best wishes,
> Much love
> C U all then

2 a Find at least two examples of the following in the messages.

1 words being missed out to make the message shorter
2 use of special number and letter combinations
3 capital letters and punctuation for extra emphasis
4 simplified 'incorrect' spellings
5 use of abbreviations
6 punctuation being missed out

b Which messages are formal? Which are informal?

3 Write an appropriate message for each of the following situations.

- Send a card congratulating an old friend and her partner, who have just had their first baby.
- Send an e-mail suggesting possible travel details, from London to your city, for someone who is attending an international conference.
- Write a note to put under someone's door to complain about the loud music coming from their flat most evenings.
- Write a note for your flatmate or a member of your family explaining why you will be out when he/she gets home, when you'll be back and what the arrangements for the evening meal are.

1

Claire,
Just heard your great news!
CONGRATULATIONS!! (a) _____ (Mind you, it is about time!) When can we get together to celebrate? Let's fix something up soon.
(b) _____

2

Previous ▼ ⬇ Next ▼ | 🖉 Reply 🖉 Reply All 🖉 Forward | 🏳 Flag | 🖨 Print 📝 Edit 🗑 Delete | 📋 Rewrap A̲ | 📥 Inbox ▼

Dear Simon,
We can now confirm available flights for your trip to Milan on 25th May. The times closest to those you requested are:
Depart: LONDON LHR 06:10   Arrive: MILAN MALPENSA 09:15
Return 28th May:
Depart: MILAN MALPENSA 10:15   Arrive: LONDON LHR 11:15
(c) _____
Either myself or Teresa Zanetti will be there to pick you up at the airport.
(d) _____ but will be back on Mon if you wish to discuss any further details.
(e) _____
Mary O'Connell

3

While you were out your dog was howling and kept the whole street awake until 5 a.m. when he finally stopped. As a result of this, we all suffered a sleepless night (f) _____
James Taverner (No. 46)

4

Hey evry1
im arrangin a little get 2gether 4 the group. The plan is 2 meet after skool on fri @ coffee republic @ 4.30 plz email me bck if u can go cos I dnt wana b the only 1 2 turn up! Tell n e 1 who doesn't check their e-mail and dnt b l8.
(g) _____

5

Marco
(h) _____ Gone to supermarket to get sthg for dinner. Pasta OK? Back about eight.
(i) _____ at 7:30 p.m.? Channel 4 'His'n'Hers ... I think it's on till 8:30 p.m, but could you check? Ring me if any problem.
Thanx!! See you later
L XX

Real life
Dealing with problems on the telephone

1 Discuss the following questions in small groups.

- Do you spend a lot of time on the phone? Who with?
- Do you enjoy chatting or do you prefer to keep your calls short and to the point?
- Have you ever got annoyed or frustrated when making a phone call? Why?

2 **T10.4** Listen to three telephone conversations. Answer these questions for each conversation.

a Who is speaking to who?
b What problem occurs?
c How does the conversation end?

3 a **T10.5** Listen and complete the sentences.

1 _____ I ringing at a _____ time?
2 Could you speak _____ a bit, please? Your voice is very _____ .
3 I _____ a message _____ .
4 If you'll just _____ with me ...
5 Sorry, you're _____ up.
6 Thanks for _____ back to me.
7 I'll have to _____ you _____ to another department.
8 It's _____ your flights to Istanbul next week.
9 When _____ be a _____ time to ring?
10 Can I just _____ your name and _____ , please?

b Discuss with a partner who said each sentence and when you would use it. Then look at the tapescript on page 173 and underline any other useful phrases for telephoning.

c Practise saying the phrases. Use the recording to help you.

4 Work in pairs. Prepare a conversation of your own, using the ideas below to help you. Practise your conversation. If possible, act it out for the rest of the class.

1 Who is speaking?	**2 What problem occurs?**
a boyfriend/girlfriend	a it's a bad time to call
b customer/telephonist	b keep getting the wrong person
c two colleagues	c problems on the line
d two friends	d other
e other	

3 Why/What about?	**4 How is the problem resolved?**
a to arrange a business meeting	a you arrange to phone back
b to arrange a night out	another time
c for a friendly chat	b you get cut off
d to make a complaint	c you hang up
e other	d other

STUDY ...

Using the Internet (1): Key Pals

Key pals are friends you keep in touch with via e-mail. It's an excellent way to practise your English! Here are some tips on how to get started, and how to make the most of your key pal.

Getting started

- Plenty of websites will help you find key pals. You can also try the *Cutting Edge* website at www.longman.com/cuttingedge/students/onedge.

- You will need to fill out a short form to become a registered user: you will need an e-mail address, a user name and a password, which you should keep secret.

- You will probably get a list of matches. Find someone who has more or less the same age and interests as you, and a similar level of English (if they are not native speakers).

- Give some information about yourself – but do not reveal your address or fix up a face-to-face meeting.

Making the most of your key pal

- The details of your life may seem ordinary, but they will be interesting to someone from a different culture – comparing lifestyles is fascinating!

- Ask questions to give your key pal something to write about.

- Do not reply to e-mails which you feel are aggressive or rude.

- Check your spelling and grammar before you send your e-mail.

- If you don't get a reply after a few days, someone else will probably be glad to hear from you!

PRACTISE...

1 Future forms ☐

Match the sentences in A to the explanations in B.

A

a I'm going to give up smoking.

b I'll phone and ask what's going on.

c Our friends are arriving tomorrow.

d Our plane leaves at 10.45 tomorrow.

B

1 a decision at the moment of speaking

2 an intention for the future

3 regular timetable

4 an arrangement in the future

▶ **Need to check? Language summary A, page 154.**

2 Making predictions ☐

Choose the correct alternative.

a She will almost certainly / definitely / likely come with us to the party.

b There may definitely / well / will be a thunderstorm later on today.

c It's likely / possibly / probably to be a fascinating evening.

d There's a good chance / opportunity / probability that the shops will still be open.

e You'd better take a coat in case it gets / got / will get cold later.

f Rosa is certain / definite / probably to win the competition.

▶ **Need to check? Language summary B, page 154.**

3 Future continuous or Future perfect ☐

Write the correct form of the verbs in brackets.

a At 9.30 a.m. tomorrow, I _____ (travel) to work – I normally get there about 10 a.m.

b Some people say that the Earth's oil resources _____ (run out) by the end of the century.

c The party _____ (finish) by midnight, so try to get there about 10 p.m.

d The children _____ (have) their dinner when you arrive – so don't worry about the noise!

e When she retires next year, Miss Tindall _____ (be) head of the school for exactly twenty years.

▶ **Need to check? Language summary D, page 155.**

4 Getting together ☐

Choose the most appropriate combination.

a an appointment with your boyfriend / at the dentist's / with your friends

b a speaker at a conference / date / dinner party

c a housewarming conference / meeting / party

d a school conference / reunion / relatives

e go on a conference / date / meeting

f business associates / classmates / relatives

▶ **Need to check? Vocabulary, page 106.**

5 Words that go together ☐

Match A and B to make phrases.

A

a arranged

b blind

c candlelit

d leisure

e wedding

B

1 activity

2 anniversary

3 marriage

4 date

5 dinner

▶ **Need to check? Reading, page 107.**

6 Phrases for problems on the telephone ☐

Put the words in the box in the correct position in the sentences.

about bad put up would

a Am I calling at a time?

b Could you speak a bit, please? Your voice is very faint.

c I'll have to you through to another department.

d I'm calling your flight to Prague next month.

e When be a good time to ring back?

▶ **Need to check? Real life, page 114.**

Pronunciation spot

'Hard' and 'soft' letters

The letters 'c' and 'g' can be pronounced in different ways.

- 'c' can be pronounced as /k/ (usually before 'a', 'o', 'u', 'r' or 't') or as /s/ (usually before 'e' or 'i')
- 'g' can be pronounced as /g/ (usually before 'a', 'o', 'u', 'l' or 'r') or as /dʒ/ (usually before 'e' or 'i')

a How do you pronounce the words below? Which of the words follow the rules above, and which are exceptions? What other ways are the two letters pronounced?

ctivities **g** ngered **g** ngel **c** ndlelit
c ndidates **c** elebrate **c** olleague **c** urious e **g** er
embra **c** e **g** ives marriage on **c** e re **g** istered
si **g** ned so **c** ial

b **T10.6** Listen and check. Then practise saying all the words, paying attention to the sounds in bold.

REMEMBER!

Look back at the areas you have practised. Tick the ones you feel confident about. Now try the MINI-CHECK on page 160 to check what you know!

Interfering with nature

▶ Hypothetical situations in the present and the past
▶ **Reading and vocabulary:** *Big questions facing modern medical science*
▶ **Real life:** Giving and reporting opinions
▶ **Pronunciation:** Sentence stress
▶ **Task:** Make the right decision
▶ **Writing:** For and against essay

Reading and vocabulary

1 Check the words in bold below in your mini-dictionary. Then mark the ideas:

1 = I think this happens already.
2 = I think this will happen in the future.
3 = I don't think this will ever happen.

a   an average **life expectancy** of over 100 years
b   the replacement of **damaged organs** using **cells** from human **embryos**
c   human **immortality**
d   the **cloning** of plants and animals
e   the cloning of human beings
f   the **eradication** of **infectious diseases** such as malaria
g   a **vaccination** against AIDS
h   the prediction and **treatment** of **hereditary diseases**
i   **cosmetic surgery** to make your hands look younger
j   **genetic engineering** of embryos to make them grow up slim, athletic, etc.

Compare your answers in pairs.

2 Read the article and check your ideas. Don't worry about the gaps at this stage.

3 a `T11.1` Can you guess what these numbers refer to in the text? Listen and check.

2,000	1 million	20th	75	35
1980s	1997	6	24-hour	2010

b Complete the text with the numbers.

4 Find words or phrases in the text that mean the following.

a   unlikely (section a)
b   without an end in sight (section a)
c   almost (section b)
d   looking exactly like (section c)
e   acceptable reason (section c)
f   remove (section d)
g   to get worse (section d)
h   a group of people considered superior to others (section d)

5 Discuss the following questions in small groups.

• Which things do you feel are positive developments?
• Which do you think are wrong or dangerous?

BIG QUESTIONS FACING MODERN MEDICAL SCIENCE

a Will we be able to live forever one day?

Scientists predict that the average female life expectancy in the developed world will be more than 150 by the year 2070 (it is currently (1) _____). But it's doubtful whether the dramatic increases in life expectancy occurring in the (2) _____ century – thanks to better housing, diet and the eradication of many diseases – can be continued indefinitely.

Perhaps our best chance of living forever lies with stem cells. Stem cells are present in embryos for a limited period in their early development. They have the potential to develop into any tissue type in the body – skin, blood, muscles, nerves, etc. – and scientists have already begun cloning embryos and using them to grow matching tissue to replace damaged organs in the body. Theoretically it could be possible to continue replacing organs indefinitely – creating the prospect of immortality, as long as there are enough stem cells to grow the necessary organs!

b Will we ever eliminate disease?

Until the (3) _____ , humanity seemed to be winning the war against the world's major diseases: the use of vaccination and the development of powerful antibiotics had seen killer diseases such as smallpox and polio all but eliminated. But since then, world-wide epidemics such as AIDS have raised a whole new set of questions about the world's health.

Disturbingly, with the exception of AIDS, little has changed in developing countries since the nineteenth century: for example, malaria is still estimated to kill approximately (4) _____ people a year. Poverty is the greatest cause of disease world-wide, so until serious efforts are made to tackle that problem, the future looks bleak.

Even in the developed world, wealth and progress create their own health problems. As we move towards a pressurised '24/7' lifestyle, there are more diseases associated with stress and depression; an over-rich diet brings an increase in heart disease and cancer; and global warming means that disease carriers such as mosquitoes may migrate further north.

All is not lost, however. The discovery of the human genome – the set of DNA instructions for human life – should make it far easier to predict and treat hereditary diseases, which may be the way forward in the future.

c Will it be possible to clone human beings?

Cloning – making a copy of a plant or animal by extracting a cell and developing it artificially – has been used on plants and animals for a very long time. The Ancient Greeks cloned plants more than (5) _____ years ago. Dolly, the world's first cloned sheep, was born in (6) _____ and the world's first cloned kitten (CC or 'Copy Cat') appeared in 2002.

For those expecting millions of identical cloned sheep and cats, all has not gone totally according to plan however: CC – though resembling her mother – was no more a 'copy' than a cat born normally. More worryingly, Dolly the Sheep suffered arthritis from an early age and died aged (7) _____ – half the age of a normal sheep. One scientist has claimed 'Cloning can and does go wrong, and there is no justification for believing that this won't happen with humans.'

Theoretically, the technology exists to clone humans too, and though the process remains illegal in all but a few countries, there have been several claims that cloned babies have already been created for infertile couples.

d Will we be able to buy the perfect body?

With plastic surgery to alter the shape of your nose, botox to remove wrinkles from your forehead, collagen to make your lips fuller, liposuction to remove fat from your stomach and dental surgery to give you perfect teeth, it seems that there is no part of the body that cannot be improved … except one. Strangely enough, until recently, there was one area that plastic surgeons could do nothing to rejuvenate: the hands.

Not for much longer. A new technique pioneered in America promises to get rid of wrinkles, by injecting fat from the stomach into the hands. 'After the age of (8) _____ , the quality of your skin starts to deteriorate and the fat over them becomes thinner,' says Jeff Hoeyberghs of the Wellness Kliniek in Belgium. 'We gently put the fat back in.'

However, Dr Lee M. Silver, of Princetown University predicts that by (9) _____ it will be possible to go much further than plastic surgery ever will. At a price, he believes, parents will be able to have (10) _____-old embryos genetically engineered, so that the child grows up slim, more athletic, or even more intelligent. In time, he believes there will be two species of human being: the 'natural' version, and a genetically engineered elite, as different from ordinary humans as we are from chimpanzees.

Language focus 1
Hypothetical situations in the present

1 **a** Look at the photos. What similarities and differences are there between them? What is the connection between the two pictures?

b Read the text and check.

Until 1988, Cindy Jackson was just an ordinary-looking farm girl from Ohio in the United States. Then, on inheriting some money from her father, she decided to re-invent herself through cosmetic surgery. She spent $100,000 on face-lifts, nose jobs, chin reductions, implants and liposuction to remove fat from her knees, thighs and waistline. 'I wanted to be Barbie,' says the forty-eight-year-old. 'Now I am.' She now runs a business in London advising other people on cosmetic surgery. She has written two books, and has made a video about her life and transformation.

'Twenty years ago I didn't exist,' she says. 'Now life is more than I ever dreamed it would be. But I have worked very hard for everything. Having said that, I'm not interested in designer clothes – with the right face and body you can look good in anything. I live very modestly. I have a flat in London, a second-hand Mercedes and three adorable cats. I value my friends and family far above material things. Anyone who criticises my choices probably has way too much time on their hands and not nearly enough fulfilment in their own personal lives.'

2 **a** Do you think there's anything wrong with what Cindy Jackson has done?

b Which of the statements below do you most/least agree with?

1 If I had $100,000 to spare, I'd probably do the same thing myself!

2 I wish people would think less about their appearance and more about what really matters in life!

3 What if everyone went out and did the same thing? We'd all end up looking like Barbie dolls!

4 It's time people changed their attitude to plastic surgery: it's everywhere nowadays so just accept it!

Analysis

1 Look at the past forms in the sentences below. Which of them refer to the past? Which of them refer to an imaginary or hypothetical situation?
  a *If (only) I **had** $100,000 to spare …*
  b *She **was** just an ordinary-looking farm girl from Ohio.*
  c ***What if** everyone **went out** and **did** the same thing?*
  d *She **spent** $100,000 on face-lifts.*
  e *It's time people **changed** their attitude …*
  f *I wish I **had** a nicer nose.*

2 The hypothetical Past simple is used in conditional sentences with *would*. Find an example in the quotes in exercise 2b.

3 Look at the sentences below. Is there a difference in meaning between them?
  *I wish **you spoke** English.*
  *I wish **you'd speak** English.*

▶ Read Language summary A on page 155.

Practice

1 a Look at picture 1 and complete the sentences below with the correct form of the verbs in brackets.

1 I wish I _____ (be) twenty-one again.
2 It's time I _____ (go) on a diet.
3 If I _____ (lose) some weight, I _____ (look) younger.
4 I wish someone _____ (invent) a cure for middle-age!

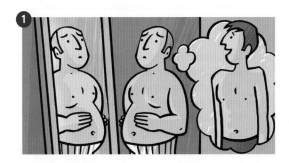

b What do you think the people in pictures 2, 3 and 4 are thinking or saying? Write similar sentences starting like this:

If …   If only …   I wish …   It's time …

2 a Look at the Wishful thinking quiz. Complete the questions in Section A with the correct form of the verbs in brackets.

WISHFUL**THINKING**

Section A

1 If you _____ (have) the opportunity to change one thing about your appearance, what _____ (you change)? Or _____ (you prefer) to stay the same?

2 Do you ever wish you _____ (can) play a musical instrument? Which one?

3 If you _____ (can) change places with a celebrity for a day, who _____ (you choose)?

4 Do you ever wish you _____ (have) a different name from the one you have? What name _____ (you choose) instead?

5 If you _____ (can) be any animal, what animal _____ (be)?

6 Is there a foreign language that you wish you _____ (can) speak?

Section B

1 It's really time that I …

2 I wish my parents/friend/partner/children would/wouldn't …

3 I wish I could …

4 I wish I had …

5 I wish I was/wasn't …

b Answer the quiz questions. Then compare with a partner.

3 a Complete the sentences in Section B of the quiz with as many ideas as you can.

b Compare your sentences with a partner.

119

Language focus 2
Hypothetical situations in the past

1 Are tattoos popular in your country? Do you know anyone who has one? What do you think of tattoos?

2 [T11.2] Listen to the story of Stuart's tattoo. Why did he have it done? How and why has his attitude towards the tattoo changed?

3 Listen again and complete the sentences.

a Everyone said it was the best tattoo _____, and I was really pleased.

b Yeah, that's right. The cards _____ up by accident.

c If I _____ with a Japanese person before I got the tattoo done!

Analysis

1 Which Past perfect verb in exercise 3 is used

a to refer back to an event that happened earlier?

b for reported speech?

c to talk about a hypothetical or unreal situation in the past?

2 Compare the groups of sentences below. Which refers to the past and which is general in each case? Which verb forms are used?

• *I wish / If only I **didn't have** this tattoo.*
  *I wish / If only I **had checked** what the card said.*

• *If he **had checked** with a Japanese person, he **would have got** the right name.*
  *If it **wasn't** so expensive and painful, he **would get** rid of it.*
  *If he **hadn't met** the girls, he still **wouldn't know** what the letters said.*

▶ Read Language summary B on page 156.

Practice

1 **a** Complete the gaps with the correct form of the verbs in brackets.

1 If I 'd checked (check) more carefully, it would never have happened (never happen)!

2 I wish I _____ (not do) it!

3 I wish I _____ (buy) it!

4 If I _____ (not meet) her, my life _____ (be) very different.

5 I wish I _____ (allow) more time.

6 If only I _____ (try) harder!

7 It _____ (be) much better if I _____ (not open) my mouth!

8 I wish I _____ (never go) to that party!

9 If only I _____ (can) turn the clock back five minutes!

10 I wish I _____ (never set) eyes on him!

b Have you ever felt regrets like these? Choose three situations and describe them in more detail. Write about what would have happened / would be different now, if you hadn't done these things.

Example:
I wish I had allowed more time to get to the party last Saturday, because I got stuck in really bad traffic and when I got there it was nearly over. If I'd left home earlier, I wouldn't have missed all the fun.

Jenny

I lived to regret it!

Real life
Giving and reporting opinions

1 **T11.4** Six people were asked their opinion about the following issues.

- Should smoking in the workplace be banned?
- Should it be illegal to use surrogate mothers?
- Should experiments on animals be banned?

Listen and make a note of which issue they were asked about and what they said.

2 **a** Match A and B to make phrases.

	A	B
1	As far as	convinced that
2	I haven't really	doubt that
3	If you ask	honest
4	I'm absolutely	I'm concerned
5	I've no	me
6	It's	often said that
7	Many people	thought about it
8	To be	would say that

b Which of the phrases are used to:

1 introduce your own opinion?
2 report someone else's opinion?
3 say you're not sure about something?

2 **a** **T11.3** Three guests are appearing on the daytime TV programme *Jenny* where members of the public discuss personal issues with the host and the studio audience. Today's edition is called 'I lived to regret it'. Listen to what they say and answer the questions.

Jade **Jack** **Phoebe**

1 Who does each person talk about?
2 How did they meet this person?
3 How did this person cause them problems?

b Who do you feel most sorry for? Who do you think acted most foolishly?

c Write sentences about each person.

She wishes she had/hadn't …
If he had/hadn't … he would/wouldn't (have) …

3 **a** Work in pairs. Think of a story for another guest on Jenny's *I lived to regret it* show. (It can be based on a real story or completely fictional.)

b Student A: You are Jenny. Decide what questions to ask. Student B: You are a guest. Decide how you will explain the story. Practise the interview.

c Take turns to act out your interviews. The rest of the class is the studio audience. At the end they can give their opinions, either supporting or criticising the guest.

Pronunciation

1 **T11.5** Listen and write the phrase used at the beginning of each sentence. Which words are stressed?

a _____ we should go ahead!
b _____ , I don't care one way or the other.
c _____ , there's nothing more to say.
d _____ that what you say is true.
e _____ the answer is obvious.

2 Listen again. Practise saying the sentences, paying attention to the stress and intonation.

3 Look at the tapescript (Recording 4) on page 173 and underline other phrases for giving your opinion.

Task: Make the right decision

Preparation: reading and listening

1 The details of the cases on the right are imaginary, but they are based on real ones. Check the words in bold in your mini-dictionary. Then read and summarise the dilemma in each case.

2 **T11.6** Listen to two people discussing one of the cases and answer the questions.

a Which case are they discussing?
b What are the main arguments for and against?

3 **T11.7** Listen and complete the phrases they use for disagreeing with each other.

a I can _____ but …
b The _____ of it is …
c I know _____ but …
d I know but _____ …

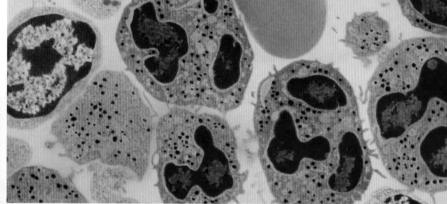

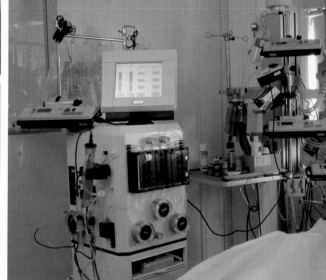

Mr and Mrs A have three children aged twelve, ten and eight. The youngest has a rare hereditary disease, from which he will die, unless a suitable **bone marrow donor** can be found. So far, no match has been found and the boy has been given two more years to live.

Mr and Mrs A want the right to be given **IVF treatment** so that an embryo with the correct bone marrow can then be selected, and Mrs A can have another baby who will save its older brother's life. The genetic selection of embryos is at present illegal in the country where the A family live. The As have appealed to the European Court of Human Rights.

QUESTION: Should the As be allowed to have a baby in this way?

A year ago Miss B was living a normal life as an administrator in a large hospital. She then suffered a **severe stroke**, which left her **paralysed** from the neck down. Now the forty-three-year-old cannot be moved from her hospital bed: she is kept alive only by a **ventilator** and the tubes that deliver food into her body. She has been told that there is a less than a one percent chance of her condition ever improving. Her mental abilities are unaffected, but she is severely depressed. Miss B, who is single with no children, has asked the doctors to turn off the ventilator so she can die a peaceful death. The doctors have told her that they are not allowed to fulfil her request.

QUESTION: Should the doctors be allowed to do what Miss B asks?

Two years ago C, a thirty-eight-year-old woman, was diagnosed with cancer, which needed to be treated with **chemotherapy**. She was told she would be unable to have children after the treatment so, using **sperm** from her partner D, she was given IVF treatment, and the embryos were then frozen, until C was well enough to have the child.

However, shortly after her treatment was completed, D left C for another woman. C is now applying to the courts for the right to have the child. However, D says he does not now want to have a child with C, and wants the embryos to be destroyed.

QUESTION: Should C be allowed to have the child?

Task: speaking

1 a Work in pairs. Choose the case that most interests you. Then look at the question at the end of the case and make notes under the following headings: arguments for and arguments against.

b Think of three or four arguments for each. Ask your teacher for any words or phrases you need.

▶ Useful language a

2 Compare your arguments for and against in groups, giving your own opinion on what should happen. Try to reach an agreement on what should be done.

▶ Useful language b and c

3 Present the arguments for and against, and your conclusions to the class. What do the rest of the class think?

Useful language

a Arguments for and against

What if ... (he/she became ill again)?

How would (the baby) feel when he/she grew up?

What about the rights of (the father/baby)?

b Giving your opinion

He/She should(n't) be allowed to ...

I think people should have the right to ...

In my opinion it's morally wrong to ...

It's a question of whether or not ...

I think you have to be practical ...

I feel really sorry for ... but I feel that ...

c Agreeing/disagreeing

I see what you mean, but ...

I totally agree (with ...)

I don't agree (at all).

Writing
For and against essay

1 Read the article and find one argument in favour of banning smoking and one argument against.

> Doctors today voted overwhelmingly for a total ban on smoking in public places. They want it outlawed in shops, bars, restaurants and at work to cut deaths from lung cancer and heart diseases. The call follows a decision by the Irish government to make smoking in public illegal.
>
> Several cities and countries, including Finland, South Africa and Thailand, already have the legislation. But critics say a ban is difficult to enforce and has sparked chaos in New York. Evidence suggests that passive smoking increases the risk of lung cancer by up to thirty percent and heart disease by twenty to twenty-three percent.

2 Here are some more arguments about the issue. Are they for or against the idea that 'Smoking should be banned in all public places'?

a Everyone should have the right to choose whether they smoke or not.
b You can't force people to stop if they don't want to.
c Banning smoking would only force people to smoke in secret.
d Treating people with smoking-related illnesses costs millions of dollars a year.
e The case that passive smoking harms people seems very strong.
f The police have better things to do than enforcing a smoking ban.

3 Look at the plan for a 'For and Against' essay. Put the phrases in the box below in a suitable section.

- **Introduction:** a short introduction to the topic and why it's interesting
- **Arguments for:** two or three arguments in favour of the statement
- **Arguments against:** two or three arguments against the statement
- **Conclusion:** your own opinion

One argument against … is	In my opinion	Firstly,
Another point in favour of … is	It is certainly true that	Secondly,
Many people nowadays think that	On the other hand	To sum up,
There are two main reasons why I think	Over the last few years	In conclusion,

4 Write an essay of about 200 words about one of the titles below using the plan in exercise 3.

a What are the arguments for and against banning smoking in all public places?
b What are the arguments for and against making it compulsory to wear seat belts in all forms of motorised transport (including buses and taxis).
c New fertilisation techniques make it possible for women to have babies in their fifties, or even sixties. Should they be allowed to have children at this age?
d Should people be allowed to have cosmetic surgery before the age of eighteen?

STUDY...

Using the Internet (2): Ideas for using online news

You can find English-language news anywhere thanks to the Internet, e.g. from *The Times, Ananova.com*. (Ask your teacher for other suggestions.) You can often browse through the day's news free of charge. Here are some ideas if you have access to English-language news online.

- Compare how two newspapers deal with the same story: Make a list of information which (1) only appears in one newspaper and (2) appears in both newspapers.

- Make a list of the different sections you would expect to find in a newspaper, e.g. political news, TV listings, arts reviews, etc. How many of the sections can you find? Make a brief note of what is covered in each one.

- Read one article in detail with a good dictionary. Make a list of ten to twelve useful words or phrases that you found in the article. Try to summarise the main points of the article yourself.

- Choose an area you are interested in, e.g. sports, fashion, music, etc. Print out a selection of articles on your chosen topic and make a list of new factual information you have got from the articles.

- Get a translation of an article into your own language (many websites offer a 'translate this article' service). See if you can do anything to improve the translation yourself!

PRACTISE...

1 Hypothetical situations in the present ☐

Choose the best way to complete the sentences below.

a If I had enough money I'll buy a new motorbike. / I'd buy a new motorbike.

b When I was younger I'd learn how to swim. / I used to go swimming every day.

c I wish we had more time to discuss it but unfortunately I have to go now. / last night, but unfortunately I had to go.

d It's time you started looking for a job. / will start looking for a job.

e I wish you wouldn't interrupt me all the time. / when I was talking to my mother.

▶ **Need to check? Language summary A, page 155.**

2 Hypothetical situations in the past ☐

Choose the correct alternative.

a If you / you've / you'd told me you wanted one, I would have bought you a ticket.

b I wish I had / I'd have / I've had enough money to buy you a lovely present!

c If we'd arrived earlier, we had / would / would have got to the restaurant before it closed.

d If he hadn't failed his exams, he 'd be work / 'd be working / would have been working now.

e He will / should / would never have done it if his friends hadn't encouraged him.

▶ **Need to check? Look at Language summary B, page 156.**

3 Giving and reporting opinions ☐

Change the words in bold so that they are correct.

a As far as I'm **concern** ... _____

b Many people would **said** that ... _____

c I'm absolutely **convince** that ... _____

d To be **honestly** ... _____

e I've **not** doubt that ... _____

f I haven't really **thinking** about it ... _____

g If **you'd** ask me ... _____

h It's often **saying** that ... _____

▶ **Need to check? Real life, page 121.**

4 Verb forms ☐

Complete the sentences with the correct form of the verbs.

a He will die, unless a suitable bone marrow donor can _____ (find).

b Should they be allowed _____ (have) a baby in this way?

c There isn't much chance of her condition ever _____ (improve).

d She was told she _____ (be) unable to have children after the treatment.

e The embryos _____ (freeze), until she was well enough to have a baby.

▶ **Need to check? Task, pages 122 and 123.**

5 Word building ☐

Write the noun, verb or adjective form of the words.

a immortal (adj) _____ (n)

b doubt (v) _____ (adj)

c justified (adj) _____ (n)

d elimination (n) _____ (v)

e poor (adj) _____ (n)

▶ **Need to check? Reading, page 117.**

6 For and against ☐

Match A and B to make phrases.

A	B
a Another point	1 conclusion
b In	2 in favour of this is
c There are two	3 is certainly true that
d It	4 other hand
e On the	5 main reasons why

▶ **Need to check? Writing, page 124.**

Pronunciation spot

Rhyming sounds

a Look at the words on the left, paying attention to the pronunciation of the letters in bold. Which word in each group rhymes with the word?

a bleak	ache / take / week
b blood	food / mud / would
c disease	face / keys / kiss
d elite	sit / sweet / white
e enough	cough / laugh / stuff
f forehead	bed / need / made
g heart	earth / hurt / part
h year	bear / hear / wear

b (T11.8) Listen and check. Then practise saying all the words, paying attention to the sounds in bold.

REMEMBER!

Look back at the areas you have practised. Tick the ones you feel confident about. Now try the MINI-CHECK on page 160 to check what you know!

Media mania

► Reporting people's exact words
► Verbs that summarise what people say
► **Vocabulary and speaking**: Types of media
► **Pronunciation**: Word stress, stress patterns
► **Speaking and listening**: The media game
► **Reading and speaking**: *Giving up TV*
► **Wordspot**: *speak* and *talk*
► **Task**: Prepare a questionnaire about the media
► **Writing**: A film review

Vocabulary and speaking
Types of media

1 **a** Work in groups. Which group(s) below do the words in the box belong to?

chat shows	comics	documentaries
live sports coverage	sitcoms	soaps
tabloids	phone-ins	traffic reports
current affairs programmes		

1   radio programmes   3   TV programmes
2   magazines/newspapers

b Think of four more examples for each group.

2 Think of an example of each type of programme, film, etc. Which types do you most enjoy? Are there any that you don't like?

3 **a** Which of the programmes you talked about in exercises 1 and 2 would you describe as

1   informative?   7   addictive?
2   controversial?   8   harmless fun?
3   influential?   9   mindless rubbish?
4   sensational?   10   usually worth watching?
5   often biased?   11   aimed mainly at men?
6   entertaining?   12   aimed mainly at women?

b Compare your opinions in small groups.

> ## Pronunciation
>
> **T12.1** Listen to the pronunciation of the adjectives in 1–9 above and mark the stressed syllable. Practise saying the words, paying attention to the stressed syllable.

Speaking and listening
The media game

1 Work in groups. Check the words on the board in your mini-dictionary. Then play the game. Each put a coin on the start square. Roll a dice to move around the board. You must talk about that topic for one minute. If you can't, you miss a turn. The first player to reach the finish is the winner.

2 **T12.2** Listen to four people talking about the topics in the game. Then answer the questions.

a Which topic were they talking about?
b What were the main points they made?
c Do you agree with what they say?

FINISH	Go back four spaces.	Miss a turn.	Talk for one minute about the 'paparazzi'.	Go to FINISH.
Talk for one minute about TV programmes aimed at men.	Talk for one minute about the programmes you liked best when you were a child.	You have thirty seconds to list ten famous cartoon characters.	Go on two spaces.	Talk for one minute about the things you read / don't read in the newspaper.
Talk for one minute about sport on television.	Talk for one minute about listening to the radio.	Go on one space.	You have twenty seconds to list five famous television crime series.	Talk for one minute about the weather forecast on the television in your country.
Talk for one minute about violence on television.	Go on two spaces.	Talk for one minute about your favourite film.	Talk for one minute about the advantages of having satellite television.	Go back to START.
Go back two spaces.	You have thirty seconds to name three stories that are in the news at the moment.	Miss a turn.	Talk for one minute about magazines aimed at women.	Talk for one minute about television commercials that you really like or hate.
START	Talk for one minute about your favourite television programme.	Talk for one minute about your favourite newspaper or magazine.	Go on three spaces.	You have twenty seconds to list four different ways you can find out the news.

Language focus 1
Reporting people's exact words

1 Read the unfortunate quotes that people have given in the media. Which ones do you like best? Do you know any other quotes like this?

That wasn't what I meant!

When people speak to the media, sometimes the words don't come out quite right. Here are some of our favourite 'stupid quotes'.

a 'We are unable to report the weather this evening, because we depend on weather reports from the airport, which is closed due to the bad weather. We don't know whether we will be able to give you a weather report tomorrow, it depends on the weather.'
TV weather forecaster

b 'Traffic is very heavy at the moment, so if you are thinking of leaving now, you should set off a few minutes earlier.'
UK radio traffic report

c 'Do you run the risk of failure if you don't succeed?'
Journalist interviewing UK Prime Minister

d 'Smoking kills – if you're killed you've lost a very important part of your life.'
Anti-smoking campaigner

e 'For every fatal shooting, there are roughly three non-fatal attacks. Folks, this is unacceptable in America – we're going to do something about it.'
US President speaking about gun crime

f 'Our main strength is that we don't have any weaknesses. Our main weakness is that we don't really have any strengths.'
American football coach

g 'Most cars on our roads have only one occupant who is usually the driver.'
BBC news reporter

h 'Mao Tse Deng's health is now failing, so many matters have been passed to Wan Li, who, despite his age, is still alive.'
TV News Report about China

i 'The streets of Philadelphia are safe, it's only the people that make them unsafe.'
Police Chief of Philadelphia

j 'The word genius isn't applicable in football. A genius is a guy like Norman Einstein.'
American footballer

k 'If history repeats itself tonight, we can expect the same thing to happen again.'
England football manager

l 'Sometimes journalists write what I say and not what I really mean.'
Baseball player

2 Look at the reported versions below of the direct speech in exercise 1. Underline the differences between the direct and reported versions.

a The weather forecaster told viewers that they were unable to report on the weather, because they depended on weather reports from the airport, which was closed due to bad weather. He said they did not know whether they would be able to give a weather report the next day, as it depended on the weather.

b The newsreader said that traffic was heavy, and that if people were thinking of leaving home at that moment, they should set off a few minutes earlier.

c The journalist asked the Prime Minister if he ran the risk of failure if he didn't succeed.

d She said that smoking kills, and that if you are killed, you have lost an important part of your life.

e The President said that for every fatal shooting in America there were roughly three non-fatal attacks. He said that this was unacceptable in America, and that they were going to do something about it.

f The coach told reporters that the team's main strength was that they did not have any weaknesses. However, he added that their main weakness was that they didn't have any strengths.

Analysis

Look at the reported speech in exercise 2 above and answer the questions.

1 What generally happens to verb tenses in reported speech?
2 In which quote above do verb tenses stay the same? Why?
3 Which verbs are used to introduce reported speech?
4 Which conjunctions follow the reporting verbs? Why is *that* repeated in e above?
5 What is the difference in the use of *say* and *tell*?
6 What happens to pronouns and time words in reported speech?
7 What happens to interjections like 'folks' in reported speech?
8 What is the difference in word order between direct and reported questions?

▶ Read Language summary A on page 156.

Practice

1 Put the remaining quotes from exercise 1 on page 128 into reported speech.

2 Correct the mistakes underlined in the reported speech.

a The journalist <u>told</u> the Prime Minister <u>did he know</u> anything about the scandal.

b The minister <u>said</u> journalists last year he <u>will</u> resign if his policy <u>is</u> not successful, but he is still in his job.

c The manager <u>told</u> that his team had done their best <u>yesterday</u> but <u>if</u> the other side had simply played better.

d Journalists <u>added</u> the minister when <u>will he make</u> his decision.

e The President said he <u>is</u> speaking to other leaders later <u>this</u> day to discuss how they <u>will</u> react.

3 **a** In everyday life people often report what other people have said ... but not always accurately! Answer the following questions for each picture.

1 What's happening?
2 What do the speakers claim were the original words?

b T12.3 Listen to the actual words and correct what was said. You do not have to report every single word, as long as the content is correct.

Actually, she said ...

Pronunciation

1 T12.4 Listen to two people reporting what another said. Who thinks Debbie is telling the truth: A or B? What is the difference in the stress pattern?

2 T12.5 Listen to eight more people reporting what others said. Which did not think the speaker was telling the truth?

3 Look at the tapescript on page 175. Practise saying the sentences, paying attention to the stress patterns.

1 Earlier on I chatted to Tammy Beauregard, the star of the film, about rumours that she is expecting a baby. She told me this was nonsense and that she will never have children because of her film career.

2 Your mother phoned about half an hour ago. She said it was nothing important and that she'd ring back later this evening.

3 She said I'd taken some money from her purse!

4 Do you know what? My boss asked me if I wanted to go out for dinner this evening. I told her to get lost!

It's my turn.

5 Mum said I could play as long as I like and that you've got to wait till I'm finished.

Reading and speaking

1 Discuss the following questions in small groups.

- How important is television to you personally? How many hours of TV do you watch in an average week?
- Do you consider yourself, or anyone you know, a 'telly addict'?
- Why might someone decide to give up TV?

2 Read the text quickly. Which sentence best describes the attitude of the writer towards television?

a He adores TV, but decided to give it up because it was dominating his life.

b He's found it virtually impossible to reduce the amount of TV he watches.

c He finds himself less and less devoted to television, but still can't stop watching it completely.

d He's totally disillusioned with television and has lost all interest in it.

3 Read the text again. Tick the things the writer did.

a He slowly reduced the amount of television he watched.

b He spent more than an hour looking for something interesting to watch.

c He watched television twenty-four hours a day as a child.

d He found it hard to find other things to do instead of watching TV.

e He stopped following the news on TV.

f He stopped watching his favourite TV programme, *The Simpsons*.

4 The writer uses colourful, figurative language to describe his relationship with TV. Check the literal meaning of the words in bold in your mini-dictionary. Then answer the questions.

a Why does he talk about '**gorging** himself on news' (paragraph 2), and '**devouring** a whole book' (paragraph 9)? What impression does this create?

b What impression does the phrase '**flicking listlessly**' give (paragraph 3)?

c Why does he talk about 'falling out of love' with TV (paragraph 4)?

d What does he mean when he says 'television needed frequent breaks from me' (paragraph 4)?

e Why does he feel that 'television had come to hate me personally' (paragraph 8)?

f What comparison is he making when he says he feels '**sour** at how he was **betrayed**' (paragraph 9)?

5 Discuss the following questions in small groups.

- Do you think the writer will ever give up TV totally?
- Should, and could, you give it up?
- What would you do instead?
- Do you think people generally watch too much TV?

Giving up TV

First off, I have to admit the falseness of the title. You can't give up television. You might want to. You might try. You might even succeed for about tweny-four hours. But, eventually you will go back. I know. I've spent the last three years trying to wean myself off the box in the corner.

It started simply. I have satellite TV, and therefore have, at the best guess, some 200 or so channels available, eighty percent being completely devoted to shopping. Of the remainder, some I felt I couldn't live without. There were channels offering comedy, a host of BBC entertainment programmes I had previously enjoyed, drama, a huge choice of instant headline news to gorge upon, historical documentaries ...

Then one day I found, with an audible start, I had been sitting for over an hour flicking listlessly through all seven million or so channels, resting on each programme for no more than thirty seconds or so.

A thought suddenly occurred to me. I was falling out of love with television. I've been in love with television now for almost my entire life. When I first fell in love, television needed frequent breaks from me. Then came twenty-four-hour television. The satellite revolution brought more delights I couldn't get enough of. More awful talk shows. More cheap adverts. More 'straight to video' movies. A twenty-four-hour diet (though most go off between three and six a.m., thus giving me a chance to grab some sleep) of television without limits.

And we both lived happily ever after.

Until that day, when I had wasted an hour of my life on television without actually finding anything to entertain, inform or educate me.

Never mind. The next night, I was back, lying in front of The Box in the corner, idly flicking. And finding nothing. At that point, I decided to give up television. It's been nice knowing you, but it's over. So long, and thanks for all the eyestrain.

But it isn't possible. I didn't manage to give up. But I did manage to detach. If I missed a programme I had read about I didn't mourn or worry. I let the programme go. Next, I gave up surfing. Easy. It was never rewarding – proof not only that television had fallen out of love with me at the same time I had fallen out of love with television, but that television had come to hate me personally. Finding other things to do was easy.

I went back to reading, devouring a whole book in an evening. Finally came news. I love news, possibly more than I love television. So this was the hardest to give up. But television actually helped. Ceefax gave me instant, always-on news at any time, better written and more succinct than television or radio has ever managed. But that leaves a single gap. *The Simpsons*. I can't tear that final link. The equivalent of keeping a wedding album years after the divorce is, for me, *The Simpsons*. Whilst every other programme has dropped away, *The Simpsons* remains. One day, I know I'll give that series up too. At that point television will be part of my history. I'll remain forever fond of the good times, and sour at how I was betrayed. But I'll be free.

Some time after the next episode of *The Simpsons*.

Wordspot
speak and *talk*

1 **a Complete the gaps with the correct form of either *speak* or *talk*.**

1 'Actions _____ louder than words' means that what you do is more important than what you say.
2 Someone who _____ their mind isn't afraid to say exactly what they mean.
3 It's rude for work colleagues to _____ shop when outsiders are present.
4 He knows what he's _____ about: he's an expert on gardening.
5 If you _____ well of someone, you say good things about them.
6 A _____ point is a subject lots of people want to discuss.
7 _____ radio has phone-ins and interviews rather than music.
8 If your voice is very quiet, people may ask you to _____ up.
9 _____ to yourself is often considered to be a sign of eccentricity.
10 Small _____ is polite, friendly conversation about unimportant topics.
11 They had a huge argument. Since then they haven't been on _____ terms.
12 Peace _____ are negotiations between the two sides in a war.
13 A _____ show features interviews with celebrity guests.

b **T12.6** **Listen and check.**

2 **a Add the phrases with *speak* and *talk* from exercise 1 to the diagrams.**

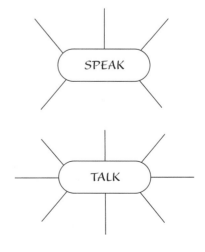

b **Spend a few minutes studying the phrases. Then answer the questions on page 141.**

Language focus 2
Verbs that summarise what people say

Read the following quotes which were given to the press. Who do you think said them: a film star, the manager of a sports team, or a politician?

a 'Yes, you're right. It was a disappointing game, but I'm fairly happy with the result.'

b 'The minister is lying now, he has lied in the past, and he will continue to lie in the future.'

c 'No, I won't answer any questions about my relationship with Shana Lane. I want to make that absolutely clear.'

d 'Speak up, please. All that shouting I did in the second half has made me a bit deaf.'

e 'Why don't you stop criticising the government and write about its achievements?'

f 'I'm sorry I hit the photographer at the Oscar ceremony. He was only doing his job, I guess.'

g 'No, I did not swear at the referee. I was only giving him a little advice.'

h 'Despite what has been written about my future, I am very happy here and have no intention of leaving the club.'

Analysis

1 Look at the way the first three quotes are reported below.
*The manager **admitted that** it had been a disappointing game, although he was happy with the result.*
*The politician **accused** the minister **of** constantly **lying**.*
*The film star completely **refused to** answer any questions about his relationship.*

The verb in bold summarises what the person is saying, without repeating every word. What construction is used after each verb?

2 a Match these verbs to the other quotes in exercise 1 above.
apologise deny insist suggest tell

b What pattern(s) above do each of these verbs follow? Use your mini-dictionary, if necessary. Then re-write the quotes above, using the verbs. Pay attention to the prepositions needed.

▶ Read Language summary B on page 157.

Practice

1 Is there a state lottery in your country? Have you, or anyone you know, ever won anything on it?

2 Read about the case of Martyn and Kay Tott on page 133 and answer the questions.

a Why hadn't the couple claimed their prize originally?
b What reasons did the lottery company give for not paying them?
c How did the Totts respond?
d What role did the media play in the story?

3 Complete the gaps with the correct form of the verbs in brackets. Use your mini-dictionary, if necessary.

Lottery couple lose fight for €millions

When Kay Tott got in tired from work one evening she just wanted to watch a video, but husband, Martyn, suggested (a) _____ (watch) the news first. Now they must wish they hadn't.

The TV news bulletin said that someone in their area of north-east England (b) _____ (fail) to claim a National lottery prize of €4,334,496 and warned the winner that, if they (c) _____ (want) the money, they had better appear quickly, because the six-month period in which to claim was nearly up. The numbers were 5–8–17–25–39–41. Kay jumped up and screamed 'We've won! They're our numbers!' Martyn went silent, then admitted (d) _____ (throw) the tickets away several weeks earlier.

Kay persuaded (e) _____ (her husband / get in touch) with the lottery organisers, Camelot, and explain what had happened. Officials agreed (f) _____ (investigate) the matter, and soon rang back to tell (g) _____ (the Totts / they / have) no doubt their claim was genuine, and that it would be investigated further.

The next day, a lottery investigator came to their house and warned (h) _____ (the couple / not / inform) any newspapers about what was happening. Six weeks later he returned to tell them that they (i) _____ (break) the rules which stated that lost tickets must be reported within thirty days. Camelot were refusing (j) _____ (pay out). Furious, Kay ordered (k) _____ (him / leave) their tiny flat. The next day, a desperate Martyn decided (l) _____ (inform) the media. Interest was immediate: a tabloid offered (m) _____ (put) the Totts up in a five-star hotel in return for an exclusive interview. Several TV companies invited (n) _____ (the couple / appear) on daytime TV. In an angry confrontation, a Camelot official apologised (o) _____ (cause) the couple so much disappointment, but insisted (p) _____ (they have to follow) their rules. The couple angrily accused (q) _____ (Camelot / ruin / their lives) by raising their hopes and putting them through 'torture'. They even threatened (r) _____ (sue) the company over the mental stress they had suffered. Officials, however, denied (s) _____ (make) any false promises.

In the end, the Totts got little except a brief taste of tabloid fame. Two years later the couple divorced. Kay blames (t) _____ (the media / raise) their hopes of a millionaire lifestyle: 'Before this happened, we were quite happy. Between them, Camelot and the newspapers turned our lives into a living hell.'

4
Here are some of the original quotes from the characters in the story. Re-write them using the reporting verbs in brackets.

a 'Remember to put the ticket in a safe place, love.' (remind)
   Kay reminded her husband to put the ticket in a safe place.
b 'Shall we have a quiet night in and just watch a video?' (suggest)
c 'I'm so sorry, love. I threw the ticket away the other week.' (apologise)
d 'We'll investigate the matter most thoroughly, Mr Tott.' (promise)
e 'You mustn't even tell your family about this.' (warn)
f 'We won't answer any questions about the investigation itself.' (refuse)
g 'We never had any problems in our marriage before this happened.' (deny)

5
a Discuss the following questions in pairs.

* Were Camelot right?
* Do you think the media were at fault or not?
* Do you feel any sympathy for Martyn and Kay?

b Imagine you are one of the characters in the story (a Camelot official, Kay Tott or Martyn Tott).

Roleplay an interview with a TV journalist, giving your version of what happened. Include some phrases in reported speech.

Task: Prepare a questionnaire about the media

Preparation: listening

1 **T12.7** You will hear five people answering questions about various aspects of the media. In each case, write the question you think they were asked.

2 Which topic below does each question answered in exercise 1 relate to?

– films and the cinema
– how people use the Internet
– newspaper and magazine reading habits
– radio
– sex and violence on the screen
– the influence of American films and TV
– the influence of the media in your country
– the quality of the media in your country
– TV viewing habits
– other

Task: writing and speaking

1 Work in pairs. You are going to prepare a questionnaire about one of the topics in exercise 2 above. Choose a topic (or two related topics) and decide what general issue you want to find out about.

2 Spend about fifteen minutes preparing eight to twelve questions. If you need help, look at the types of question on page 142. Ask your teacher for any words or phrases you need.

Make a copy of the questionnaire each, leaving plenty of space to make notes.

▶ Useful language a

3 Interview other students individually using your questionnaire. Talk to as many of the class as you can, but do not answer the same questions twice!

4 Compare your answers in your original pairs. Decide how you will summarise your questionnaire and the results to the rest of the class, focussing on the things that are most interesting.

▶ Useful language b

5 Listen to the results of some of the other pairs' surveys. Does anything they say surprise you?

Useful language

a Preparing questions

Where / At what time of day / Which / How often / What kind of ... do you ...?

What are some of your favourite...?

Which of these ... do you / have you ever / listened to / watched / read?

How do you feel about ...?

b Summarising

We wanted to find out whether ...

We asked people if/what ...

We were quite surprised that / Surprisingly / Not surprisingly ...

About a quarter / half / two-thirds said that ...

People had very mixed feelings about ...

Most people feel that ...

Hardly anybody likes ...

Writing
A film review

1 Have you seen any good films recently either in the cinema or on video/DVD? Tell your partner about what you have seen.

2 Read a review of the film *Bend It Like Beckham* and complete it with phrases from the box.

A film I've enjoyed	It was directed
Things get really complicated	is set
all ends happily	it stars
What made me want to see it	played by
I would recommend this film	The problem is that
The soundtrack	Eventually
there are a number of things	

a) _____ recently is *Bend It Like Beckham*. It's a British film, and it's nice to have a change from Hollywood movies! (b) _____ was the title first of all, and I was also interested to see what it's like for an Indian teenager growing up in England.
(c) _____ by someone called Gurinder Chadha and (d) _____ two young British actresses, Parminda Nagra and Keira Knightley.

The film (e) _____ in present-day London. The main character is an Indian girl called Jess. She comes from a very traditional Indian family, who all want her to learn to cook and get married like her elder sister. (f) _____ Jess is only interested in playing football, which her parents won't allow her to do as they think it's an unsuitable sport for a girl. Encouraged by her friend, Jools – (g) _____ Keira Knightley – she starts playing for a local girls' football team, but tells her family she has got a part-time job in a shop.

(h) _____ her parents find out, of course, and try to stop her. (i) _____ when it turns out that both she and Jools are in love with Joe, the team's young (male) coach. So Jess is forced to choose between her family, her friend and the man she loves. However, it (j) _____ and Jess is allowed to continue with her footballing career.

Although sometimes the film is a bit slow-moving (and the dialogue is quite difficult to understand at times) (k) _____ I really liked about this film. There is quite a lot of humour in the film, and there are some amusing characters, especially Jools's mum, who is always worrying about her daughter. The scenes showing Jess's sister's wedding were very warm and colourful. (l) _____ is good too,

3 Make brief notes under the following headings.

Title: *Bend It Like Beckham*
Reasons for going to see it:
Director:
Stars:
Where/when it's set:
Brief summary of the plot:
Positive points:
Negative points:
Who it would appeal to:

4 Make similar notes about a film you have seen recently. Include as much information as possible. Use your notes to write your own film review.

5 **a** Display your reviews on a wall or desk. Read other students' reviews.

b Which films have you already seen? Do you agree with the writer's comments? Which films would you like to see?

with a mixture of rock and Indian music. (m) _____ to anyone who has an interest in football, or in family life, or just wants something a bit different from the usual Hollywood blockbuster!

135

CONSOLIDATION

A Speaking: Future forms

1 Work in pairs. Choose one of the following topics.

- An important trip which will be happening soon
- A sporting event in the near future
- Your holiday plans for this year

2 Prepare a conversation lasting about a minute. Try to include some of the phrases in the box as naturally as possible.

I'll be watching …	I'll probably be riding on a …
I'll have done my …	I'll probably be sitting on a …
I'll have gone to …	We'll have finished our holiday …
By then …	We're going somewhere …
By the time …	We'll be going to …

3 Act out your conversation to the class.

B Grammar and speaking: Modals and hypothetical forms

1 The people below are imagining themselves in the following situations. Read the texts and decide which person is imagining the following things.

- being in prison for a crime they didn't commit
- they (or people they know) have won the lottery
- they were one of the first astronauts in space, back in the 1960s
- what it would be like to have missed in a vital penalty shoot-out

a You (1) _must feel_ (feel) absolutely terrible, all those millions of people watching you, and you're bound to think, oh I (2) _____ (hit) it harder, or if I (3) _____ (put) it on the other side, the goalkeeper (4) _____ (be able) to save it. All those things running through your mind – what a nightmare. Thank goodness it'll never happen to me!!

b It (5) _____ (be) unimaginably frustrating – the sense of unfairness and helplessness … stuck in there knowing you haven't done anything … I think I (6) _____ (get) a bit depressed in that situation. I (7) _____ (even go) a bit crazy.

c They (8) _____ (be) incredibly brave. There (9) _____ (be) an accident at any moment, and they (10) _____ (blow) to pieces in space, with no chance of survival.

d It (11) _____ (be) very strange. I imagine that at first you (12) _____ (feel) fantastic, knowing that you can buy whatever you want, that you don't have to go to work, or whatever … but your life (13) _____ (change) an awful lot. You (14) _____ (end up) with a lot of new problems.

e If I (15) _____ (be) one of their wives or children, I think I (16) _____ (be) terrified, knowing that the person you loved was all that distance away, in such a completely unknown situation, and maybe I (17) _____ (feel) a bit angry too, because they had chosen to risk their life like that.

f I think if it (18) _____ (happen) to a member of my family or a close friend, it (19) _____ (be) quite difficult. I (20) _____ (get) jealous, you just don't know. I (21) _____ (feel) as if I had a right to some of their money. Who knows what (22) _____ (happen) to our relationship?

2 Complete the gaps in the texts with the correct form of the verbs in brackets. (There may be more than one possibility.)

3 Imagine one of the situations above happening to you. Tell your partner how you would feel in that situation and what you or other people might do.

C Listening and grammar: Reported speech

1 Look at the pictures. What do you think is the relationship between the two people? What is happening in each picture?

2 a **C1** Listen to the two conversations. What was the problem in each case? How was the problem resolved?

b Summarise the first conversation by completing the sentences below. You do not have to report the exact words.

1 'How will you be paying?'
The receptionist asked the guest *how she would be paying* .

2 'You are obliged to pay for the telephone calls, madam.'
The receptionist told _____
_____ .

3 'I'm not paying anything until I see the manager.'
The guest refused _____
_____ .

4 'I said I want to see the manager and I want to see him now.'
The guest insisted _____
_____ .

5 'Perhaps you might like to make an appointment to see the manager.'
The receptionist suggested _____
_____ .

c Look at the sentences from the second conversation. Who said each one, the angry driver or Andrew Clark?

1 'You did that on purpose, didn't you? You deliberately backed into me!'
2 'It wasn't on purpose. It was an accident.'
3 'My wife thinks you're wonderful.'
4 'I wonder if you'd mind giving me your autograph.'
5 'Well, okay, if you insist.'
6 'Sorry I lost my temper just now.'

d Summarise the second conversation using the verbs in the box.

ask	~~accuse~~	agree	apologise	deny	tell

The angry driver accused Andrew Clark of deliberately backing into him.

D Vocabulary: Alphabet quiz

1 Work in pairs. Complete the gaps with words from Modules 9–12. (The first letter of each word is given, and the number in brackets refers to the module in which the word appears.)

a An a _ _ _ _ _ _ _ _ _ _ is a meeting at a particular time or place, e.g. with a doctor or dentist. (10)

b A newspaper or TV channel which favours one side more than the other can be described as b _ _ _ _ _ . (12)

c A c _ _ _ _ _ _ _ is a TV programme where the host interviews celebrity guests. (9)

d A d _ _ _ _ _ _ is an illness usually caused by infection. (11)

e An e _ _ _ _ _ _ _ _ _ _ _ TV programme or show is amusing and interesting. (12)

f If a piece of clothing f _ _ _ you, it is the correct size. (9)

g G _ _ _ _ _ are people you invite to a party. (10)

h A h _ _ _ _ _ _ _ _ _ _ _ party is to celebrate moving into a new home. (10)

i Someone who is i _ _ _ _ _ _ _ _ _ _ can change the way you think about something. (12)

j The j _ _ _ _ _ _ _ _ _ _ _ _ for something is the reason for it. (11)

k L _ _ _ coverage of an event is shown as it is happening. (12)

l If you speak your m _ _ _ , you are not afraid to express your opinion. (12)

m N _ _ _ _ _ _ _ _ _ are people who live near or next to you. (10)

n If you p _ _ someone through, you connect them by telephone. (10)

o If you r _ _ _ _ _ _ _ someone, you look like them. (11)

p A s _ _ _ _ is a mark on clothing which is difficult to remove. (9)

q The t _ _ _ _ _ _ _ _ _ _ _ _ is a TV or radio report telling you about conditions on the road. (12)

r An u _ _ _ _ _ _ _ murder is one where the killer has not been identified. (9)

s A v _ _ _ _ _ _ _ _ _ _ is an injection which protects you against illness. (10)

t W _ _ _ _ means strange and difficult to explain. (9)

2 Work in pairs. Find five more words and write clues for them. Take turns to read out your clues and see if the other students can guess the words.

COMMUNICATION

Module 1: Language focus 1, page 10

Answers

1 a Past simple   d Present perfect
   b Past perfect   e Present continuous
   c Past continuous   f Present simple
2 a Formula One driver
   b Taxi driver
3 Sentences b and h are incorrect
4 a broke, was ice-skating
   b were sitting, went out
5 a diagram 3 (action continues until the present)
   b diagram 1 (action is finished / completed period in the past)
6 Sentence b
7 a … before they started going out.
   b … but they don't get on very well.
8 Sentences a and c
9 Sentences b and c

Grammar genius rating?

0–6 You definitely need to read the Language summary on page 144!

7–13 There are still quite a few gaps in your knowledge. Have a look at the Language summary on page 144.

14–20 You have a good knowledge of English verbs, but it's probably still worth checking the Language summary on page 144.

Module 1: Wordspot, exercise 3, page 13

Student A

Read the questions below to Student B for him/her to answer using a phrase with *get*. (Suggested answers are shown in red.) Then answer Student B's questions.

a What phrase with *get* means 'to improve'? get better
b What happens if it rains and you don't have an umbrella? you get wet
c If you can't deal with a problem yourself, what should you do? get help
d What expression means 'understand a hint'? get the message
e What phrasal verb means 'to continue with'? get on with
f What do people hope to get on their birthday? (lots of) presents
g What can you get if you don't have a map? get lost
h Why do people sometimes not laugh at a joke? (because) they don't get it
i What's the opposite of 'leave the house'? get home

Module 2: Language focus 2, page 22

The blanked-out word is 'smile'.

Module 4: Task, page 42

Quiz B

1 Are you generally a neat and tidy person?
   a yes   **b** no

2 If you buy a new piece of equipment (for example, a mobile phone) do you start using it straightaway or do you read the manual carefully first?
   a read the manual   **b** start using it straightaway

3 If you're hanging a picture on the wall, do you measure carefully first, or put it where it looks straight?
   a measure carefully   **b** put it where it looks straight

4 When reading a magazine do you start at page one and read your way through, or jump around to what looks interesting?
   a start at page one   **b** jump around

5 Do you make a list of things you have to do and enjoy ticking things off as you do them?
   a yes   **b** no

6 When speaking, do you use your hands a lot, or only a little?
   a only a little   **b** a lot

7 There is going to be a big change in your life (new job, a move, etc.) How do you feel?
   a worried   **b** excited

8 Which of these areas most attract you?
   a maths and science   **b** philosophy and religion

9 When making a decision, what do you do?
   a think carefully about each option before you decide
   b follow your intuition

10 If someone tells you a story, do you visualise it in your head?
   a no   **b** yes

Number of a answers _____

Number of b answers _____

Module 4: Writing, exercise 5, page 46

EasyLingua

- Learn a new language in just 28 days!
- Clear easy-to-follow course with modern illustrations and photographs.
- Twelve top quality CDs/cassettes with native speaker models
- High quality CD-roms
- Twenty-four-hour helpline with qualified teachers to advise you!

Choose from over thirty languages including:

French	Russian	Japanese	Portuguese
Spanish	Italian	Chinese	Korean
German	Turkish	Polish	Czech

Only €295 P&P

Module 7: Vocabulary and speaking, exercise 2, page 72

1. In which country do you think the photo of the wedding was taken? Why?
2. In which photo did you see an audience?
3. How many photos featured a crowd?
4. In which photo were people carrying placards?
5. What was the actor in photo 4 doing?
6. In which country do you think the photo of a football crowd was taken? Why?
7. What was written on the big banner in photo 2?
8. In which photo were people dancing in the street?

Module 7: Study, exercise 2, page 82

The big lesson

On April 9th, 2003, children and adults all over the world broke the record for the largest simultaneous lesson ever taught. Over 1.8 million children in more than 100 countries from the UK to Uganda, Sweden to Senegal took part in the Big Lesson. In addition thousands of signatures were collected, along with special radio and TV programmes and public events aimed at raising awareness over lack of access to education (particularly for girls) and the prevalence of child labour in many parts of the world. The event, organised by the Global Campaign for Education (GCE) was part of a campaign to get every child in the world into school by the year 2015. 450,000 people across Bangladesh and at least 100,000 people in Brazil participated, and in the UK, 2,500 took part in one massive lesson at London's Wembley Arena. 'Let this be not only the world's biggest lesson, but a lesson the world will never forget,' said the UN Secretary Kofi Annan.

Module 9: Wordspot, exercise 2, page 99

a Nobody seemed to notice that the painting was hanging **with the bottom at the top**.
b The new computer system **stopped working** just a few hours after it had been installed.
c I thought I'd really enjoy this new job, but I **made a very big mistake**!
d He looked such an idiot wearing his baseball cap **with the back at the front**.
e My Walkman **isn't working properly**. I'll have to get it fixed.
f Make sure you don't put the knives and forks away **where they shouldn't be**, like last time.
g You seem very quiet this evening. **Is there a problem**?
h Jack went to see the doctor. He was greatly relieved to hear **he's absolutely fine**.
i I was expecting a call from Melanie, but instead it was just **someone had dialled incorrectly**.

Module 6: Practice, exercise 4, page 66

Team A Quiz
Complete with correct articles. (The correct answer to each question is circled.)

1. When do ... Americans celebrate their independence day?
   ⓐ On ... fourth of ... July.
   b On ... fourteenth of ... July.
   c On ... fourteenth of ... August.

2. What is ... capital of Australia?
   a ... Sydney.
   b ... Melbourne.
   ⓒ ... Canberra.

3. If you are 'incarcerated', where do you go?
   a To ... school.
   b To ... church.
   ⓒ To ... prison.

4. Which of these is not ... natural river?
   a ... Danube.
   b ... Mississippi.
   ⓒ ... Suez.
   d ... Nile.

5. Where is ... Tokyo?
   a In ... north of ... Japan.
   ⓑ In ... east of ... Japan.
   c In ... west of ... Japan.

Module 8: Task, exercise 1, page 91

Entertainment: Stalking the stars

Stardom has always guaranteed wealth and abundant media attention, but now, it seems, it attracts something more sinister: stalkers. Stalkers are fans whose relationship with their idol becomes obsessive: they know everything there is to know, including where the celebrities live, where they go to relax and how they spend their days. But some go even further than that. In January this year, a woman was arrested after she was found in actor Brad Pitt's Santa Monica home. She wanted to be close to him and dressed up and slept in his clothes. But this is just another list in a long list of similar cases: Madonna, Nicole Kidman, Steven Spielberg and Ricky Martin are just a few of the stars who have been targeted in recent years.

Celebrity stalking is not new, but the issue came to the world's attention in 1980 when Mark David Chapman shot John Lennon and later said: 'I was Mr Nobody until I killed the biggest somebody on earth.' The tactics used by celebrity stalkers can vary, from sending letters, to a full scale break-in of their home.

Dr Sandy Wolfson, Lecturer in Psychology at the University of Northumbria, believes that the seeds of stalking are deep-rooted and that it may only take something small – like a family row – to push a potentially obsessive fan over the edge. She adds, 'When an obsessed fan becomes violent, it is because something has made them lose their grip on reality and control of what is happening around them.' However, most fans, says Dr Wolfson are level-headed, responsible individuals.

It seems that stalking can happen to all sorts of people in all walks of life. In the UK, more than 2,500 stalking cases were brought before the courts and research carried out in the USA estimated that over one million women and 370,000 men were stalked each year.

A NATION OF SHOPAHOLICS

It's the sort of thing men joke about in the pub. 'My wife's addicted to shopping,' they'll say, while their mates grin and nod sympathetically.

A study suggests however, that the compulsion to buy may be a growing problem, affecting as many as one in five people, and in extreme cases leading to family breakup and financial ruin.

The number of people who confess to being shopaholics has grown from fifteen percent to twenty-two percent of the population in five years. And while twenty-nine percent of women admit to being addicted, so do fifteen percent of men. Shopping is no longer simply a way of providing essentials for the family, say market researchers, to many women it is more like a hobby.

True, many people have more money to spend these days. Personal disposable income has risen by seventy-five percent in twenty years.

However, what they buy is not necessarily what they can afford.

Over the same period, the number of people using credit cards has increased by four times, and consumer debt has trebled.

Spending sprees can be a symptom of serious personal problems, according to researchers who have studied the subject. There are 'revenge shoppers', who want to spite their husbands or boyfriends because they are unhappy with their relationships. There are those who need shopping trips to add excitement to their lives. Dr Helga Dittma, of the University of Sussex, believes habitual shopping – particularly for designer clothes and jewellery – is a symptom of a collapse of self-esteem. 'Addicts want not only the latest fashions, they want to feel like the sort of person who would normally own them, and to feel important, glamorous and loved.'

Woman banker stole €150,000 for clothes

A bank executive stole more than €150,000 from her employers and blew it on clothes and make-up to 'escape the stresses of being a working mother'. Lyne Harding hid her purchases from her husband, who had no idea of what she was doing. And she got away with it for four years, until Lloyds Bank became suspicious of the assistant branch manager and called in auditors.

Now the thirty-one-year-old mother of two is facing a jail sentence. A court heard that Harding would open bank accounts using fictitious names, and authorise loans of up to €15,000 a time.

Harding went on huge spending sprees, sometimes spending thousands on designer make-up in one day. The only other luxury she allowed herself was a car paid for with a cheque from a bogus account.

'It was a vicious circle. I couldn't stop spending,' she told police after her arrest in February. 'It all started as a way of escaping the demands of a full-time job, combined with looking after a home and two children,' she said. 'Although I had a boss, he did not take a very active part in running the bank. I dealt with almost everything, and was finding it extremely difficult.'

She awaits sentence at Southwark Crown court.

The show must go on for pop diva

Serbian pop star Goca Trzan got the shock of her life when she walked onstage for her sell-out show at the Sava Concert Hall in the capital city of her country, Belgrade.

Imagine Goca's horror, then, when she walked out to find … one person in the audience, sitting alone in row twenty, the middle of the auditorium. A thirty-year-old businessman had bought all the tickets for the show in order to have his own private performance. After she had initially refused to perform, her manager persuaded her to carry on with the show, on the grounds that her 'audience' had paid an estimated €20,000 for the pleasure of seeing her, and deserved value for money … and perform she did … although it seems that tears and singing were served up in fairly equal measure during the two-hour spectacular.

It seems that the show was a big hit with her Number One fan, because at the end, he presented her with 101 roses, a diamond ring, a one-way air ticket to Switzerland … and an offer of marriage!

Module 12: Wordspot, exercise 2, page 131

a   What are the main talking points in the news at the moment?
b   If you're not on speaking terms with someone, how do you feel towards them?
c   According to the saying, what speaks louder than words?
d   Do you ever listen to talk radio? Why / Why not?
e   Do you tend to speak your mind about things, or do you keep your opinions to yourself?
f   If someone spoke highly of you, would you be angry or pleased?
g   What reasons might there be for someone to talk to himself/herself?
h   Do you think you know what you're talking about when it comes to cooking?
i   If people are talking shop, what are they talking about?
j   Can you name a popular talk show host in your country? Do you like him/her?
k   What kind of people would probably take part in peace talks?
l   On what kind of occasions do you hear a lot of small talk?
m   Have you got a loud voice or do people ask you to speak up?

Module 1: Wordspot, exercise 3, page 13

Student B
Answer Student A's questions. Then read the questions below to Student A for him/her to answer using a phrase with *get*. (Suggested answers are in red.)

a   If it's too far to walk, and you can't afford a taxi, what can you do? get the bus
b   What phrasal verb means 'have a good relationship'? get on well (with someone)
c   If you are promoted, what does this mean? you get a better job
d   What do you get if something unexpected and unpleasant happens? you get a shock
e   What can happen if a child misbehaves at school? he/she'll get into trouble
f   What phrase is the opposite of 'get better'? get worse
g   What will probably happen if you walk for ten kilometres? you'll get tired
h   If you are travelling in a lift and it stops between floors then it …? gets stuck
i   What's the opposite of 'leave work'? get to work

Module 6: Practice, exercise 4, page 66

Team B Quiz
Complete with correct articles. (The correct answer to each question is circled.)

1   Where is … highest range of mountains in … world?
a   … Andes.
ⓑ   … Himalayas.
c   … Rockies.

2   What is 149.6 million kilometres?
ⓐ   … distance from … Sun to …Earth.
b   … distance from … Moon to … Earth.
c   … distance from …Sun to … nearest star.

3   Which of these is not in … Africa?
a   … Lake Victoria.
b   … Johannesburg.
ⓒ   … Ecuador.
d   … Nile.
e   … Madagascar.

4   If a baby is born at 1.00 p.m., what time of … day is it born?
a   in … morning?
ⓑ   in … afternoon?
c   in … evening?
d   at … night?

5   If you are 'discharged', what do you leave?
ⓐ   … hospital.
b   … university.
c   … home.

Module 12: Task, exercise 2, page 134

TV/video

1 Are there any TV programmes which you, or someone in your family, try never to miss? What are they? When are they on?

2 At what time of day do you usually watch TV? Is there a time when you never watch?

3 Which TV channel do you watch most? Do you ever watch satellite TV? What kind of programmes do you watch and where do you watch them?

4 How many televisions are there in your house? Of the people you live with, who watches the most television and who watches the least?

5 About how much television do you watch in a typical day? At what time(s) do you usually watch TV?

6 Have you ever appeared on television, or watched a TV show being made? Tell me about it.

7 How often do you rent a video or DVD?
   a two or three times a week
   b once a week
   c less than once a week
   d never

Print media – Books, magazines, newspapers

1 Do you read a particular newspaper? Which one(s)? Do you have a particular reason for reading it?

2 What would you say is the most popular newspaper in your country? What are the reasons for its success?

3 Which section of the newspaper do you read first? Second? Which section(s) do you never read?

4 How many magazines do you buy in an average week? Are there any magazines you buy regularly? What is it that you like about them?

5 Name three or four magazines which are popular in your country.

6 Can you remember the titles of any books you read as a child? What were they about?

7 What was the last book you read? Tell me about it.

8 Do you think people read less nowadays? Why do you think this is?

9 If you could have only one book, which would it be?

Radio

1 How many radios do you own (including car radios)?

2 Do you have digital radio?

3 Do you ever listen to sports commentaries on the radio? Which sport(s)?

4 How often do you listen to the radio news?
   a every day
   b most days
   c occasionally
   d never

5 How many radio stations can you name? Which ones do you listen to regularly?

6 Which of these types of music do you listen to on the radio?
   – classical   – dance music   – jazz   – pop   – rap
   – rock   – other

7 Where do you listen to the radio?
   a in your bedroom
   b in the car
   c in the kitchen
   d other

8 Have you ever been on the radio? Tell me about it.

9 Do you ever listen to radio phone-ins? Would you ever take part in one?

10 Do you ever listen to radio over the Internet? What stations have you listened to?

Module 5: Wordspot, exercise 3, page 60

What expression with *first* ...

a has the same meaning as 'mother tongue'?

b means that you know someone well enough to use their first name?

c means 'initially'?

d is the opposite of 'last thing at night'?

e means the thing or place that you choose first?

f means of the very best quality?

g means you fall in love with someone as soon as you meet them?

h means that you are in the leading position?

i is the idea of people or things that you get when you first see them?

j is a type of simple medical care?

k is the slowest speed on a car or racing bike?

l means 'before everything else?'

Module 4: Language focus 1, exercise 1, page 44

Answers to IQ test

a 2   b 2   c 67, 61   d Rocket

Verb	Past Simple	Past Participle
be	was / were	been
beat	beat	beaten
become	became	become
begin	began	begun
bend	bent	bent
bite	bit	bitten
blow	blew	blown
break	broke	broken
bring	brought	brought
build	built	built
burn	burned / burnt	burned / burnt
burst	burst	burst
buy	bought	bought
can	could	been able
catch	caught	caught
choose	chose	chosen
come	came	come
cost	cost	cost
cut	cut	cut
dig	dug	dug
do	did	done
draw	drew	drawn
dream	dreamed / dreamt	dreamed / dreamt
drink	drank	drunk
drive	drove	driven
eat	ate	eaten
fall	fell	fallen
feed	fed	fed
feel	felt	felt
fight	fought	fought
find	found	found
fly	flew	flown
forget	forgot	forgotten
forgive	forgave	forgiven
freeze	froze	frozen
get	got	got
give	gave	given
go	went	gone / been
grow	grew	grown
hang	hung	hanged / hung
have	had	had
hear	heard	heard
hide	hid	hidden
hit	hit	hit
hold	held	held
hurt	hurt	hurt
keep	kept	kept
kneel	knelt	knelt
know	knew	known
lay	laid	laid
lead	led	led
learn	learned / learnt	learned / learnt
leave	left	left
lend	lent	lent

Verb	Past Simple	Past Participle
let	let	let
lie	lay	lain
light	lit	lit
lose	lost	lost
make	made	made
mean	meant	meant
meet	met	met
must	had to	had to
pay	paid	paid
put	put	put
read /riːd/	read /red/	read /red/
ride	rode	ridden
ring	rang	rung
rise	rose	risen
run	ran	run
say	said	said
see	saw	seen
sell	sold	sold
send	sent	sent
set	set	set
shake	shook	shaken
shine	shone	shone
shoot	shot	shot
show	showed	shown
shut	shut	shut
sing	sang	sung
sink	sank	sunk
sit	sat	sat
sleep	slept	slept
slide	slid	slid
smell	smelled / smelt	smelled / smelt
speak	spoke	spoken
spend	spent	spent
spill	spilled / spilt	spilled / spilt
spoil	spoiled / spoilt	spoiled / spoilt
stand	stood	stood
steal	stole	stolen
stick	stuck	stuck
swim	swam	swum
take	took	taken
teach	taught	taught
tear	tore	torn
tell	told	told
think	thought	thought
throw	threw	thrown
understand	understood	understood
wake	woke	woken
wear	wore	worn
win	won	won
write	wrote	written

Module 1

Ⓐ Overview of past and present verb forms

1 Names of tenses

	Simple	Continuous	Perfect simple	Perfect continuous
Present	I work	I'm working	I've worked	I've been working
Past	I worked	I was working	I had worked	I had been working

2 Present simple versus Present continuous

While the Present simple is used for things that happen **regularly** or that we see as **permanent**, the Present continuous is used for things that we see as **temporary** or are happening over a **limited period of time**.

*Normally I **take** the train to work ...* (= this is what I usually do)
... but this week I'm coming by bicycle. (= for a limited period)

3 Verbs not normally found in continuous forms

A number of verbs (state verbs) describe states rather than actions. They are rarely found in continuous forms. These include:

a verbs that describe thought processes and opinions:
agree, believe, disagree, forget, know, remember, think
b verbs that describe emotions:
adore, detest, like, love, hate, want
c verbs that describe the five senses:
feel, hear, see, smell, taste
d others:
be, belong, have, seem

4 Verbs that can describe both states and actions

Some verbs can describe both states and actions, but there is a change of meaning.

STATE: He**'s** very friendly. (= this is his character)
ACTION: He**'s being** very friendly. (= he is behaving this way, he is not usually like this)

STATE: They **have** an apartment near the town centre. (= possess)
ACTION: They**'re having** a coffee. (= taking)

STATE: I **think** you're absolutely right. (= this is my opinion)
ACTION: I**'m thinking** about what you said. (= considering, it is in my mind)

5 Past simple and Past continuous

a The Past simple is used to describe actions or states in the past that we see as **complete**. The time when the action happened is often stated or understood.
*Jane **went** to visit her aunt in hospital **yesterday**. She **got** home about eight.*

b The Past continuous is used to describe actions or states that were **in progress** at a point of time in the past, or that we see as in some way **incomplete**.
*I **was driving** along when suddenly a dog ran into the road.*

6 Present perfect and Past simple

a The Present perfect is used when an action happened in the past, but is linked to the present. It is still relevant or important **now**.
*She**'s broken** her leg.* (= her leg is broken now)
*I **haven't read** 'War and Peace'.* (= I am unfamiliar with it now)

b The Past simple is used for actions or states which we see as being **completely in the past**.

7 Present perfect and Past simple with periods of time

If an action continues over a period of time up to the present, we use the Present perfect. To describe a finished period of time in the past, we use the Past simple.

*I**'ve worked** in Singapore for two years.* (= I still work there now)
*I **worked** in Singapore for two years.* (= completely in the past, I don't work there now)

8 Present perfect and Past perfect

a The Present perfect is used for things which continued **up to the moment of speaking**, or ended a short time before.
*They**'ve been** together for years.* (= and are still together)

b The Past perfect is used for things which continued **up to a point of time in the past**, or ended a short time before.
*We**'d been** there for over an hour when the taxi finally arrived.*

9 *used to*

We use *used to* for describing habits and states in the past. We can always use the Past simple instead of *used to*, but we cannot use *used to* for actions that happen only once.

*I **used to** go to my grandmother's every Sunday.*

10 Past forms to express hypothetical meaning

We often use past forms to talk about situations which are hypothetical or imaginary. These verbs do not refer to past situations, but to the **present**.

*If only I **knew** the answer to your question.*

Ⓑ Different uses of auxiliary verbs

Auxiliary verbs often emphasise things, show interest, or avoid repetition. If they are used alone, remember they must agree with the tense and person of the main sentence.

1 to emphasise

A: Are you hungry?   B: Yes, I am!
A: I don't think you want to go.   B: I do want to go, but ...

2 in questions

a You can show interest in what someone said by responding with a short question using an auxiliary verb.
A: Yes, I've got six grandchildren.   B: **Have you**? How lovely!
A: We didn't like the film at all.   B: Really, **didn't you**, why not?
Notice here that positive questions are used with positive sentences, and negative questions are used with negative sentences.

b Question tags at the end of a statement encourage the listener to respond. Here negative questions are used with positive sentences, and positive questions with negative sentences.
*You've remembered (+) your keys, **haven't** (–) you?*
*It isn't (–) a very nice day, **is** (+) it?*

If there is no doubt about the statement, the voice goes down.
*It isn't a very nice day, **is** it?*

If there is an element of doubt, the voice goes up.
*You've remembered your keys, **haven't** you?*

3 to avoid repetition

We also use auxiliary verbs to avoid repeating whole phrases.
*I enjoyed the film very much, but most of my friends **didn't**.*
(= enjoy the film very much)
*The other students in the class don't understand Italian, but
Alexandra **does**.* (= understand Italian)

This is common in answers to *yes/no* questions.
A: Have you done your homework yet?
B: Yes, actually, I **have**. (= done my homework)

Module 2

Ⓐ Common suffixes for nouns

-ance, -ence

Often used to form abstract nouns from adjectives ending in *-ant*
or *-ent*.
  patient → *patience*
  tolerant → *tolerance*

-ee

Used to describe a person on whom an action is performed.
  employee (= person who is employed)
  trainee (= person who is being trained)

-er, -ian, -or

Often used for people or things that do a particular job.
  act → *actor*
  football → *footballer*
  music → *musician*
  can opener

-hood

Used to form abstract nouns, especially those concerned with
periods of life or relationships between people.
  child → *childhood*
  mother → *motherhood*

-ism

Often used to describe particular religions or ideologies, and with
some abstract nouns.
  Buddhism, Liberalism, criticism, cynicism

-ist

Used to describe people's beliefs and sometimes their occupation.
  communist, journalist, pianist

-ity, -iety, -y

Used to form nouns from adjectives.
  anxious → *anxiety*
  immune → *immunity*

-tion, -(s)sion

Often used to form nouns from verbs.
  imagine → *imagination*
  admit → *admission*

-ment

Often used to form abstract nouns from verbs.
  enjoy → *enjoyment*
  move → *movement*

-ness

Often used to form abstract nouns from adjectives.
  happy → *happiness*
  nervous → *nervousness*

-ship

Used to form abstract nouns, usually about relationships.
  friend → *friendship*
  member → *membership*

> **REMEMBER!**
> Many other nouns are exactly the same as the verb form.
>
> *to comment* → *a comment*
> *to decrease* → *a decrease*
> *to drive* → *a drive*
> *to study* → *a study*

Ⓑ Gerunds

The gerund (*-ing* form) is used in the same way as a noun, either
as the subject or object of the sentence, or alone. It is commonly
used:

1 to describe general activities or abstract ideas.
   ***Trusting** your children is very important.*
   ***Walking** and **swimming** are my favourite forms of exercise.*

   We cannot use the infinitive here.

2 when there is no single noun to describe that idea.
   ***Going to the dentist's** makes me really nervous.*

3 when ideas or activities are not put into complete sentences.
   This can be in written lists:
   Our priorities for next year are:
   – cutting costs.
   – expanding into new markets.

   or in conversation:
   A: *So, what's your idea of relaxation?*
   B: ***Having** a nice long bath and **reading** my book.*

C Common suffixes for adjectives

suffix	examples
-able, -ible *This suffix sometimes means 'can be', e.g. washable (= can be washable)*	miserable, responsible
-al	physical, psychological
-ant, -ent, -ient,	pleasant, violent, efficient
-ed*	depressed, talented
-ful	powerful, successful
-ic	enthusiastic, scientific
-ing*	exciting, interesting
-ive	aggressive, intensive
-less	hopeless, penniless (= without)
-ious, -ous,	anxious, nervous
-y	healthy, wealthy

> *** REMEMBER!**
> Many adjectives to describe feelings have both an *-ing* and an *-ed* form.
> *annoyed / annoying   depressed / depressing   excited / exciting*
>
> The *-ed* form describes how you feel.
> *I'm very **tired** this morning.*
>
> The *-ing* form describes what makes you feel that way.
> *Looking after babies can be very **tiring**.*
>
> However, not all *-ed / -ing* adjectives have both forms.
> *Ben is a very **talented** musician.*
> *Fortunately, her illness isn't **catching**.*

D Prefixes used to form opposites

prefix	example
dis-	disloyal, displeased*
il-	illegal, illiterate
im-	immature, impossible
in-	inexperienced, insecure
un-	unhappy*, unpopular

* Note that these prefixes can also be used with some verbs, e.g. **dis**agree, **un**lock.

E Other prefixes which change meaning

prefix	examples	meaning
anti-	anti-social, anti-war	against
mis-	misunderstood, mismanaged	badly, in the wrong way
non-	non-stop, non-smoking	without, not
over-	over-cooked	too much
post-	post-war	after
pre-	pre-war	before
pro-	pro-European	in favour of
re-	re-united, re-charged	again
self-	self-confident	relating to itself
under-	under-cooked	not enough

Module 3

A Narrative tenses

Past simple	I work**ed**	verb + **-ed** (regular verbs)
Past continuous	You **were** work**ing**	**was / were** + **-ing**
Past perfect simple	She **had** work**ed**	**had** + past participle
Past perfect continuous	She **had been** work**ing**	**had** + **been** + **-ing**

1 Past simple and Past continuous

The Past simple describes the **main events** in a past narrative.
*I **called** the police and they **arrived** more or less straightaway.*

The past continuous describes **actions in progress** at the time that time that the main events happen.
*When they **got** home, everyone **was waiting** to greet them.*

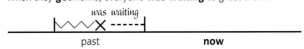

2 Past perfect simple and Past perfect continuous

Both these tenses describe events **before** the events in the main narrative. They are 'the past of the past.'
*The suspects **had disappeared** when the police arrived.*

The Past perfect continuous emphasises the duration of an event, and often describes actions which continue up until the main past events.
*He **had been waiting** for hours when we **got** there.*

B Continuous aspect

Continuous verb forms can:

1   emphasise that an action **lasts for some time**.
    *We **were waiting** for ages!*

2   emphasise that an action is **repeated**.
    *I **rang** you this morning.*
    *I **was ringing** you all morning!*

3   describe an action that is in progress at a particular time.
    *He **was** just **having** breakfast when the postman came.*

4   describe a situation which is temporary.
    *They**'d been staying** at their sister's house for a few days.*

C Continuous aspect in other tenses

Present continuous	He **is** work**ing**	**be** + **-ing**
Present perfect continuous	She **has been** work**ing**	**have / has** + **been** + **-ing**
Future continuous	We **will be** work**ing**	**will** + **be** + **-ing**

The points in section B above are also true of continuous tenses with the Present perfect and the future.
Compare the following pairs of sentences:
I've cut my finger! (= action lasts for only a moment)
I've been cutting firewood. (= action lasts for some time)

She's visited her relatives in Canada. (= one visit)
She's been visiting her relatives in Canada. (= she's visited several different people)

We'll have dinner at eight. (= the meal will begin then)
We'll be having dinner at eight. (= the meal will be in progress)

Module 4

A The active and the passive

1   In active sentences the subject is the agent (or 'doer') of the verb.
    *The two fire fighters **rescued** the child.*
        (subject)   (verb)   (object)

2   In passive sentences the subject is **not** the agent of the verb.
    *The child **was rescued** by the two fire fighters.*
      (subject) (verb)   (agent)

3   The passive is formed with *be* + past participle.

	Active	Passive
Present simple	It makes	It **is made**
Present continuous	It is making	It **is being made**
Present perfect	It has made	It **has been made**
Past simple	It made	It **was made**
Past continuous	It was making	It **was being made**
Past perfect	It had made	It **had been made**
Future simple	It will make	It **will be made**
Infinitive forms	make to make	**be made** **to be made**
-ing form	making	**being made**

B Reasons for using the passive

1 The agent is unknown, unimportant or obvious.

*My bicycle **has been stolen!*** (= we don't know who did this)
*The mice **are kept** in cages.* (= it's not important who does this)
*A man **was arrested**.* (= it's obvious the police did this)

2 The main topic of the sentence is not the agent.

In English, the main topic of the sentence normally comes at the beginning, and the new information about the topic comes at the end.
Roman Polanski directed 'The Pianist'.
(In a profile of Polanski, who is the main topic of the sentence.)
If the agent is not the main topic of the sentence, we use the passive.
'The Pianist' was directed by Roman Polanski.
(In an article about *The Pianist*, which is the main topic of the sentence.)

> **REMEMBER!**
> If we include the agent in the sentence, we use *by*.

C Formal and informal texts

1   In more formal texts, the passive is preferred because it is less personal. This is especially true in scientific, technical or academic writing.

2   The following passive constructions are particularly common in this kind of formal writing:
    It is said that …   It is thought that …   It is believed that …
    It has been proved that …

3   In informal speech, we can avoid using the passive by using a subject like *we, you, they, people, someone,* etc. This sounds more personal and friendly.
    Compare the following pairs of sentences.
    *Gregor **is said to be** interested in living abroad.*
    ***They say** Gregor is interested in living abroad.*

    *The Gold Label credit card can **be used** all over the world.*
    ***You can use** the Gold Label credit card all over the world.*

    *More computers **are being** bought than ever before.*
    ***People are buying** more computers than ever before.*

D Passive forms with *have* and *get*

a   The passive form *have* + object + past participle is used to talk about something we pay other people to do for us.
    *She **had her nose pierced** when she was a teenager.*

    We use *get* + object + past participle when it was difficult to have something done.
    *After many years of trying, he finally **got his book published**.*

b   We use *get* + past participle for things that happen by accident, or things which happen to us that are unpleasant.
    *It's common for things **to get broken** when you move house.*
    *My luggage **got stolen** somewhere at the airport.*

Module 5

Ⓐ Overview of perfect tenses

	Simple	Continuous
Present perfect	I have worked	I have been working
Past perfect	I had worked	I had been working
Future perfect	I will have worked	I will have been working

All perfect tenses link two points in time. They show actions **before** a particular time in the present, past or future.

1 Present perfect

a   The Present perfect links actions in the past to the present. This can happen in a number of ways:

* the action is not finished, but continues into the present.
  *We **have lived** here all our lives.* (= and we still live here now)

* the action took place in a period of time which is not finished.
  *We**'ve** all **been** ill this year.* (= this year is not finished)
  *I**'ve been** to Italy several times.* (= in my life)

* the action happened very recently and is still 'news'.
  *They**'ve** just **had** a baby.*

* the results of a past action are still important now.
  *I**'ve lost** my mobile phone!*

b   If you relate the action to a past time you must use the Past simple.
  *I first **met** John **when I was twenty-one / in 2004**.*

c   The Present perfect is often found with these time phrases:
  already   ever   for   just   never   since   so far
  this month/morning/week   today   yet

2 Past perfect

The Past perfect links a point in the past with a time further in the past. It describes actions that happened 'before the past'.
  *She **had been** ill for some time before she **died**.*
  *When I **got** home the cat **had escaped**.*

a   Many of the time phrases often used with the Present perfect are also used with the Past perfect.
  ***Had** you **ever seen** the man before that night?*
  *Mary **hadn't** been **abroad for** many years.*

b   Other common phrases often used with the Past perfect are:

1   *by* + past time phrases
  ***By eight o'clock** last night, they **had managed** to clear all the roads.*

2   Clauses with *by the time, when,* etc.
  *The **party had finished by the time** I arrived.*
  *We went on holiday **when** we**'d finished** our exams.*

3   Notice that when we use *before* and *after*, the order of events is obvious, so the Past perfect is not always necessary.
  *I **remembered** to lock up before I **went** to bed.*

3 Future perfect

The Future perfect links two actions or times in the future.

We use the Future perfect when we look forward to a time in the future and then think about something that will be completed before that time. It is often introduced with *by* + future time phrase.
  *Come over about ten. We**'ll have eaten by then**.*
  ***By the time I'm fifty**, I hope I**'ll have earned** enough money to retire.*

Notice the word order of Future perfect questions.
  1   2   3
  ***Will you have finished** by tomorrow?*

Ⓑ More about the Present perfect simple and continuous

1 What they have in common

Both the Present perfect simple and the Present perfect continuous link the past and the present as described above. Sometimes there is no important difference in meaning between the two.
  *He**'s been living** here for a long time.*
  *He**'s lived** here for a long time.*

However, in most cases there are differences in emphasis which mean we choose a particular form.

a   **'Long' / repeated and 'a moment'**

If an action lasts only for a moment or a very short time, the simple form is used. The continuous form emphasises that the action continues for a period of time, or was repeated.
  *Oh no! I**'ve broken** my glasses!* (= lasts only for a moment)
  *Be careful. It**'s been snowing**.* (= lasts some time)
  *I**'ve been phoning** all my friends to tell them the news.* (= I've made several calls)

b   **'Complete' actions and 'incomplete' actions**

If we see the action as completed, we tend to use the simple form. The continuous form emphasises that the action is incomplete, or we could continue it later.
  *I**'ve done** my homework. Can I go out now?* (= completed)
  *He**'s been working** on his assignment.* (= it's not necessarily finished)

c   **Activities and results**

The continuous form often describes an activity. It answers the question 'How have you spent your time?' We use the simple form when we emphasise the result of an activity. It answers the question 'What have you achieved?'
  A: *What **have** you **been doing** today?*
  B: *I**'ve been mending** my bike.* (= interested in activity)

  A: *What **have** you **done** today?*
  B: *I**'ve fixed** my bike!* (= interested in result)

If you give a number, the simple form is always used because we are emphasising completion / results.
  *I**'ve been** to the gym three times this week.*
  *I**'ve sent** fifteen e-mails so far today.*

2 State verbs

Remember that some verbs describe states and are therefore not usually used in the continuous form.

Module 6

Ⓐ Use and non-use of articles

1 Basic rules

a Indefinite article

We use *a / an* when 'we don't know which one' because the thing or person:

*   is one of many.
    *He's **an** artist.* (= there are many artists)

*   is not unique.
    *I've just bought **a** Ferrari.*

*   has not been mentioned before.
    *There was **a** new student in class today.*

b Definite article

We use *the* when 'we know which one' because the thing or person:

*   is unique (or unique in that context).
    The Australian Prime Minister. (= there is only one)
    I looked inside – the engine was in a terrible state. (= there is only one engine, in this case)

*   has been mentioned before.
    *The man gave me a ticket. I looked at it, and saw that **the** ticket was a single.*

*   is defined by the phrase which follows it.
    *What's **the** new student's name?*

c No articles

We do not use an article when we talk about things in general:
*   using plural or uncountable nouns
    Do you like sport?
*   with the names of people or places, but there are many exceptions (see 3a and b).
    *a book by **Professor Jones***

d Fixed phrases

There are many fixed phrases with and without articles. It is best to learn these individually. These include:

*a few at home at work at **the** beginning at **the** end go to bed go to **the** cinema/shops/station in **the** world once **a** week sixty kilometres **an** hour **the** next **the** other **the** other day **the** same*

2 Areas that often cause problems

a Jobs

If there are many people doing a particular job, we use *a / an*.
    *My husband is **an** architect.* (= there are many architects)

But if a job is specific to one person, we use *the*.
    *He is having talks with **the** French foreign minister.* (= there is only one)

b Superlative

We use *the* with superlative adjectives.
    *She's **the** best person for the job.*

c *last* and *next*

These adjectives can be used with or without *the* but there is a change of meaning.
    *I saw James **last** night.* (= the one before this one)
    *It's **the last** night of our holiday.* (= the final one)
    *I'll see you **next** week.* (= the one after this one)

d Institutions: school, prison, university, church, home, hospital

With words like *prison, university, church,* etc., we use no article when we are thinking about the **institution**, and the normal purpose we use it for.
    My sister had to stay in hospital overnight.

However, if we are thinking about the **building**, we use *the*.
    *Our flat is opposite **the** hospital.*

3 Use and non-use of definite article with phrases of time and place

a Phrases of time

Some time phrases take *the*.
    Dates: **the** 25th of December / December **the** 25th
    Parts of the day: in **the** afternoon, in **the** evening, in **the** morning (but *at night, at lunchtime*)
    Decades / Centuries: **the** 1980s, **the** 21st century

Other time phrases take no article.
    Years / Seasons: *in 2002, in summer*
    Months / Days: *in August, on Friday, see you tomorrow*

b Place names

1   The names of most countries, continents, islands, states, provinces, towns and cities do **not** take an article.
    in Asia   to Sydney   from Texas   in Turkey

    Exceptions:
    ***the** Czech Republic, **the** Netherlands, **the** UK, **the** Arab World, **the** USA*

2   If we talk about a region we do **not** use an article.
    North-west India, Northern Europe

    But:
    *in **the** east of the country, in **the** south of Italy, on **the** coast*

3   Most roads, streets, parks, bridges, shops and restaurants do **not** take an article.
    Central Park, Harrods, Oxford Street, Tower Bridge

4   The names of theatres, cinemas, hotels, galleries and museums take *the*.
    ***the** Hermitage, **the** National Theatre, **the** Odeon, **the** Ritz*

5   The names of particular mountains and lakes do **not** take an article.
    Lake Victoria, Mount Everest

6   Mountain ranges, rivers, seas and canals take *the*.
    ***the** Atlantic, **the** (River) Danube, **the** Himalayas, **the** Panama Canal*

Ⓑ Different ways of giving emphasis

1 Intensifiers

a   *absolutely, completely, really, so*
    We use these words to add emphasis to adjectives.
    *Her new book is **absolutely** brilliant.*
    *It's **so** annoying.*

Absolutely and *completely* are usually used only with ungradable adjectives (for example *fantastic, awful,* etc.) which already describe an extreme or absolute quality.
    *The weather was **absolutely perfect**. (not ~~completely good~~)*
    *The second half of the match was **completely awful**. (not ~~completely bad~~)*

b *far*
Far is used for emphasis with *too* + adjective or *too much /
many* + noun.
It's **far too much** trouble.

We also use *far* with comparative adjectives.
You're **far** taller than I'd expected.

2 Use of auxiliary verbs

We often add an auxiliary verb in the positive for emphasis.
Your father **does** make me laugh.

We also use auxiliary verbs in the positive to emphasise a
contrast.
Donna is a vegetarian, but she **does** eat fish.

Adding *really* before the auxiliary also adds emphasis.
I **really do** apologise for what happened.

3 Cleft sentences

The usual word order for a sentence in English is:
subject + verb + object   + (adverbial phrase)
I   like   your sense of humour (most of all)

However, if we want to emphasise that we like his sense of
humour (more than anything else about him), we can use a cleft
sentence that begins with a *what* clause and the verb *be*.
What I like most (about you) is your sense of humour.
His rudeness annoys me. **What annoys me is** his rudeness.

Similarly, if we want to emphasise a particular person (more than
anyone else), we use a cleft sentence with *it + be + who*.
Both my children like fashion, but **it's my son who** spends most of
his money on clothes.

If a pronoun is used, the object pronoun is more usual than the
subject pronoun, though some consider this incorrect.
It was me who found it.

4 Emphatic questions

Informally, we can use the phrase *on earth* after a *wh-* question
word to emphasise surprise, annoyance, or the fact that we do not
know the answer to a question.
You're over two hours late – **where on earth** have you been?
What on earth is that girl wearing?

5 *so* and *such*

So is used before adjectives to intensify them.
You were **so** lucky!

Such is used before an adjective + noun.
We're having **such beautiful weather**!

A / An are used after *such*.
It was **such a** long journey!

Notice that with *much / many* + noun we use *so*.
We've had **so many problems**!
It takes **so much time**!

Module 7

Ⓐ Revision of relative clauses

Relative clauses give us information about things, people,
possessions, places and times using a relative pronoun *(which,
that, who, whose)*.

1 Things *(which, that)*

It's a shop **which / that** sells electronic goods.

> *REMEMBER!*
> It is incorrect to use **what** here.
> ~~It's a shop what sells electronic goods~~.

2 People *(who, that)*

A spectator is a person **who / that** watches a public event.

> *REMEMBER!*
> In 1 and 2 above, the relative pronoun is the subject of the clause.
> If a person or thing is the object of the relative clause, you can
> omit *which, who* or *that*.
> A ring is a metal thing *(which)* you wear on your finger.
> Look! There's the man *(who)* I met at that party the other night.

3 Possessions *(whose)*

A widow is a woman **whose** husband has died.

4 Places *(where, which / that + preposition)*

This is the room **where** Leo sleeps.
This is the room **which / that** Leo sleeps **in**.

5 Times *(when)*

A public holiday is a day **when** all the shops close.

Ⓑ Relative clauses with and without commas

1 Defining relative clauses (without commas)

Sometimes the relative clause is necessary to tell us which thing /
person we are talking about. In this case, there are no commas.
That's the man **who offered me a lift home**. (= we need the
relative clause to know which man we are talking about)
I've just finished the book **you gave me for Christmas**. (= we need
the relative clause to know which book we are talking about)

2 Non-defining relative clauses (with commas)

Sometimes the relative clause gives us extra information. It is not
necessary to tell us which thing / person we are talking about. In
this case, there are commas before and after the clause.
Christmas Day, **which is on a Thursday this year,** is always a
public holiday.
He gave me a photograph, **which I keep in my wallet.**

C Quantifiers

Nouns in English are either countable or uncountable. If a noun is uncountable, it does not have a plural form.

Some countable nouns in English have countable and uncountable forms.
*Colombia exports a large amount of **coffee**.* (= uncountable)
*I've ordered three **coffees**.* (= cups of coffee)

Some uncountable nouns have a plural form which is different in meaning.
*The bomb caused over €1 million worth of **damage**.*
(= uncountable: physical harm)
*The court awarded him €5,000 in **damages**.* (= plural: financial compensation)

1 Quantifiers with countable nouns

a several, a few, quite a few, very few

Several and *a few* refer to countable nouns. *Several* means 'more than a few'.
*Natasha speaks **several** languages.* (= perhaps three, four or more)
*There are only **a few** tickets left.*

Quite a few emphasises the positive.
*I know **quite a few** Australian people.*

Very few emphasises a small number. Note that *a* is not normally used here.
*There are **very few** people here who speak English.*

b many, a number of, loads of, hundreds of, dozens of

These are all used with plural countable nouns. *Many* and *a number of* are used in more formal situations to talk about a non-specific number. *Loads of, hundreds of* and *dozens of* are all used in conversation and informal contexts.

c too many

Too many is used with countable nouns to mean 'more than we need or is good'.
*I've eaten **too many** cakes.*

2 Quantifiers with uncountable nouns

a a little, very little, (quite) a bit of

A little and *a bit of* refer to uncountable nouns. *A bit of* is more used in conversation and informal situations.
*There's still **a bit of** wine left. Would you like it?*
*There's **a bit of** cheese in the fridge.*

Very little emphasises a small quantity.
*There's **very little** time left.*

Quite a bit of is used to emphasise the positive. We **cannot** say ~~quite a little~~.
*There's **quite a bit of** interest in his new book.*

b much, a great deal of

Much is used to talk about large quantities. It is used with uncountable nouns and is mainly used in questions and negatives.
*Hurry up, there isn't **much** time!*

A great deal of is used in positive sentences in more formal contexts.
*There is **a great deal of** concern about the new proposals.*

c too much

Too much is used with uncountable nouns to mean 'more than we need or is good'.
*I can't sleep. I think I drank **too much** coffee.*

3 Quantifiers with countable and uncountable nouns

a a lot of, lots of

A lot of is used with both countable and uncountable nouns. It is mainly used in informal situations. It is not usually used in negative sentences and questions. *Lots of* is used in the same way.
***A lot of** people arrived late.*

b enough, plenty of

Enough is used with both countable and uncountable nouns to mean 'as much as we need'. *Plenty of* means 'more than we need'.
*Have you got **enough** money to pay the bill?*
*Don't worry, we've got **plenty of** time to get to the airport.*

c some and any

Some and *any* are both used with plural and uncountable nouns, and in positive and negative sentences.

1 *Some* refers to a limited quantity or number. It can be followed by the phrase 'but not all'.
***Some** (but not all) people like getting up early.*
*I don't like **some** of his music.*

2 *Any* refers to an unlimited quantity or number. With a positive verb it means 'all' and with a negative verb it means 'none'.
*You can get online at **any** cybercafé.* (= all of them, it doesn't matter which)
*I can't think of **any** reasons to ask him to stay.* (= none)

Module 8

Ⓐ The use of gerunds

1   Grammatically, gerunds (*-ing* form of the verb) are used in the same way as nouns/pronouns. (See Module 2 for a comparison between the use of gerunds and nouns.)

    a   As the subject or object of the sentence.
*Too much **sunbathing** is bad for your skin.*
*I hate **being** late.*

    b   After a preposition.
*She's very good **at organising** things.*
*He acted **without thinking**.*

> **REMEMBER!**
> Notice the negative form of the gerund.
> *I want to achieve immortality through **not dying**.*

2   Certain verbs are followed by the gerund. These include: *admit, can't stand, consider, deny, enjoy, hate, imagine, like, dislike, love, (don't) mind, miss, practise, risk, suggest.*

3   There are also some noun phrases which take a gerund, for example, *have difficulty, have trouble.*
*We're **having trouble recruiting** new staff.*

4   There are also a number of useful patterns with *It* + gerund.
***It's worth seeing** the gardens in summer.*
***It's no use talking** to her – she won't change her mind.*

Ⓑ The use of infinitives

Infinitives are not generally used as the subject of sentences. We sometimes use infinitives with *to* and sometimes without *to*.

1   Infinitives with *to*

These are most commonly used in the following constructions.

a   Verb + infinitive

Certain verbs are followed by the infinitive with *to*. The most important include: *afford, agree, decide, expect, hope, manage, offer, plan, pretend, promise, refuse, seem, tend, threaten, want.*
*He has **agreed to come** into the studio and do an interview.*
*She **refused to answer** any questions about her engagement.*

b   Adjective + infinitive

Many adjectives are followed by an infinitive with *to*.
*It's **easy to see** why she's been so successful.*
*He was the **first to suggest** a new approach.*

Three common constructions with adjective + infinitive are:

•   *too* + adjective + *to*
*He's **too experienced to make** such a simple mistake.*

•   *not* + adjective + *enough* + *to*
*Maria isn't **old enough to go out** on her own.*

•   adjective + *for* + person + infinitive
*It's **easy for people to get** information over the Internet.*

c   Noun + infinitive

The following nouns are followed by infinitive forms: *chance, decision, effort, opportunity, time.*
*Their best **chance to win** the game came in the second half.*
*They really made an **effort to make** us feel at home.*

d   *Something* / *Nowhere*, etc. + infinitive

We often use infinitive forms after words like *no one, nothing, nowhere, something, somewhere, what, where,* etc.
*There was **nowhere to buy** a newspaper at that time of night.*
*Would you like **something to eat** before you go?*

e   Infinitive of purpose

We use an infinitive with *to* to explain why someone does something – to express purpose.
*Helen's gone out **to buy** a newspaper.*

In more formal English we use *in order to*.
*Taxes have been increased **in order to reduce** inflation.*

> **REMEMBER!**
> We form the negative infinitive with *not* + *to* + verb
> *I told you **not to do** that.*

2   Infinitives without *to*

Infinitives without *to* are used:

a   after modal verbs.
***I can't wait** for the weekend.*
*You **must have been waiting** for a long time.*

b   after *'d better* and *'d rather*.
***We'd better go** home now.*
***I'd rather watch** a video than go to the cinema.*

c   after *let, make* and *help.*
*She's the kind of person who really **makes you laugh**.*
*When I was a teenager, my parents never **let me stay out** late.*
*Can you **help me carry** the suitcases to the car?**

(* The infinitive with *to* is also possible here.)

Ⓒ More complex infinitive and gerund forms

1   Passive forms

Infinitives and gerunds can be used in the passive form:
*I just want **to be left** alone. (passive infinitive with* to*)*
*He'd rather **be given** money than a present. (passive infinitive without* to*)*
*She hates **being told** what to do. (passive gerund)*

2   Perfect forms

We use the Perfect infinitive (*to have* + past participle) when the infinitive clause refers to a time before the main clause. Compare the following sentences.
*I'd like **to visit** Rome while I'm in Europe.*
*I'd like **to have visited** Rome while I was in Europe, but unfortunately I ran out of money.*

Notice the perfect infinitive form without *to*.
*I would rather **have known** the truth.*

The perfect gerund is also possible, but sounds very formal and is often avoided.
*I remember **having seen** them before.*
*I remember **seeing** them before.*

3   Continuous forms

We use continuous infinitives instead of the Present continuous in infinitive constructions.
*The weather seems **to be getting** better. (= I think the weather is getting better)*
*I'd rather **be lying** on a beach than working! (=now)*

The gerund is not used in the continuous form.

D Different types of linking words

Two types of phrase are used to link together ideas and arguments.

1 Conjunctions: *although, despite, even though, in spite of, whereas, while*

These ideas link two ideas or clauses in the same sentence. *Although, even though* and *whereas* can go before either clause. The emphasis is on the clause without the conjunction.

> *Although he's terribly famous, he lives an ordinary lifestyle.*
> *He's terribly famous, although he lives an ordinary lifestyle.*

> *Whereas at one time, he lived in luxury, he now lives in a tiny apartment.*
> *He now lives in a tiny apartment, whereas at one time he lived in luxury.*

> **REMEMBER!**
> *Despite* and *in spite of* are prepositions and are therefore not followed by a subject or verb. They are followed by a noun, pronoun or *-ing* form.
> *Despite his achievements, he still feels insecure.*
> *He still feels insecure, in spite of his achievements.*
> *In spite of being so successful, he's very mean with money.*

2 Adverbial phrases: *besides, for this reason, furthermore, however, nevertheless, on the other hand, therefore, what is more*

These adverbial phrases link ideas in two different sentences (or even different paragraphs). The adverbial phrases always go in the second sentence, usually at the beginning.

> *Money can't buy happiness. **However**, it certainly makes life more comfortable.*

They can go at the end or in the middle of the second sentence and are separated from the rest of the sentence by commas.

> *The Prime Minister no longer has the support of Parliament. He has, **therefore**, called an immediate election.*

Module 9

A Overview of modal verbs

1 *should / shouldn't*

Should is used for obligations that are not strong – it is not necessary to do something but it is 'a good idea' or the right/correct thing.

> *You **should** be in bed by now. (= this is the right thing)*
> *You **shouldn't** eat so much chocolate. (= it's not a good idea)*

> **REMEMBER!**
> 1 *Should* can be followed by a continuous form.
>   *You **shouldn't be carrying** that heavy suitcase. (= now)*
>
> 2 *Ought to* has the same meaning as *should*.
>   *You **ought to be** in bed by now.*

2 *must / mustn't*

Must expresses necessity. There are two types of necessity:

a obligation
> *I **must** go home now. I've got to be at work early tomorrow.*

Mustn't means 'obliged not to' / 'not allowed to'.
> *You **mustn't** smoke in here! You could start a fire!*

> **REMEMBER!**
> *Have to* and *have got to* also express obligation. *Must* often expresses an obligation that comes from the speaker while *have to / have got to* express an obligation that comes from someone or something else.
> *I **must** go home now. It's late. (= I have decided this)*
> *I**'ve got to** be at work early tomorrow morning. (= my boss decided this, I have an early meeting, etc.)*
>
> The idea that something is not necessary is expressed by *don't have to*.
> *You **don't have to** buy a ticket if you don't want to.*

b logical necessity
> Here *must* means 'from the evidence I am sure this is true'.
> *He's not answering his phone. He **must** be in a meeting.*

> If we want to say that something is logically impossible, we use *can't*.
> *Surely he **can't** be sixty, he only looks about forty!*

3 *can*

Can expresses possibility in three ways:

a ability
> *She **can** speak fluent German. (= she is able to speak German)*

b permission
> *Can I interrupt for a moment? (= is it possible to interrupt?)*

c general possibility
> *It's very hot in summer, but it **can** be freezing in winter.*

Notice that *can* is not used to talk about specific possibilities either in the present or in the future.
> *Look in the cupboard. It ~~can~~ / **could** / **may** / **might** be in there.*

4 *could*

Could also expresses possibility in three ways:

a ability (as the past of *can*)
> *He **could** already walk on his first birthday.*

b permission
> *Could I interrupt for a moment?*

c present / future possibility
> *Of course, I **could** be wrong.*

5 *may*

Generally, *may (not)* expresses possibility in two ways:

a permission (mainly in first person: formal)
> *May I speak to you for a moment?*

b present / future possibility
> *There **may** be a storm later.*

6 *might*

Might expresses:

a   present/future possibility.
*We **might** see you later. We'll see what happens.*

b   permission (rather old-fashioned).
***Might** I ask you to speak up a little?*

c   in reported speech, as the past of *may*.
*'It **may** rain'. → He said it **might** rain later.*

> **REMEMBER!**
> 1   The different degrees of probability expressed by modal verbs can be summarised like this:
>
> | sure / logically certain → | must |
> |---|---|
> | possible, but not certain → | may, might, could |
> | sure / logically certain not to happen → | can't |
>
> 2   These modal verbs can be followed by a continuous form to talk about things happening now.
> *Have a look outside. Someone **might** / **may** / **could** be waiting for me.*
> *There's a lot of noise. They **must** be having fun.*

B Past modals

Modals sometimes have different past forms according to the meaning.

1 *had to*

When *must* expresses obligation, the past form is *had to* and the negative is *didn't have to*.
*When I was at school, I **had to** / **didn't have to** wear a uniform.*

2 *could*

The past of *can* is *could* or *was able to*.
*   *Could* is only used to talk about general abilities, not specific occasions.
    *We **could** come and go whenever we wanted.*

*   *Was able to* is used to talk about what you managed to do on a specific occasion.
    *Although he was badly injured, he **was able to** crawl to safety. (= he managed to do this)*

*   In the negative form, *couldn't* and *wasn't able to* can be used in all cases.

*   The past form *could have* is used when it was possible for something to happen, but it didn't.
    *It was very stupid of you to throw it out of the window. You **could have** killed someone!*

3 *can't have, could (not) have, may (not) have, might (not) have, must have*

All these modal verbs of probability have equivalent past forms. (modal + *have* + past participle)
*You **must have been** worried when you heard what had happened. (= logically it seems certain that this happened)*

*They **may** / **might** / **could have got** in through the window. (= logically it is possible that this happened)*

*They **can't have climbed** over that wall without a ladder. (= logically it seems impossible that this happened)*

4 *should have* and *ought to have*

The past form of *should* is *should have* + past participle.
*You **should have locked** the door before you went out. (= this was a good idea, but you didn't do it)*

*You **shouldn't have left** the door unlocked! (= this wasn't a good idea, but you did it)*

The past of *ought to* is *ought to have* + past participle.
*We **ought to have booked** in advance – there are no tables left.*

Module 10

A Plans and decisions in the future

1 *going to*

We use *going to* to express present intentions for the future. The action may be distant or in the near future.
*I'm never **going to** get married.*

2 *will*

We use *will* for a decision made at the moment of speaking.
*I'll **phone** you later.*

3 Present continuous

We use the Present continuous to talk about something we have arranged for the future.
*I'm **meeting** Henry for lunch on Friday.*

> **REMEMBER!**
> 1   The use of *going to* and the Present continuous is very similar. You can always use *going to* instead of the Present continuous to talk about the future.
> *I'm **going to meet** Henry for lunch on Friday.*
>
> The use of the Present continuous is more limited. You only use it to talk about definite arrangements.
> *I'm **going** to get married before I'm 30. (= general intention)*
> *I'm **getting married** in June. (= this has been arranged)*
>
> 2   When the main verb is *go*, the Present continuous is often preferred to the *going to* form.
> *We're **going** (to go) to Greece for our holiday.*

4 Present simple

When action in the future is part of a regular timetable, the Present simple is used.
*The show **begins** at eight o'clock.*

B Predictions

1   We can use both *going to* and *will* to make predictions about the future. When the prediction is based on some evidence in the present, we usually use *going to*.
*Watch out! You're **going to drop** those plates if you're not careful! (= I can see you're not carrying them properly)*
*All the opinion polls suggest that the government **is going to win** with a large majority.*

2   When the prediction is based on our own beliefs and expectations rather than present evidence, we use *will*.
A: *I wonder where Anna is?*
B: *Don't worry. I'm sure she'll **get** here soon.*

3 In many cases there is no important difference in meaning and both forms are possible.
*Who do you think **is going to win / will win** the Champion's League this year?*

> **REMEMBER!**
> There are many other ways of making predictions about the future using modal verbs, adverbs and phrases such as *certain to, I bet, likely to, there's a good chance that,* etc.
> *Economists are saying that inflation **may (well)** rise this year.*
> *My mother **will almost certainly buy** me a pair of socks for Christmas.*
> *In this heat, it's **likely to** be an uncomfortable journey.*
> ***There's a good chance that** I'll be accepted.*

C Future clauses with *if, in case, when,* etc.

We use a present tense in many future subordinate clauses. Notice that the main clause uses a future form. Words that introduce such clauses are: *after, as soon as, before, if, in case, once, when, unless, until.*

__Will__ you __be__ there to meet me __when I get__ to the airport?
(main clause)   (subordinate clause)

D Future continuous and Future perfect

1 Future continuous

Positive form	Negative form	Question form
I'll (= will) + be + *-ing*	I won't (= will not) + be + *-ing*	Will I + be + *-ing*?
I'll be working	*I won't be working*	*Will I be working?*

a As with all continuous tenses, we use the Future continuous for an action in progress at a particular time.

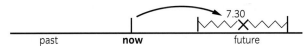

__I'll be driving__ home at seven o'clock this evening.

Compare the following sentences.
*We**'re having** dinner at eight o'clock this evening.* (= the meal will start at eight o'clock)
*We**'ll be having** dinner at eight o'clock this evening.* (= the meal will be in progress at 8 o'clock)

b We also use the Future continuous for something that will happen without any particular plan or intention, but as part of the normal course of events.
*I expect you**'ll be going** to the swimming pool tomorrow.*

This form is also used when we make requests, to suggest that something will not cause trouble to other people.
*I**'ll be turning** off the electricity for a while later. Is that OK?*
__Will__ you __be going__ past the supermarket when you go out? It's just that we need some milk.

2 Future perfect

Positive form	Negative form	Question form
I'll (= will) + have + past participle	I won't (= will not) + have + past participle	Will + have + past participle
I'll have done it	*I won't have done it*	*Will you have done it?*

a We use the Future perfect to talk about an action which will be completed **before** a point of time in the future.

*We**'ll have had** our dinner by the time you get home.*

Compare the following sentences.
*We**'ll have finished** painting by Monday.* (= **before** Monday)
*We**'ll finish** painting the flat on Monday.* (= **on** Monday)

b There are many phrases often used with the Future perfect with *by* and *by the time.*
***by** dinner time / one o'clock*
***by the end of the** decade / month / week / year*
***by the time** we go to bed / get home / I retire / I'm thirty*
***by this time** next month / next week / next year / tomorrow*

Module 11

A Hypothetical situations in the present

1 Hypothetical situations with *if*

a When talking about hypothetical or imaginary situations in the present, we go back one tense into the past.
*I **don't have** a cat, but if I **had** one I'd call it Henry.*
*It**'s raining** now; if it **wasn't raining** we could eat outside.*

This is sometimes called the 'unreal past'. The unreal past is often used after *if* in conditional sentences, as above. In the main clause we often use *would* or other modal verbs.
*If I **had** more time,   I **would start** going to the gym.*
*   I **could** learn to drive.*

b In certain phrases with the unreal past, we can use *were* with *he / she / it* with the first and third person.
*If Rachel **were** here, she'd know what to do.*

Some people consider this too formal and old-fashioned. However it is still common with the phrase *If I were.*
*I'd tell her about it **if I were you**.*

2 Imaginary situations with *wish* and *if only*

a We also use the unreal past after *if only* and *I wish* because they both describe imaginary situations.
*I wish I **could** speak Spanish.* (= I can't speak Spanish, but I'd like to)
*If only we **had** a map with us!* (= but we don't have one)

b We can also use *wish + would(n't)* to refer to things that you would like to happen (but you don't think they will happen).
*I **wish** my boss **would** give me a pay rise.*

I wish + you would(n't) is often used to express annoyance.
*I **wish you'd** hurry up.* (= you are being very slow)

c If there is no possibility of change, we must use the Past simple.
*I **wish you were** taller.* (= you cannot change this)
*I **wish you'd** be more helpful.* (= you can change this)

d We cannot use *wish + would* when the subject of the two clauses is the same.
I wish I would know the answer.

e The unreal past is also used after the phrase *It's time.*
*It's time people **changed** their attitude towards plastic surgery.*

B Hypothetical situations in the past

1 When we talk hypothetically with *if, if only* and *I wish*, the Past simple becomes the Past perfect.
   *If only / I wish I **had thought** about it more carefully!* (= but I didn't)
   *If you**'d told** me about the problem earlier, I would have done something about it.* (= but you didn't tell me about it)

2 In conditional sentences, if the main clause also refers to the past, *would have* + past participle is used.
   *If our best player **hadn't got** injured, we **would have won**.*

> **REMEMBER!**
> As with present hypothetical situations, *might have* and *could have* are often used instead of *would have*.
> *If he **hadn't been** injured, we **might/could have** won.*
>   'IF' CLAUSE   MAIN CLAUSE

3 Notice that in the sentences in 2 above, both the *if* clause and the main clause refer to the past. It is also possible to have a sentence where the *if* clause refers to the past and the main clause refers to the present.
   *If we**'d set off** earlier, we**'d be** at the hotel now.*
        'IF' CLAUSE   MAIN CLAUSE

Alternatively, the *if* clause may refer to the present, and the main clause to the past.
   *If my father **wasn't** the boss, he **wouldn't have got** the job.*
        'IF' CLAUSE   MAIN CLAUSE

Module 12

A Reporting people's exact words

1 Change of tense

When we report what someone said, the verb forms generally move one tense into the past.
   *'I **believe** that what I **am doing** is right,' she said. 'I **will** continue to fight for justice.'*
   *She said she **believed** that what she **was doing was** right, and that she **would** continue to fight for justice.*

Verb forms change in the following way:

Direct speech (the actual words)	Reported speech (indirect speech)
Present simple (*I do*)	Past simple (*I did*)
Present continuous (*I am doing*)	Past continuous (*I was doing*)
Present perfect (*I have done*)	Past perfect (*I had done*)
Past simple (*I did*)	Past perfect (*I had done*)
Past continuous (*I was doing*)*	Past perfect continuous (*I had been doing*)
Past perfect (*I had done*)	no change possible
Past perfect continuous (*I had been doing*)	no change possible
will	would
is going to	was going to
can	could
must	had to

* This frequently does not change in reported speech.

> **REMEMBER!**
> 1 The change of tense often happens because what the person said is now in the past.
>   *His teachers at school said he **would** end up in trouble, but now he's a successful businessman.*
>
> 2 If what the person says is still true/relevant now, we often don't change tenses.
>   *'I'll probably be late for the meeting.'*
>   *Pippa says she'll probably be late.* (= the meeting is still in the future)
>
>   It is possible to change tenses in such cases, but it is often done in more formal contexts.
>   *'Today's agreement **is** a historic opportunity,' the Prime Minister said.*
>   *The Prime Minister said that today's agreement **was** a historic opportunity.*
>   (Probably in a newspaper or on the news).
>
> 3 Notice that if the reporting verb is in the present tense, then there is no change.
>   *Mum **says** I **can** borrow the car tonight.*

2 Reported questions

Because reported questions are not real questions, the word order is the same as in statements.
   *'**Will you** continue to fight this case?' the journalists asked.*
   *The journalists asked if **they would** continue to fight the case.*

3 Some common reporting verbs and the constructions used after them

a Statements

say	He **said (that)** he was enjoying his new job.
tell	He **told me (that)** he was enjoying his new job.
answer	She **answered that** she had no intention of resigning.
reply	She **replied that** she had no intention of resigning.
add	She **added that** she wanted to thank her supporters.

b Questions

The verb *ask* is most commonly used to report questions, but *wonder* and *want to know* are sometimes used too. After *wh-* questions, the question word is used as a conjunction.
   *The police **asked (him) where** he had been.*
   *They **wanted to know what time** he had arrived home.*

With *yes/no* questions *if* or *whether* are used.
   *Ben **wondered if/whether** you wanted to come round for dinner.*

> **REMEMBER!**
> Say does not take a direct object, but *tell* always does:
> *He **said** ~~me~~ (that) he'd be here about nine o'clock.*
> *He **told me** (that) he'd be here about nine o'clock.*
> In both cases *that* can be omitted.

4 Other changes in reported speech

a When we report what someone said we need to show any changes in the situation, e.g. a change in the speaker, the time or the place.
   Direct speech: *'I'll help you clean the car later on today.'*
   Reported speech the next day: *You said you would help me clean the car yesterday.*

b Here are some typical changes of time phrases in reported speech. Notice that they do not happen automatically, it depends on the situation.

Direct speech	Reported speech
now	then / at that time
today	that day / last Tuesday, etc.
yesterday	the day before / the previous day
tomorrow	the next day / the following day
this week	last week / that week
last year	the year before / the previous year
next month	the month after / the following month
an hour ago	an hour before / an hour earlier

c However, we often omit the time reference if it is not important.
'We are unable to report the weather this evening.'
The announcer said that they were unable to report the weather.

B Verbs that summarise what people say

There are a large number of verbs which summarise what people say without reporting every word. The patterns that follow these verbs vary and have to be learned separately. With some verbs more than one pattern is possible. Here are some of the most important ones.

1 Verb + *(that)*

agree   *We **agreed (that)** we would meet again soon.*
(Also: *complain, explain, insist, recommend, say, suggest*)

2 Verb + object + *(that)*

warn   *My parents **warned me (that)** this would happen.*
(Also: *assure, persuade, tell*)

> **REMEMBER!**
> Here *that* can be omitted.

3 Verb + gerund

deny   *He **denied making** any threatening phone calls.*
(Also: *admit, recommend, suggest*)

4 Verb + preposition + gerund

apologise   *The minister has **apologised for making** the remarks.*
(Also: *insist on -ing, object to -ing*)

5 Verb + object + preposition + gerund

accuse   *They **accused me of lying**!*
(Also: *blame someone for -ing, congratulate someone on -ing, suspect someone of -ing*)

6 Verb + infinitive

refuse   *The young man **refused to give** his address.*
(Also: *agree, decide, demand, offer, promise, threaten*)

7 Verb + object + infinitive

tell   *The police **told the man to put** the gun down.*
(Also: *ask, invite, order, remind, warn*)

> **REMEMBER!**
> Negative gerunds and infinitives can also be used.
> *I decided **not to accept** the job.*
> *She blamed him for **not helping** her.*

MINI-CHECKS

Module 1

A Choose the correct tense – simple or continuous.

1 This week, Kate is looking after / looks after the shop for the owner.

2 What are you thinking / do you think of our new neighbours ?

3 Teresa is being / is a very calm person – it's part of her character.

4 Can I call you back later? We 're having / have lunch right now.

5 Did it rain / Was it raining when you last looked outside?

6 I read / was reading the newspaper the other day when I saw an interesting job advertisement.

B Choose the correct alternative.

7 I'd definitely buy a car if I had / had had / was having enough money.

8 When I was younger, I have played / play / used to play football on the beach with my friends.

9 In his twenties, Michael has lived / lived / used to live abroad for a year.

10 Unfortunately, the concert had started / started / used to start when we got there so we missed the first song.

11 I have seen / saw / used to see Neil the other day.

C Complete the sentences with a preposition.

12 He's very upset, but I'm sure he'll get _____ it soon.

13 E-mail had not been invented _____ those days.

14 _____ that time, the country was still not completely independent.

15 It's important that everyone in the group tries to get _____ with each other.

D Choose the correct alternative.

16 Well, I'd better get back / getting back / to get back to work.

17 The number of accidents decreased at / during / on the 1980s.

18 At that time / In those days / These days it's quite common for people to have two jobs at the same time.

19 Sorry about / for / to disturb you.

20 Leave me alone, are you? / do you? / will you?

/20

Module 2

A Complete the table.

Noun	Adjective
1	happy
2	critical
health	3
patience	4
science / scientist	5
6	developing / developed

B Complete the sentences with the correct form of the word in bold.

7 Were you happy when you were a **child**?
Did you have a happy _____ ?

8 To do this job, you need to be very **creative**.
To do this job, you need to have a lot of _____ .

9 A balanced diet has many benefits for your **health**.
A balanced diet is very _____ .

10 Roy and I have always been very close **friends**.
Roy and I have a very close _____ .

11 I can understand your **anxiety**.
I can understand why you are so _____ .

C Choose the correct alternative.

12 It was a very excited / excitement / exciting game.

13 There's no point in get / getting / to get upset about it.

14 Thinking about all the work I have to do before my exams makes me very depress / depressed / depressing.

15 Try not to / to don't / to not worry about it.

D Write an appropriate prefix for each group.

16 _____ -centred, -confident, -employed

17 _____ -smoking, -stop, -violent

18 _____ -government, -social, -war

19 _____ -confident, -cooked, -paid

20 _____ -graduate, -war, -2001

/20

Module 3

A Choose the correct alternative.

1 By the time she'd thought of the answer to the question, she'd got / lost / missed / run out of time.

2 A car drew in / off / out / up outside the house and two men got out.

3 Our car broke / fell / ran / stumbled down last night.

4 As I was running along the street, I slipped / spilled / stuck / stumbled on some ice and fell flat on my back.

5 It was only when we got to the airport that we realised we'd forgotten / left / lost / missed our passports at home.

B Complete the sentences with the correct form of the verbs.

By the time they 6_____ (arrive), we 7_____ (wait) for several hours.

As I 8_____ (travel) home on the train, I remembered I 9_____ (promise) to phone my parents.

It was obvious that someone 10_____ (break) a window in order to enter the house.

I'm tired! I 11_____ (run) up and downstairs all morning.

C Complete the sentences with a suitable word.

12 _____ that moment, we heard a cry from somewhere above us.

13 This is the third time this week you've been late _____ school!

14 It took a long time to persuade him but _____ the end he agreed.

15 _____ a shame you can't come to Marianne's party on Saturday!

16 _____ of a sudden, there was a loud crash and everyone looked up.

D Choose the correct form.

17 I heard someone to whisper / whispered / whispering behind the door.

18 'Have you heard that Max and Karine are getting married?'
'You joke! / You're joking! / You've been joking!'

19 The witness insists telling / that he's telling / to tell the truth.

20 It had been snow / snowed / snowing for several hours when we arrived.

/20

Module 5

A Choose the correct alternative.

1 Oscar has done / made / set excellent progress.

2 I wish you wouldn't do / have / take so many risks when you're driving!

3 After such hard work, it's good that she's beaten / gained / won an award.

4 They are hoping to overcome / raise / rise money to build a hospital.

5 Let's hope they do / make / set a good example.

B Complete the sentences with the correct form of the verbs.

6 The grass was extremely dry, as it _____ (not rain) for weeks.

7 We _____ (sit) at the table for about twenty-five minutes before anyone came to take our order.

8 Gwen _____ (work) on her presentation all morning – she must be nearly finished now.

9 By the time he was five, Joe _____ (learn) to play the guitar.

10 At the end of next month, we _____ (live) in this flat for exactly one year.

11 It was no good trying to persuade him: he _____ (make) up his mind a long time before.

C Choose the correct alternative.

12 I think I've left / I've been leaving my bag at the restaurant.

13 Have you been finishing / Have you finished with that DVD I lent you?

14 He's been trying / He's tried to fix his motorbike for ages.

15 I've written / I've been writing her ten e-mails but she never answers them.

16 I've never seen / I've never been seeing such an untidy room!

D Complete the sentences with a preposition.

17 Neil was a little shy _____ first, but he soon got used to the class.

18 Many people have found it hard to cope _____ so many changes.

19 As a result _____ this, we've had to cancel the party.

20 They promised it would be delivered first thing _____ the morning.

/20

Module 6

A Complete the gaps with the correct article: *a / an, the* or –.

1 My car is _____ most expensive thing I've ever bought.

2 All _____ people we met during our stay were extremely kind.

3 Although he has _____ Italian passport, Joe was born in the UK.

4 _____ people generally welcome strangers around here.

5 We have had _____ number of problems with the car.

B Choose the correct form.

6 I didn't enjoy the starter very much, but I did / have / was like the main course.

7 Have you thought in booking / of booking / to book your holiday on-line?

8 You should take every opportunity of practising / for practising / to practise what you have learnt.

9 You may find it difficult at first if you're not used doing / to do / to doing regular exercise.

10 If I am / were / would be you, I'd look for somewhere cheaper to stay.

C Cross out the extra word in each sentence.

11 No place is completely safe from a lightning.

12 Do not touch or not put anything on the wound.

13 Wait for the storm to pass on.

14 If you are indoors, stay in there!

D Complete the sentences with a suitable word.

15 It was _____ a boring journey we were happy to stop for lunch.

16 How _____ having a walk by the river before we go home?

17 _____ I really liked about the book was the surprise ending.

18 _____ you ask me, you can't find a better beach than this one.

19 _____ was you who wanted to spend the weekend camping!

20 There's a bus stop just opposite _____ hospital.

/20

Module 7

A Complete the sentences with a relative pronoun, where necessary.

1 That's the man _____ photo was in the paper the other day.

2 Chiang Mai, _____ is one of the biggest cities in Thailand, is in the north of the country.

3 This is the place _____ a new library is going to be built.

4 For dinner we had *bouillabaisse*, _____ is a kind of fish stew.

5 Sunday's the day _____ we all go and visit my grandmother.

6 Cate Blanchett's first film *Paradise Road*, in _____ she played a young nurse, was released in 1997.

B Choose the correct alternative.

7 The demonstrators were silent as the leader of the movement did / had / made / put his speech.

8 The next meeting is due to take off / part / place / out in March.

9 People were cheering and carrying / moving / shaking / waving their flags as the King's car drove slowly along.

10 We decided not to go swimming because the water was absolutely / extremely / rather / very freezing.

C Write extreme adjectives that mean:

11 very frightening _____

12 very hungry _____

13 very tired _____

14 very small _____

D Cross out the incorrect word or phrase in each sentence.

15 There are a bit of / a few / quite a few / several things to tell you.

16 There is a bit of / a little / very little / very few money left.

17 There were a bit of / a great deal of / hundreds of / loads of people waiting for the team at the airport.

18 Someone put enough / much / plenty / too much salt in the soup!

19 I foolishly didn't follow all / any / no / some of the advice I was given.

20 I knew some of the people in the room, but a few / any / many / some of them I'd never met before.

/20

159

Module 9

A Choose the correct alternative.

1 It's the wrong way down / round / over / up – the stripe should be at the top.

2 I'm afraid we couldn't agree about / for / to / with the answer to this.

3 There's anything / nothing / something wrong with my printer – the copies are very poor quality.

4 The CD was so badly burnt / chipped / scratched / shrunk it wouldn't play properly.

5 This jacket doesn't fit / go with / suit / work with me. It's too small.

B Replace the words in bold with a suitable modal verb.

6 **It's not necessary for you** to do anything right away.

7 **I'm sure that he isn't** serious.

8 **Is it possible for me to** borrow your newspaper?

9 **It's forbidden to** talk about what happened here.

10 **It's not a good idea to** wear that colour.

C Complete the sentences with a suitable word.

11 When I was a teenager, I _____ stay out as long as I wanted as long as I phoned home.

12 There was hardly any traffic on the road, so we didn't _____ to rush to get to the station on time.

13 I'm sure hearing the news was a terrible shock: it _____ have been an awful experience for you.

14 David _____ have left the house any time he wanted to. No one forced him to stay.

15 You _____ have paid more attention when they were giving you your instructions.

16 We don't know what's happened to Nicola. She may _____ got lost somewhere.

D Complete thee table.

Noun	Verb	Adjective
17	disappear	
suspect suspicion	suspect	18
mystery		19
20 explain		

/20

Module 10

A Complete the sentences with the correct form of the verb.

1 We'd better keep the door locked in case he _____ (try) to escape.

2 The TV programme _____ (finish) by the time we get back, so we'll have to set the video.

3 At this time tomorrow, David _____ (fly) back from Spain.

4 We'd better set off early in case the weather _____ (get) worse later.

5 I _____ (take) my nephew to his first football match on Sunday.

B Complete the sentences with the correct form of the verbs.

6 It's likely _____ (get) fairly cold once the sun has gone down.

7 By the middle of the next decade, most people will only be _____ (work) three days a week.

8 I think he would be a really interesting person _____ (talk) to.

9 It's likely that prices will have _____ (fall) by next year.

10 We'll get started as soon as the rain _____ (stop).

C Choose the correct alternative.

11 I'm afraid Jane can't come to the phone. She's in a conference / meeting / reunion.

12 Apparently, the former dictator is alive / live / living and well and living abroad somewhere.

13 Helen was hoping that Ed would ask her for a(n) appointment / date / meeting, but he doesn't seem to be interested in her.

14 We couldn't hear what she said as her voice was rather faint / loud / quietly.

15 She is certain / definite / surely to do well if she continues to work hard.

16 There were a hundred associates / guests / invitations at the wedding.

D Choose the correct preposition to make a phrasal verb.

17 put _____ = connect someone by telephone

18 get _____ with = have a good relationship with

19 go _____ = attend (a date, etc.)

20 speak _____ = speak louder

/20

Module 11

A Complete the sentences with the correct form of the verbs.

1 If I _____ (know) you were here I would have bought you a drink.

2 I wish I _____ (can) translate this for you, but I can't.

3 If I had the photos to show you, you _____ (be) absolutely convinced.

4 It's time you _____ (make) an effort to understand how serious it is.

5 I wish you _____ (hurry up).

6 If we hadn't lost the tickets, we _____ (watch) the show now.

B Complete the sentences with the correct form of the verbs.

7 _____ (be) honest, I haven't really thought about it.

8 We believe that a cure for this disease can _____ (find) before long.

9 Do you think that people under eighteen should be allowed _____ (get married)?

10 It is often _____ (say) that there is no solution to this problem.

C Complete the sentences with a suitable word.

11 _____ the other hand, there are several good reasons for staying where you are.

12 He inherited a large sum of money _____ his grandfather.

13 If we'd arrived earlier, we could _____ seen the stars arrive.

14 How much did you pay _____ that new coat?

15 You've been spending too much money _____ clothes lately.

16 If we _____ arrived any later, we would have missed the flight.

D Complete the sentences with the correct form of the words.

17 It's very _____ (doubt) whether we'll be able to do anything now.

18 As far as I'm _____ (concern) we shouldn't say anything.

19 One of the aims of the government is to tackle the problem of child _____ (poor).

20 In _____ (conclude), I think it should be banned.

/20

TAPESCRIPTS

Module 1

Recording 1

1 Um, quite an important place for my family, I think is my grandparents' house, when I was very young. Park Hill, and it was just this absolutely huge house, erm, in Lancashire up in the north of England, and it had these really really lovely gardens. That, er you know when you are a kid and you just feel like everything just goes on for ever. Just everywhere just seem so huge and, erm, I just remember the kitchen was bright yellow and this enormous table where we all used to sit round for family dinners and things. It was very good.

2 I think one of the teachers that I will never forget is a teacher that was called Miss Brown, and she used to teach, er, sports at school. And I used to absolutely loath her. She is … she's lived with me for the rest of my life, I think, because I … she just used to make my life hell. Erm, when I went swimming with the class she used to give us ten seconds to get dressed and dried after the class. So she would count down from ten and we'd have to arrive in the next class by the time she got to one. So you can imagine we'd all arrive with wet hair and half dressed and I hated her.

3 Well, er, my favourite day of the week is Monday, which I know may seem a bit strange, but it's because I like going out on Monday evenings and it always feels a bit naughty because you've got work the next day.

4 An important date in my family is the 6th June, because both my parents were born on the 6th June, and also one of my cousins was born on that date.

5 An important place in er, my family history is the village of Glengareth in, er, Cork in Southern Ireland 'cos em, that's where my mother was born and most of my family come from. I always used to go back there as a child to visit my grandmother's house for the summer and somewhere I'll always remember with great love.

6 An important person I haven't seen for quite a while is my friend Emma who moved to San Francisco years ago, so I haven't really seen much of her for a long time. She was at college with me and very, very close friend. Umm, yeah, I'd like to see her again.

7 Er, the number of the house that's really important to me is 3042. It was the house that I was born in in Buenos Aires, and my parents went back about ten years after I was born and found some builders pulling the house down and they took the number plate from the front of the house and we now have it in, on our fireplace at home.

8 An important date for me is the 4th September 1993 cos that's the day I got married and, erm, it was the best day of my life I think. It was really nice to have all the people that I know in one place at the same time, cos that's so unusual.

9 An important person when I was growing up was my brother, Tony. He was, er, ten or eleven years older than me, so we never had any of that um sort of brother and sister jealousy that you often get, and, er, he was always a good friend, as well as a brother to me.

10 An interesting place that I have been to quite recently, is er, Berlin. I thought that it was just amazing how, erm the city was completely divided by this war. I just couldn't imagine how people lived there, erm, during the cold war.

Recording 2

(answers only)

1	was born	10	was growing up
2	lived	11	used to talk
3	left	12	had never been
4	had moved	13	doesn't seem
5	went	14	've always thought
6	spoke	15	have
7	lived	16	want
8	remember	17	're planning
9	influenced	18	are looking forward

Recording 3

(answers only)

1 Have they?
2 is it?
3 isn't.
4 does
5 she has

Recording 4

a A: I've got some really interesting news, do you want to hear it?
   B: Of course I do!
b A: John, you're not listening to me, are you?
   B: I am listening, darling.
c A: Was the party good on Saturday night?
   B: No, to be honest, it wasn't.
d A: Are you still going out with your sister tonight?
   B: I think I am, she hasn't phoned yet.
e A: Have you heard? Annie and Phil have got engaged!
   B: Really, have they?
f A: We had a terrible journey home last night; we were nearly two hours late!
   B: Oh no, were you?
g A: I know you don't believe me …
   B: I do believe you!
h A: Listen, the neighbours are having an argument! Can you hear what they're saying?
   B: No, I can't!
i A: You didn't tell me you were moving house!
   B: I did, didn't I?
j A: I've had the most awful day at work!
   B: Oh dear, have you? Why?

Recording 7

F = FIONA; R = HOTEL RECEPTIONIST; S = SEAN

F: … right, so I'll pick that up in the morning, then.
R: Right, Madame.
F: Okay, thank you.
S: Hi, excuse me, I couldn't help overhearing. Is that a Scottish accent there? I thought I noticed …
F: Um, yes, it is. I am Scottish, yes.
S: Oh, that's great.
F: Yes. Well …
S: Mm … which part of Scotland are you from? I haven't actually been there myself, but …
F: I'm from a place called Dunoon. It's just outside Glasgow.
S: Right. Mmm. So are you over here for long?
F: No, I just arrived, in fact … just come from the airport.
S: I see. So you haven't had a chance to look round yet?
F: No, not really.
S: So are you here on holiday?
F: No, I'm here for work actually … just for a couple of days … then I'm off back home.
S: Oh, right. So what kind of work do you do?
F: I'm a researcher. I work in television research. We're doing a programme about the elections here.

s: Oh, sounds interesting. You must get to travel a lot …

f: Well, not all that often actually. Well, if you'll excuse me, I have to er …

s: Oh, right. Don't let me keep you.

f: Okay.

s: My name's Sean by the way.

f: Hello. Nice to meet you, Sean.

s: Nice to meet you. Sorry, I don't know your name.

f: Er … Fiona.

s: Fiona, right. That's a nice name.

f: Thank you. So, I must be getting on, really. I've got to unpack. It's been nice talking to you.

Module 2

Recording 1

1	happiness	7	movement
2	researcher	8	evidence
3	depression	9	society
4	employees	10	criticism
5	friendships	11	feeling
6	scientists	12	behaviour

Recording 2

(answers only)

a	happiness	n	lonely
b	health	o	Companionship
c	getting	p	important
d	balance	q	interaction
e	fitness	r	Membership
f	enjoyable	s	political
g	satisfaction	t	stress
h	doing	u	frustration
i	creative	v	Joining
j	painting	w	supportive
k	cooking	x	social
l	gardening	y	beneficial
m	solitary		

Recording 3

1 a: … and most of the people there seem very friendly, so, yeah, all that side of things is fine.

   b: Good.

   a: It's just that … well, I don't want to sound as if I'm moaning already or anything, but I've got a bit of a problem with my boss somehow. It's a bit hard to explain. When you first meet her, she seems perfectly nice, you know, good fun, and young and everything, but I don't know. She's got this way of kind of ignoring whatever I say. She doesn't actually criticise me, not openly, but she just doesn't seem to take any of my suggestions very seriously.

   b: Oh dear, how annoying.

   a: Yeah, well, I'm supposed to be her assistant manager, not some junior who doesn't know anything about the job.

   b: That sounds awful. Have you tried talking to anyone else about it? Or to her, even?

   a: Well, I don't know. I don't feel as if I'm really well enough established there yet.

2 a: … well, if we hurry we might just get there. Oh, no!

   b: What's the matter?

   a: Look! Look at the traffic! It's just solid. Oh I don't believe it. I mean how is anyone supposed to get around …

   b: Okay, okay. Calm down, calm down.

   a: Will you stop telling me to calm down? It is SO annoying … (BANGS ON HORN) Come on, will you!!

   b: Look, there's no point in getting upset about it. It's rush hour. There's bound to be a lot of traffic.

   a: Yes, and when we turn up an hour late, I can imagine they're gonna be really happy about it.

   b: OK, come on, we're not going to be an hour late. I tell you what, I'll give them a ring to tell them we're stuck in traffic, okay?

   a: Yeah, okay, I mean there's not much else we can do is there, short of buying a private helicopter. I mean the traffic in this town is just …

3 a: Hello?

   b: Helen? It's Linda here.

   a: Oh, hi. Nice to hear from you. How's it going?

   b: There's a bit of a crisis, actually. That's why I'm ringing. I don't know what to do.

   a: Oh, dear. You've not locked yourself out again, have you?

   b: No, no, it's … it's Tony.

   a: Oh, Tony.

   b: He should have been back hours ago. I mean he's always here when I get in from work, always, and he's just not here. He's disappeared!

   a: Well, never mind. I'm sure he'll come back. He always does, doesn't he?

   b: Yeah, but, you never know what might've happened. I mean he's not used to being out on his own.

   a: Have you looked under the bed? That's where he was last time.

   b: Of course, I have. No, he's not in the flat. He's gone. I just don't know where.

   a: Look, Linda, try not to worry about it. He's probably out with one of his girlfriends or something. Have you called him? He could be in the garden.

   b: Yeah, I've looked everywhere. He's not in any of his usual places.

Recording 4

1 Never mind.

2 Don't take any notice of him.

3 Don't worry. It doesn't matter.

4 That sounds awful!

5 You must be really worried.

6 Try not to worry about it.

7 What a shame!

8 Come on! Pull yourself together!

9 Just ignore them.

10 There's no point in getting upset about it!

11 Calm down!

12 How annoying!

Recording 5

1 One thing that I often do actually, that always makes me feel really embarrassed is I say the wrong thing at the wrong time to people and I end up getting myself into situations that it's just because of my big mouth, and I open my big mouth and say something and there it is. Oh, said something really stupid, again.

2 There's only one thing that really stresses me, and that's the sound of the telephone ringing and nobody answering it. Especially at work, it just sends me completely crazy. I can't concentrate with that noise.

3 Something that always makes me feel depressed in the winter, is getting up in the morning and it's still dark and you go to work in the cold and then you are at work all day and by the time you come out of work, go home again, trotting down to the station in the cold, it's dark again already. So you hardly ever see the daylight except at weekends.

4 What helps me relax? Well, I chant, which is slightly unusual for a western person, and I do Buddhist chanting

in the morning and in the evening and that really helps me relax.

5   What makes me laugh is, well actually almost anything. I erm, I find all sorts of strange situations quite funny, and it can be embarrassing as well, but I do have perhaps an odd sense of humour.

6   The thing that frightens me the most is watching horror films or thrillers on TV or at the cinema, cos I believe everything that I see. So it becomes completely real to me. I get terrified.

7   What makes me really happy is when I wake up on a Saturday morning and I know that I can just go back to bed with a cup of tea and I just listen to the radio and think ah, I've got the whole day ahead of me. I put some music on, have a dance around the kitchen, and it just puts me in a really great mood.

8   I absolutely detest snakes to the extent that I actually pass out when I see one.

9   Something that always makes me laugh is when people fall over or walk into something. I know you shouldn't laugh, but I can't stop myself from laughing when something like that happens.

10 I find it incredibly embarrassing when I'm in a social situation and somebody comes up to me and goes, 'Oh hi, how are you?' and I'm going 'I don't know who you are', but I'm thinking this to myself and I'm looking at them. And after about two minutes it's too late to say 'I'm sorry, I haven't got the faintest idea what your name is' and so it gets more and more embarrassing. Ah, I just feel terrible about it.

Recording 6

a   One thing that always makes me feel embarrassed is I say the wrong thing at the wrong time.

b   There's only one thing that really stresses me …

c   It just sends me completely crazy.

d   I find all sorts of strange situations quite funny.

e   The thing that frightens me the most is watching horror films.

f   It just puts me in a really great mood.

g   I absolutely detest snakes.

h   I know you shouldn't laugh, but I can't stop myself from laughing.

Module 3

Recording 1

1   Um, I'm a really, really deep sleeper and I used to have a habit of getting up, turning my alarm off and getting back into bed, and not actually waking up. And one time I did this on the morning of an exam so um I was about twenty minutes late for the exam. I woke up at about ten past nine and realised I had to be in the exam at nine o'clock, so I threw my clothes on over my pyjamas and cycled to the exam as quickly as I could, walked into the exam room completely out of breath and everybody was staring at me. Of course, I was really uncomfortable during the exam cos I still had my pyjamas on and I did really, really badly.

2   When I was about twelve, I was on holiday with my parents in, erm, in Denmark in Copenhagen, and we were getting onto a train to go to, I don't know, some shopping centre or something, I can't remember, and erm it was getting a bit late and my father said quick run we've got to get on the train so I ran. My parents were behind me. I jumped onto the first train I saw and as the door closed and the train pulled out, I could see my parents standing on the platform waving to me, and I ended up going to Sweden for the day.

Erm, it was okay, I mean I was old enough to get back on the train and go back again, but it was a bit scary at the time.

3   Erm well, one time I went um, for a first date with somebody, to quite a posh restaurant, and the first thing I did, I was very nervous, and after about five minutes of being there I managed to spill all of my drink over the person I was on the date with. And it was a very embarrassing moment.

4   I didn't lock myself out, but my flatmate locked me in. What actually happened was, it was a Saturday morning and my flatmate left quite early locking the door. Now it was a very important day. It was my great grandmother's ninetieth birthday. So I got up early, went to the door and er realised that my flatmate had locked me in. So at first I was quite calm 'cos I thought well I can jump out of the window, if necessary. Um, but then I realised that it was quite a drop to the ground. So I went into a state of panic because there was no way I was going to be able get out of that flat and down to my grandmother's somewhere in the country, um, you know within two hours. So I rang the fire brigade, and uh, they came after about five minutes, but by that point I had got out of the window and jumped down.

Recording 2

It was about midnight, I guess. I was coming home from a Christmas party with my friend Frank. It was very, very cold – absolutely freezing. There was thick ice everywhere and it had been snowing for several hours. Actually, maybe it was still snowing because we really couldn't see where we were going. The road we were walking down was on a really steep hill, too, so you can imagine, it was just so slippery, and we couldn't see a thing, so, well, we just kept falling over. We'd get up, and two seconds later, we fell over again. Not because we were drunk or anything, but just because it was so slippery. Anyway, for some reason, this all began to seem very funny, and we were laughing our heads off and calling to each other for help, y'know. We really didn't know how we were going to get down that hill. We weren't making any progress at all. Well, eventually we realised that the only way we could move at all was if we held on to the cars that were parked in the street for support. So, that's what we did, and slowly we were managing to move along. Except suddenly this police car drew up and two police officers got out and started shouting at us. We tried to talk to them and find out what the problem was, but they wouldn't listen to us. They just pushed us in the back of the car and drove us to the nearest police station. To be honest, I can't remember much after that, but a few hours later, I woke up in a police cell, feeling absolutely terrified, not to mention freezing cold!

Recording 3

It all happened at about one o'clock in the morning, I would say. I had gone to bed at ten, as usual, but I had to get up to go to the bathroom. As I was getting back into bed, I heard this dreadful noise outside in the street … men shouting … so of course I went to the window to see what was going on. Anyway, I looked out and saw these two young men just outside my house. They were swaying all over the place, shouting and swearing at each other. They had obviously been drinking, you could see they were drunk – very aggressive and nasty-looking types. Then I noticed that they were doing something to the cars. It was a very clear night, with a full moon, so I could see everything. They were banging on all the car windows trying to break into them. Obviously as soon as I realised what was going on, I called the police straightaway, and thank goodness, they came more or less immediately, and arrested them before they could do any damage. It was very lucky I happened to wake up and catch them, otherwise I'm sure half the cars in the neighbourhood would have been robbed, even stolen. This is a nice neighbourhood. People have expensive cars with radios and CD players and all sorts. It was very lucky that I saw it all.

Recording 4

(answers only)

1	was reading	16	were flying
2	became	17	was driving
3	was coming	18	entered
4	gave	19	had not noticed
5	looked	20	carried on
6	hadn't been	21	ran out
7	had been coming	22	was
8	was lying	23	decided
9	was travelling	24	'd only been waiting
10	had been going	25	saw
11	suddenly started	26	were wearing
12	ran	27	seemed
13	got	28	realised
14	'd been sitting	29	had driven
15	explained		

Recording 6 and 7

1 A: What have you been doing this morning?
   B: Oh, just the usual kind of things I do every morning; tidying up, washing …
   C: I've been answering e-mails all morning – mostly boring ones from my boss.

2 A: How long have you been learning to drive?
   B: Not long! This is just my third lesson, so, yeah, a couple of weeks, that's all.
   C: I've been learning to drive for about a year … I've had I don't know how many lessons. I just can't seem to get the hang of it, somehow. I don't know how I'll ever pass my test!

3 A: What will you be doing at eight o'clock this evening?
   B: Eight o'clock? Don't know, watching TV probably.
   C: Well, in fact, I know exactly what I'll be doing at eight o'clock this evening. I'll be babysitting. It's what I always do on a Friday evening!

4 A: What will you be wearing tomorrow?
   B: I've just bought this really nice black top, so I'll probably be wearing that.
   C: I've got absolutely no idea. I never think about what I'm going to wear each day. I just open the wardrobe and put on the first thing I see!

5 A: How long have you been living in your present flat?
   B: Not long, actually. We just moved in about six months ago.
   C: Let me see. We've been living in this flat for about, yeah, about eight years.

6 A: What will you be doing this time tomorrow?
   B: This time tomorrow? The same as I am now, I suppose, sitting in a classroom, studying!
   C: Well, tomorrow's Saturday, isn't it, so I can't be totally sure, but I'll probably be playing football in the park, with my friends.

Recording 8

1 A: Hello, yes, we booked a table for two. The name's Read, R-E-I-D.
   B: Right … Reid, yes. That was for eight o'clock, wasn't it, sir?
   A: Yes, it was eight o'clock, that's it.
   B: I'm afraid there is a small problem, sir, as you see we are very busy, and we have actually had to give your table … um … to someone else.
   A: What? You've given … I don't believe it! But we booked it ages ago. It was …
   B: Well, sir, I think what's happened is … um … it is nearly 8.45 and we thought you probably weren't coming so …

A: Oh, for goodness' sake. This is ridiculous! Surely there must be another table you can give us.
   B: If you give me a moment, sir, I'll see what we can do. Um, let me see. If you'd just like to take a seat at the bar …

2 C: Hello, is that Jane Parry?
   D: Speaking.
   C: Oh hi, this is Jacqui from Head Masters, the hairdresser's.
   D: Oh, hello.
   C: Um, we've got you down as having an appointment with us for eleven o'clock this morning, with Fiona.
   D: That's right, yeah.
   C: Well, I'm afraid Fiona's not in today, and we've got a couple of staff off sick.
   D: Oh, dear.
   C: Yeah, and we haven't actually been able to get anyone to cover for Fiona.
   D: Oh, what a nuisance.
   C: I wonder if it would all right to move your appointment to the same time tomorrow.
   D: Yeah. I don't see why not. Just let me get my diary. Yes, that's fine. See you tomorrow.

3 E: Excuse me, hello, we'd like two tickets, please. Do you do a discount for students?
   F: We do, but I'm afraid the museum closes in ten minutes. We stop selling tickets at 12.30.
   G: Oh, no! You're joking! Are we too late?
   F: Well, it's 12.50 now so it's not really worth it. You won't be able to get round to see everything in ten minutes.
   E: Well, couldn't you just let us in for free? Oh, we just want to have a quick look.
   F: No, I'm, sorry. You'll have to come back tomorrow. The museum opens at nine.
   G: Oh, no!
   E: Oh, what a shame!! I so wanted to see it! It's your fault! You should've checked before we came out!
   G: Well, how was I to know? It's not my fault they've decided to close early, is it?

4 H: Yes, please.
   I: Can I change these euros into Czech Crowns, please? It's 150 euros.
   H: I'm sorry, we don't have Czech crowns. You'll have to order them. It takes about twenty-four hours.
   I: Oh, that's a pity. It's just that I'm flying to the Czech Republic tomorrow. Is there any way I can get them now?
   H: Well, there's a bureau de change across the road.
   I: Oh good, well I'll try there then.
   H: But that doesn't have Czech crowns either.
   I: Right, I see. So what do you suggest then?
   H: Your best bet is probably to try at the airport, I'd say, or you could always try phoning up.

Recording 11

Like chat: approach, check, cheek
Like joke: gentle, gorgeous, jelly
Like bath: sympathy, theft, thick, thought
Like bathe: father, leather

Module 4

Recording 1

A: If you had mainly (a) answers, you are mainly left-brained. This means that you tend to think in a linear way, using information in a step by step way in order to arrive at the answer. You tend to try and work things out logically rather than rely on your intuition and feelings. You are very interested in details. Verbal communication is very important to you, and you respond to explanations and logical arguments.

B: If you had mainly (b) answers, you are mainly right-brained. This means that you tend to start with the bigger picture and think about the details later. You also rely more on emotion and feeling to arrive at the answer: the right-hand side of the brain is often connected with artistic creativity. You like to be able to visualise things. Explanations are less important to you, and when you are learning something new, you like to try it out for yourself.

A: Most people have a balance of (a) and (b) answers. Men tend to get a higher proportion of (a) answers than (b) answers.

B: Ideally, we should make use of both sides of our brain in order to learn most effectively. If you pay attention to your less dominant side, you can learn how to improve it.

Recording 2

(answers only)

a	be established	l	was published
b	is said	m	produced
c	been invented	n	been translated
d	is thought	o	claims
e	was claimed	p	are given
f	been recorded	q	succeed
g	was educated	r	Being defeated
h	soon became	s	remarked
i	wanted	t	be surprised
j	dropped	u	was written
k	had made		

Recording 3

Do you need to: Increase your concentration? Develop your powers of logic? Improve your study skills and remember thousands of facts effortlessly? Never forget a name, face or appointment again? Open up your imagination? Yes? Then you need BrainBoost! You can boost your brainpower with Professor BrainBoost's unique methods, developed over twenty-five years. All in just ten minutes a day! BrainBoost special package includes: Twelve quality booklets to take you step-by-step through Professor BrainBoost's unique methods; CD-roms with enjoyable easy-to-follow exercises; Eight CDs of classical music specially selected to stimulate your brain; Three months' supply of unique BrainBoost vitamin supplements. And all for the special price of €150 + €5.95 postage and packing. Call 0800 323 323 now and receive your BrainBoost package in forty-eight hours.

Recording 4

A: Flair Drycleaning?

B: Oh hi, I'm just phoning with a question; do you do alterations?

A: What's it for, Sir?

B: Oh, I just need to have a pair of trousers altered. They're too long. Can you do that?

A: Sure, no problem at all, just bring them in.

B: The problem is I need to get them done before Friday, because I need them for a job interview. Is that okay?

A: Don't worry, just bring them in this afternoon and they'll be ready on Thursday.

B: Brilliant, thanks.

A: Bye then.

Recording 5

(answers only)

1 speak your mind.
2 I don't mind.
3 absent-minded

Recording 6

(answers only)

1	treat	8	keep
2	love	9	hold
3	said and done	10	told you
4	took the time	11	I'm
5	Tell	12	made
6	hasn't died	13	feel
7	Give me		

Consolidation Modules 1–4

Recording 1

1 Karen
About five years ago I had my eyes lasered because I wanted to correct my short-sightedness. Um, I suppose it was for vanity reasons as well because I hated wearing contact lenses and er glasses. So I went along to a private clinic in London and I had to wait for most of the afternoon um before the doctors could see me. And of course, by the time the procedure was about to happen, I was really, really nervous, and actually now I'm surprised that I didn't faint with fear. Um, it took a few months for my eyes to heal properly and although they're not ... I haven't got sort of perfect 20:20 vision, I'm really glad that I had them done because I can do all kinds of things that I couldn't do before, and one of the best things is being able to wake up and see the alarm clock in the morning.

2 Nigel
Um, I had this tattoo done on my eighteenth birthday. Um, I couldn't decide whether I was going to have like a Celtic cross or a dolphin but in the end I decided for a dolphin. Um, I had to go into Manchester city centre to get it done. I was a bit scared about it cos I thought it might hurt but um when I was in there I just kind of breathed regularly and it was all over quite quickly. And so anyway, that was about five years ago and um I still love it.

3 Penny
When I was at university; I used to really enjoy having my hair dyed different colours. My favourite colour was having it royal blue. And when I had my hair dyed royal blue, I just felt really cool, and like I stood out in the crowd, and it just felt fabulous. And I also had blue plastic extensions put in so my hair went all the way down to my waist and it was in blue plaits, and every time I turned around my hair would swing out and hit people, and it was just fabulous. But I look back at the photos now and kind of think 'Oh, my God. What was I doing?'

Module 5

Recording 1

a Britain's oldest teacher has just celebrated her seventy-fifth year at a village primary school. Elsie Gamble, 94, set up Coteswood School in Woodthorpe, Nottinghamshire, in 1927 as a teenager to get out of doing the household chores. Then, the fees were £3 a term. Now they are £700. But little else has changed in seventy-five years. Pupils still wear uniforms, and are drilled in reading, writing and arithmetic.
'Everything goes on more or less as it did when I began it,' said Gamble. 'I always say: if you have a good beginning you can go on from there.'

b Git Kaur Rhandawa, from Hayes in West London, had more

reason than most people to feel nervous when she took her driving test a few years ago. Git Kaur had already tried forty-seven times to pass her driving test, spending more than £10,000 on driving lessons, without success. Imagine her joy when the examiner turned to her and said 'Congratulations, Mrs Rhandawa. I'm happy to tell you you've passed your driving test.'

c   James Hughes, thirty-five years old, is believed to be the world's biggest film addict. After seeing his first film at the age of six (his parents took him to see *Pinocchio* as a Christmas treat) he has seen nearly 10,000 films. He currently goes to the cinema at least six times a week, an average of about 800 films a year. He records every title he has seen in his diary (with a star rating) and, given his current rate of viewing, he hopes to achieve his ambition of seeing 20,000 films by the time he is forty. When asked for his favourite film among the films he has already seen, Mr Hughes, who is unmarried, has no hesitation. *Pinocchio,* he says.

Recording 2

1   One thing that I think has really, really made a difference to people is um having running hot and cold water, and as basic as it sounds I think that … and I just can't imagine now being able to uh, you know get washed and do the washing up without you know … I just think it's amazing that we have that constant supply of hot and cold water just coming through our houses.

2   I think one of the most important technological developments in recent years has been the Internet and er the difference that it's made to peoples lives. Not just in communications, but for example, I er do all my banking now by Internet. I used to be terrible for paying bills and er paying cheques into the bank, and things like that, and now I just sit there in front of the screen and tap away and get it all done without any of the leg work or the writing letters or anything that I used to do.

3   One person that I really admire is Steve Redgrave, the rower, and certainly the greatest Olympian ever to come out of Britain. Um, he has won five gold medals at consecutive Olympic games and I think he's um … not only his ability but also his personality is an inspiration for everybody. What makes his achievement even more admirable is that he was diagnosed with diabetes during his training um … but he's battled on and he's been a role model for many, many people.

4   One achievement I find absolutely amazing is the construction of Stonehenge because the stones were moved several hundred miles from somewhere in Wales to where they stand um and no one really knows how they did it because it was about three or four thousand years ago.

5   I think probably the most outstanding leader I've ever heard of is probably Gandhi, Mahatma Gandhi. Er the British empire was at its height – it was the most powerful empire in the world and he brought it down. And not only did he bring it down, but he did it without the use of violence. You look at how governments operate today, and how regimes and empires are destroyed, all using violence. I don't think anybody else has ever brought down such a massive empire without the use of violence.

Recording 5

1   You haven't been trying to phone me, have you? (upward)
2   They'll have finished the work by Thursday, won't they? (downward)
3   We haven't lost the tickets, have we? (upward)
4   You haven't heard this story before, have you? (upward)
5   They've moved house recently, haven't they? (downward)
6   You'll have finished with the car by six, won't you? (downward)

7   You'd forgotten it was my birthday, hadn't you? (downward)
8   They hadn't seen the film before, had they? (upward)

Module 6

Recording 1

(answers only)

a   opportunity
b   resist
c   You should
d   Always remember
e   careful
f   might
g   if you're
h   effort
i   make sure
j   Start
k   of time

Recording 2

1   A: When do Chinese people celebrate New Year?
    B: The Chinese don't celebrate their New Year on the 1st January – the exact date varies from year to year, but it's usually around the end of January.

2   A: When is it common for people in some countries to have a siesta?
    B: It is common to take a siesta – or short sleep – in many hot countries; Spain and Mexico to name but two. The normal time for a siesta is after lunch in the middle of the afternoon.

3   A: Newcastle is a city in which part of the UK?
    B: Newcastle, a city once famous for its shipbuilding but now better known for its football team, is situated 450 km north of London, in the north-east of England.

4   A: Which is the largest sea or ocean in the world?
    B: The largest ocean has an area of 166 million square kilometres … and it contains more water than all the other seas and oceans of the world put together! It is, of course, the Pacific Ocean.

5   A: Jeanne Louise Calment, who died on the 4th of August 1997, is famous for being …
    B: … the world's oldest woman. She was 122 when she died.

6   A: If you went for a boat trip on the River Vltava, and went climbing in the Sumava Mountains and went sightseeing in Prague, which country would you be in?
    B: All of these places are to be found in the Czech Republic.

7   A: Where will the next Summer Olympic Games be held?
    B: The next Summer Olympics are to be held in 2008, in Beijing, in China.

8   A: Lake Titicaca is …
    B: … not the largest lake in the world, but with an area of over 8,000 square kilometres, it is the largest lake in South America.

9   A: Austrian Reinhold Messner is famous as …
    B: … the first man to climb Mount Everest without oxygen.

10 A: When was the former President of South Africa, Nelson Mandela, released from prison?
    B: Following twenty-six years in prison, Nelson Mandela was finally released in 1990. He became President of South Africa four years later.

Recording 3

H = HANNAH; D = DAN

H: Oh, this is so annoying. Where on earth did I put my car keys?
D: Not again! Have you looked on the kitchen table?
H: I've looked everywhere.
D: Hannah, you really are hopeless.
H: Thank you. I suppose it's too much trouble for you to help

look for them. Oh, look, here they are under this magazine.

D: Well, that just goes to show! What you need is some kind of system for where you put things. You're always losing things. It's absolutely ridiculous.

H: You've got such a nerve! It was you who lost all your credit cards the other day, and it was me who found them for you!

D: Yes, I know, and I'm extremely grateful to you, but you do need to get yourself organised with keys.

Recording 4

a A: I'm absolutely exhausted. Let's stay in and rent a video.
   B: Oh, you're so boring these days. I want to go out.

b A: I really like living here because it's so near the centre of town.
   B: That's true, but it gets really noisy at night.

c A: Thanks for everything, we've had such a nice evening!
   B: You're welcome. Come again soon!

d A: I suppose you want to see Liz.
   B: No, actually it was you I wanted to see.

e A: Why on earth are we inside on such a beautiful day?
   B: Well, it was you who wanted to spend the day at a museum.

f A: Ouch! This tooth is so painful.
   B: You know you do need to go to the dentist's.

g A: What's all this broken glass! What on earth have you been doing?
   B: Don't blame me! It wasn't me who broke it!

h A: Your friend was really lovely. I do hope you'll invite him again.
   B: Yes, I will. I think he really enjoyed the evening as well.

i A: Come on, let's go to that new club.
   B: Look, I really do think it's time we went home. It's nearly three.

j A: I really think you ought to apologise to her.
   B: Why on earth should I apologise? It wasn't me who started the trouble.

Recording 5

There are a number of key principles of the so-called 'Montessori method' which are still used in Montessori schools world-wide and widely copied and adapted elsewhere. Let me summarise these briefly now.

Firstly, there is the belief that children learn better if they are placed in what is called an 'enriched environment' – that is an environment which stimulates the senses through pictures, sound, colour, touch, etc., and in which the children themselves can choose from a wide variety of activities. Children need a wide range of activities from which they can choose what they'd like to do, rather than everybody having to do the same thing at the same time.

Secondly, the idea that children learn through purposeful activity, not just play, but activities with a purpose, for example, making somthing, drawing pictures, etc. Given a choice, children will choose work rather than play. Toys which do not serve a specific purpose are therefore discouraged.

And thirdly, in order that children develop confidence and self-esteem, they should always be treated with respect and should be allowed to develop at their own pace – a sharp contrast to many of the disciplinarian attitudes which were prevalent at the time when Montessori was developing her ideas.

Having looked at those principles, let's look briefly at some of the key events in Montessori's later life before summarising her influence on the world of education today.

In her later years, Montessori travelled widely, spending several years in Spain, India and the UK. It was typical of her energy that, even in her seventies she remained as active and dynamic as ever. She was nominated for the Nobel Peace Prize on three occasions – in 1949, 1950 and 1951. She died in the Netherlands in 1952. She had previously insisted that she was buried there rather than in her native Italy as she considered herself a 'citizen of the world'.

The influence of Montessori is still widely felt today. She was among the first to put the learner at the centre of the learning process. As she wrote herself 'We teachers can only help the work going on, as servants wait upon a master.' There are now thousands of Montessori schools in more than fifty countries, and former students include Jacqueline Kennedy and the British royal princes, William and Harry.

Recording 6

1 Take my advice – go to Australia.
2 You could always try New Zealand.
3 Have you thought of coming here to Malta?
4 The most important thing is to pick the right school.
5 I'd check there if I were you.
6 If you ask me, you can't beat the USA.
7 Try logging on to the *Study in the USA* website.
8 How about coming to Ireland?

Recording 8

Like advice: discipline, experience, string, website
Like advise: choose, citizen, downstairs, visible
Like cash: discussion, international, ocean, rush

Module 7

Recording 1

1 One thing that I attended earlier this year I think was one of the most important events I have ever been to. Erm it was the Anti-war demonstration. I think it was March or April this year and erm it was one of the most moving events I've ever been to. I must have been one of about a million people and we filled the streets and the atmosphere was so positive. The idea that we all believed the same thing, that erm we could maybe change the ideas of some politicians, I don't know. Erm, but it was just incredible and I found myself crying at some points and laughing at other points. But the overriding feeling was that I was proud of myself and proud of everybody else who was there.

2 I think something I'll never forget is when I was um ... I was in Moscow and this was ... a few years ago and erm while I was there I was there for about a month, um ... they were celebrating the 800th or the 850th I can't remember which, anniversary of the founding of Moscow and erm it was absolutely amazing cos for about a week the city just completely came alive. There were loads and loads of people all over the place. They just closed off streets and they had street fairs and parties and um ... there was one evening I was standing outside em, St Basil's in em Red Square and they had this huge orchestra and, and like this choir with five hundred voices or more. Anyway thousands god knows and they did the um, 1812 overture ... Tchaikovsky and it was absolutely incredible. I mean it's not my favourite piece of music to be honest, but just standing there surrounded by these Muscovites and with all these cannons firing and the noise and these voices and the orchestra, and everybody was crying. It was absolutely incredible.

3 I think one of the best things, the most impressive thing almost that I've ever attended was when I went to see Nirvana and this would have been, gosh ages ago. 1991 maybe, 93? I can't remember. Erm and it was one of the first gigs that they did in London and I remember this place cos it had a balcony and we were sitting on the balcony. I was with um my boyfriend at the time and it was utterly spectacular because people from the audience were just going up onto the stage and just diving off the stage, all

while the band were playing and everything. Nobody took any notice of them, but there was just this constant stream of people from the audience getting up and just diving headlong into the crowd and surfing you know across on top of the crowd so all the bodies were being passed along by the other people in the audience. It was just amazing. It was just amazing.

4   Something I'll … I'll never forget is the time I went to Brazil and I actually um … arrived on the 31st December which obviously is New Year's Eve. And as soon as I got there the people I was staying with they said, 'Okay well you've got to come to a traditional Brazilian New Year's Eve Festival' which was on the beach. So we all went down, as you know it's really hot at that time of year in Brazil, so we went down to the beach and I had been told I had to wear only white and gold clothes so I had to get together white and gold clothes. We all went down to the beach and then we had to go right up to the sea and throw rose petals into the sea. And like you know ten hours previously I had been in London where it was really, really cold and suddenly I was there on the beach with all these people throwing rose petals into the … into the water and in some way it was really, really magical.

Recording 2

(answers only)

1   which used to be
2   when Japanese families
3   where the day
4   who lived away from
5   which became known
6   when children
7   which their children have lovingly prepared
8   that has special meaning
9   who have died
10 which are made into

Recording 4

a   The Cannes film festival, which takes place in May every year, attracts the biggest names in the film industry.
b   Steve Redgrave, who has won medals at five Olympic Games, is one of Britain's best-known sportsmen.
c   The Winter Olympics, which normally take place in January or February, are held every four years.
d   Madonna, who has been an international star for over twenty years, had her first hit single in 1984.
e   The annual bull-running festival takes place in Pamplona, which is a city in northern Spain.

Recording 5

There is plenty of evidence that people who eat too many burgers can become ill, whether or not that's because of something in the food itself which could be addictive in some way or whether it's just simple overeating. Well, I think there's no clear answer to that, yet.

Although it's true to say that humans can't actually survive without any salt, we actually need very little of it. About six grams a day, which is about a teaspoonful, is actually more than enough, and indeed too much salt can be extremely bad for you.

There's an old saying that an apple a day keeps the doctor away, which may or may not be true, but in fact you're more likely to have problems with the dentist. Many modern apples contain a great deal of sugar; in some cases as much as four teaspoons in one apple. So if you eat a lot of apples, it's a good idea to clean your teeth afterwards.

There are actually over 10,000 types of mushroom, and most of them, the great majority, in fact, are completely harmless but there are some varieties of mushroom which are poisonous, and a few which can actually kill you. There are a number of deaths through eating poisonous mushrooms every year, so it's best to be careful.

Recording 6

B = BELLA

a   A: Go on, have a bit more. I insist! Have the last piece, Bella!
    B: Thank you, it was lovely, but just a tiny portion. I'm rather full.
    A: Go on, I insist. Have the last piece, Bella!
    B: No really, I'm fine, thank you. It was lovely, but I couldn't possibly manage any more!
b   C: Oh dear, how clumsy of me! I'm terribly sorry! Let me get a cloth.
    B: Don't worry. It doesn't matter in the slightest.
c   D: You know Vera, don't you, Bella?
    E: Hi, there, Bella. Of course, she knows me. How are things with you, then?
    B: Hello, Vera. How lovely to see you again. It seems ages since we last met. Let me see, when was it?
d   F: You must try some of this spinach salad, Bella. It's their speciality.
    B: Actually, I'm afraid I can't eat spinach. It doesn't agree with me. Unfortunately it brings me out in a rash!
    F: Oh, dear.
e   G: It's been lovely to see you again, Bella. You must come and spend a day with us some time, mustn't she, Mary? How about next weekend, for Sunday lunch?
    B: Oh, that's really sweet of you, Uncle Geoff. It's really nice of you to think of me. I'd love to come, but I don't think I'll be able to make it then. I've got some really important exams starting that week. Perhaps some other time, when I'm not so busy?

Recording 7

a   I'm fine, thank you.
b   I couldn't possibly manage any more!
c   Don't worry.
d   It doesn't matter in the slightest.
e   How lovely to see you again.
f   I'm afraid I can't eat spinach.
g   I'd love to come.
h   But I don't think I'll be able to.

Recording 8

1   Do you normally take your time getting up in the morning?
2   Do you know anyone who's really good at taking photos? Who?
3   If someone asks you to 'take a seat', do you stand up or sit down?
4   If you took up a new sport or interest, what would it be?
5   Do you ever have to take care of small children? Who?
6   Which sports do you play? Do you take it seriously?
7   When you arrive home, what's the first thing you take off?
8   Who do you take after more in terms of appearance, your mother or your father?
9   Have you ever taken part in a concert? What was it?
10 How long did it take you to get here today?
11 Have any important historical events ever taken place in your town?
12 Have you taken any notes during this lesson? What about?

Recording 9

(answers only)

/e/ (stressed): festival, precious
/e/ (unstressed): demonstration, sensation
/ə/: flower, cookery

/ɪ/: enough, eccentric.
silent: vanished, vegetable.
/iː/: cheese, three

Module 8

Recording 2

(answers only)

a	long	k	stay
b	way	l	born
c	find	m	find
d	mind	n	Fame
e	car	o	home
f	star	p	alone
g	pass	q	blow
h	were	r	friend
i	parking	s	ride
j	space	t	wait

Recording 3

Well, this article is about something called CWS, which stands for 'Celebrity Worship Syndrome', and this is something that some psychologists at a university in the UK have discovered, and they say it affects a lot of people – as many as one in three, in fact.

A key word from the article is 'syndrome'. A syndrome is a kind of behaviour that is typical of a particular psychological problem. And another important word in the article is 'obsessed'. If you are obsessed with something it means that you think about it all the time, you can't think about anything else. The noun is 'obsession', so you can say that some people have an obsession with famous people like David Beckham or Jennifer Lopez … and finally, 'pathological'. Pathological means strong, unreasonable, uncontrollable feelings … a kind of madness really.

So as I said, according to the article one in three people in the survey have CWS in some form, and the number is apparently going up. Apparently some psychologists at the University of Leicester did some research on 700 people, and they found that twenty-two percent of people had the mild version of the syndrome (which isn't really a problem; you tend to talk about your favourite celebrity a lot and bore your friends), twelve percent have the moderate form and two percent are 'hardcore' sufferers, which means that they are really, really obsessed and can be solitary and anti-social – 'borderline pathological' is the term they use.

The article also discusses why this is happening. One theory is that it's to do with families becoming less important, and people are replacing friends and family with celebrities, people who they don't even know. I think it raises the question of the kind of TV programmes and videos people watch. In my opinion, people spend far too much time looking at screens. I think it's unhealthy, really.

What I wondered was whether this is more of a problem for men or women. It doesn't actually tell you in the article, and er I'd be interested to know what other people think about that … and another thing that might be interesting to discuss is …

Consolidation Modules 5–8

Recording 1

a Toddler Aruw Ibirum, who lives in Bradford, Yorkshire, miraculously survived after a thirty-eight-tonne lorry ran her over as she lay in her pushchair. The lorry driver, who was unaware of what was happening, pulled up after he heard an unusual scraping noise. Aruw, whose pushchair had been dragged along for nearly a kilometre, was discovered with just a few cuts and bruises. An astonished elderly woman who saw the whole thing happen told reporters, 'You wouldn't have believed a child could have come out of that alive.'

b An Australian man who has been suffering for years finally discovered the cause of his acute backache last week. It was due to a shark's tooth which had been stuck in his spine for almost forty-eight years. Leo Ryan, sixty-six, who will be having an operation to remove the tooth, had been attacked by the shark as a teenager. In the accident, which happened off the Gold Coast, where he had been swimming, he also lost three fingers and part of his arm. 'That shark was determined to hang onto me,' he told reporters.

Module 9

Recording 1

a Men go bald because of a chemical in their bodies called testosterone, which causes them to grow facial hair and have deep voices. If large amounts of this chemical occur in the body, signals are sometimes sent to the head, saying that there is no need to grow any more hair, so the head 'forgets' to replace hair which falls out naturally. Women don't usually go bald because testosterone is only present in much smaller quantities in their bodies.

b As far as we know, human beings are the only animals that laugh, and they are certainly the only animals who are ticklish! Most of us have a ticklish spot somewhere, and it's usually pretty easy to find. The feeling we get when another person tickles us is similar to what we experience when spiders or small insects are crawling over us. This same feeling sends us into a state of panic and elicits a response of uncontrollable laughter if a person tickles us. Even if we know that we are about to be tickled, the fear and unease of someone touching and possibly hurting us causes us to laugh. Some people are so ticklish that they begin laughing even before they are touched.

c No one is quite sure why people sleepwalk but it is thought that it happens when there is sudden activity in the brain during very deep sleep. Sometimes we respond to this unusual activity by getting up and walking. Sleepwalking is much more common in children than in adults. Experts believe that almost every child sleepwalks at some time, but it is especially common in pre-adolescent boys. Sleepwalking is much more worrying in adults. It can be a sign of serious stress, or even addiction problems.

d The yawn is the result of the body's need for extra oxygen. This often occurs just after we have woken up, or if we are bored or short of air in a hot, stuffy room. In most cultures, it's good manners to cover your mouth when you yawn. But the original custom may have come from fear rather than politeness. In ancient times, it was feared that the soul – and life itself – might leave the body when the mouth was open, so the hand was placed in front of the mouth to keep it in its place!

e Hiccups are actually caused by a spasm, a sudden muscle movement, in the diaphragm – the part of the body which controls our breathing. Although most attacks of hiccups last only for a few minutes, they can be extremely embarrassing and there is one case on record of an attack of hiccups lasting for sixty-eight years! There are many suggested cures: a sudden shock, holding your breath, swallowing rapidly, drinking a glass of water, but all have one thing in common – they all make you concentrate on something else, so your body then forgets to hiccup!!

f English speakers say 'Bless you', Spanish speakers say 'Jesus', German speakers say 'Gesundheit'– meaning 'health'. In many cultures, it's customary to give some kind of blessing when someone sneezes. But why is this? Some believe that the custom stems from the Middle Ages, when a deadly disease called the Bubonic Plague was common in Europe. One of the final stages of the disease was prolonged sneezing. When others heard the sneezes, they knew the person was about to die. Hence the original saying 'God bless you,' now shortened to 'Bless you'.

Recording 2

1 This is false. Over a period of time, shock or stress can turn your hair white, but it can't happen overnight.

2 This is also false. You only have to count your ribs to check this. It's a myth from the bible which people have tended to take literally.

3 This is true. Babies do have more bones than adults. They join together as the baby develops.

4 This is false. People don't normally die from tarantula bites.

5 This is also false. Elephants can't even see mice, apparently let alone be afraid of them! It is not clear where this myth comes from – possibly the children's film Dumbo!

6 This is again false. In fact, only a quarter of all people struck by lightning actually die.

7 This is true. Although they have wings, turkeys are indeed unable to fly.

8 This is also true. It is due to the different gravitational forces in the two hemispheres.

9 This is again a well-known myth, but there is no evidence in fact to support it – it's also false.

Recording 3

Part A

Paris 1889: The year of the 'Great Exhibition'. The city was packed with businessmen and tourists, and most hotels were fully booked.

A few days before the exhibition was due to start, two English ladies, Eleanor Redwood and her mother Clara, arrived in the city on their way back to London from India, where they were escaping the latest outbreak of the Plague.

They managed to book the last two rooms available at one of the most famous hotels in Paris, and after arriving at the hotel both women signed the register, and were shown up to their rooms. The mother was given room 342, a particularly luxurious room decorated with beautiful red velvet curtains.

Almost immediately however, the mother fell ill and they had to call the hotel's doctor. He examined Mrs Redwood carefully, then called the hotel manager and spoke urgently to him in French. Eleanor could only speak a little French and didn't understand what they were saying, But after a few minutes, the doctor explained in English that he couldn't leave Mrs Redwood because she was too ill, so he asked Eleanor to go and fetch the medicine her mother needed, which was available only at his surgery on the other side of Paris.

Eleanor set out in the doctor's own carriage, but the journey was frustratingly slow, and it was four hours before Eleanor finally returned with the medicine. She rushed into the hotel foyer and asked the manager anxiously how her mother was.

The manager stared at her blankly. 'What are you talking about, Mademoiselle?' he asked. 'I know nothing of your mother. You arrived here alone.' The hotel doctor too denied ever meeting her mother, and in the register, there was only the girl's signature.

Eleanor managed to persuade them to take her back to room 342, but the room was empty, and even more mysteriously, the decorations appeared to have been completely replaced, and the beautiful red velvet curtains had disappeared.

The distraught girl rushed to the British Embassy to tell her story, but officials refused to believe her, and when she returned to Britain she was put in a mental asylum. However, the girl continued to insist that her story was true, and doctors never found any other evidence that she was insane. Eventually she was released, but her mother's body was never found.

Recording 4

Part B

So what is the explanation for this strange disappearance? Many experts in historical mysteries believe that Mrs Redwood must have brought the Plague back with her from India. If this news had become widely known, it would certainly have wrecked the Great Exhibition, so the hotel manager might have conspired with the doctor to keep the terrible news a secret. The British Embassy should certainly have investigated her story more fully, at the very least. But surely they can't have disposed of the body and redecorated room 342 in just four hours? Perhaps after all Eleanor was insane. But in that case, what did happen to her mother, and why was she never traced again, dead or alive?

Recording 5

(answers only)

a managed to
b had to call
c could only speak
d couldn't leave
e managed to persuade
f must have brought
g might have conspired
h should certainly have
i can't have disposed

Recording 6

1 Twenty years ago you couldn't send e-mails and faxes. So now you can contact somebody really urgently and get a quick response, but twenty years ago you couldn't.

2 Something I could do when I was twelve that I can still do now is speak Italian. We lived in Milan for four years when I was young and I became fluent then.

3 Well, I'm the mother of um teenage children and something I didn't have to do ten years ago, which I have to do now is supervise children's homework and I must say it's one of the most frustrating tasks I could ever have imagined.

4 I shouldn't have started smoking. I started smoking when I was eleven and I'm still smoking.

5 Yesterday at work I had to talk to somebody because there'd been a complaint about them and I didn't want to do it cos I really like that person, but um I think they lost their temper.

6 Um, I should have paid a cheque into my bank account this afternoon and I remember walking right past the bank and just forgot all about it.

Recording 8

1 I shouldn't have gone out last night.
2 She should have phoned me.
3 I shouldn't have worn these shoes.
4 He shouldn't have got angry with her.
5 You should have got up earlier.

6 I shouldn't have eaten so much.
7 You should have waited for me.
8 I should have brought more money with me.

Recording 9

1 The case of Isidor Fink

The story of Isidor Fink is a classic 'locked-door' mystery. No one was ever arrested for the murder, and no motive was ever established, but it now seems clear how his death happened. Fink can't have committed suicide since no gun was found in the room, and his murderer can't have got into the room and escaped, because of the barred windows and locked doors. The only other possibility therefore is that he was shot at the door, and then somehow managed to lock the doors himself before staggering across the room and collapsing dead on the floor. This might also explain why he had a bullet hole in his wrist. The murderer shot at his hands as he was struggling with all those bolts and keys.

2 The case of the vanishing children

The farm labourer who found the children came under immediate suspicion of kidnapping them, but it soon became clear that his house was too small to hide them. There was never any evidence that anyone else in the area had kidnapped them and the children clearly had no recollection of any such thing.

It is possible that the search parties missed them, but this seems highly unlikely, and in any case is it really possible that not just one, but all three children slept for four days without waking up?

What is certain is that this case is far from unique – there have been literally hundreds of stories of individuals and groups of people apparently vanishing into thin air, either temporarily as in this case, or permanently. For many years there was a popular theory that a 'fourth dimension' existed, normally invisible, into which people occasionally 'fell' by accident. This theory has never been accepted scientifically, but neither has anyone ever come up with a better explanation for all the strange stories of people simply vanishing.

3 Supernatural happenings in the temples?

After two days of near hysteria when statues of the Hindu god Ganesha apparently drank milk in temples all over the world, on September 23rd the 'miracle' seemed to end as unexpectedly as it had started. Explanations of what exactly happened on those two days seem to depend largely on one's religious faith – or lack of it. While some scientists claimed that the milk had somehow been drawn up from the spoons, absorbed into the statues, and then trickled down the outside of the statues in an invisible film, millions believed that they had witnessed a true miracle. 'I feel that the Gods are showing their power, specially to the younger generation, who will now start believing,' said one priest.

4 Is this a photograph of the Loch Ness Monster?

The photograph claims to show the huge prehistoric monster, supposedly seen in Loch Ness in Scotland. The photograph was published in 1934 in the English newspaper, *The Daily Mail*, and immediately caused a sensation. It was widely accepted as genuine, and began a craze for monster-hunting which has continued to this day. In 1994, however, the photo was revealed as a fake. Duke Whetherill – wishing to play a trick on the press – sent his children to a toyshop to buy a toy submarine and some plastic wood. From these things they made a monster which they floated on the lake and photographed. Sixty years later, one of Whetherill's children (now an old man) decided it was time to confess to the deception he and his father had played on the world. Whether or not the Loch Ness Monster really exists is still a mystery, however.

Recording 10

Conversation 1

A: Can I help you?
B: Yes, I bought this in the sale here. A couple of weeks ago, I think it was.
A: I see, yes.
B: And I looked at it the other day and I just thought, no, I don't like it. I don't think it suits me. The colour's not really right for me, do you know what I mean?
A: Well, um, do you have a receipt? Or proof of purchase?
B: No, no, I didn't keep the receipt, sorry. Does that mean I can't change it? I've only worn it a couple of times and I've seen another one I like.
A: Well, we don't normally change goods that have been worn, you see.
B: Oh, no! Er well, can I speak to the manager, and see what he says because I would like to change it.

Conversation 2

A: Excuse me, what is this, please?
B: That's your pizza, madam.
A: Yeah, I can see that.
B: It's Pizza Napoletana, mozzarella cheese, tomato, garlic.
A: Yes, I know what it is, but it's not what I ordered.
B: Oh, oh, I'm sorry,
A: I ordered the lasagne with green salad. I think you must have the wrong order.
B: I'll just go back and check, sorry about that …
A: OK, you go and check, I think you'll find I'm the lasagne.

Conversation 3

… Yeah, I've got the delivery okay … yes, everything seems to be here but there's just one slight problem … Well I've got it all set up according to the instructions, and I managed that all right, but when I switch it on, nothing happens. The screen's just completely blank … no nothing at all … Yes, I've tried that … yes, the battery's fully charged … well, I don't know, that's why I'm ringing you … Well, is there anyone there who can help me? … I see, right. … Well, if I leave my number, can you ask that person to ring me back as soon as possible, yeah? Okay, it's 0-1-3-5 …

Conversation 4

A: I'd like to change this CD, please.
B: You'd like to change it. What exactly is the problem?
A: It was a Christmas present. I asked my mum to buy me a CD for Christmas, but this isn't the one I wanted. I wanted the new CD by Chaos Theory, and she bought me this. It's their first CD, not their latest one.
B: I see, so you'd like to exchange it for the right CD, is that right?
A: Well, no, not really, you see I don't like Chaos Theory any more. I'd like a computer game instead.
B: I see, well, if you'd like to choose which computer game you'd like, then we can probably take the price of the CD off the price of the computer game. If you have the receipt with you … do you have the receipt?
A: Yeah, it's here.
B: Okay, then. So if you'd like to choose the computer game, then we'll try and sort it out for you, okay?

Recording 12

Like here: hemisphere, severe, volunteer , weird
Like there: everywhere, hair, pair, unaware

Module 10

Recording 1

(answers only)

a   I'm going to take
b   are playing
c   we're having
d   it starts
e   won't mind
f   leave
g   I'll tell
h   she'll understand
i   Are you going to take
j   I'm going to drive
k   's dropping
l   I'll pick you up
m   is
n   likely to be
o   leave

Recording 2

1   Okay, well I'd choose Hillary Clinton. Erm she's always fascinated me cos I think in a way she was like the power behind the throne when her husband was president, as she always seemed to be the driving force behind him and I reckon she's a very tough cookie and I think a conversation with her ... with her would be really interesting. I'd like to ask her, you know, how she put up with him when he was carrying on as he did and also you never know ... em she might just run for president herself. That would be extraordinary, wouldn't it?

2   If I could invite anyone I wanted to to a dinner party, I'd definitely invite David Beckham. Not only is he extremely good looking, but I'm sure he'd also have some funny stories to tell about people he's met and places that he's been.

3   Someone I'd really like to have round for dinner would be Marge Simpson from The Simpsons, um and the reason I'd choose her is because I think she's had the most amazing experiences. When you think about what happens to them every week in those programmes, um ... the fact that she's got really strong opinions on ... on most ... most topics and I think it would be interesting to sit down and argue with her and also because she's so kind of long suffering, she kind of has this awful time with Homer and with Bart, and I think it would be wonderful just to be able to give her a good meal and a ... and a glass of wine and say 'You know Marge, it's OK. You're with friends, let's have a ... let's have a chat or something.'

4   I'd like to invite Elvis Presley for dinner, 'cos he was just a fantastic song writer and also really quite a curious human being, you know, because he was so talented and I think he got so ... he was one of the earliest ... one of the first really famous people and it would be just really interesting to know how that affected his life and you know what he thought of the whole thing about being famous and I think it would be great to talk to him.

5   The person I would like to invite for dinner is Nelson Mandela. As everyone knows he's the former president of South Africa and he spent twenty-seven years imprisoned on Robin Island for standing up for his beliefs in the equality of all people and against apartheid. Um ... I think that must have taken tremendous courage and strength of character to do what he did and to endure all those years of privation when he was in imprisoned. Um ... he comes across as a very sincere person, very down to earth and just a lovely warm human being.

6   One person I'd like to invite is Darwin, because his ideas nowadays seem so normal. Um ... I'd really love to talk to the person who thought of those ideas in the first place and to find out where he got the ideas from.

Recording 3

a   He'll have had his lunch by then.
b   I'll still be working at ten.
c   The children'll have gone to bed by then.

d   I'll be driving past the supermarket.
e   I'll be lying by a swimming pool this time tomorrow!
f   I won't be using the car this evening.

Recording 4

Conversation 1

Hello? Hello? Sorry? Yes, that's right, this is Stephen Lloyd, yes, thanks for getting back to me ... yeah, um, I left a message earlier about the furniture that you're supposed to be delivering to me at the end of this week ... and I wondered if ... sorry? ... no, no it's just that I'm on a train and I keep losing you ... we, we keep going into tunnels ... I said I keep losing you whenever we go into a tunnel ... could you speak up a bit, please? No, your voice is very faint ... yeah, yeah, that's better yeah ... yeah, I can hear you perfectly, yeah ... sorry, you said that you'll be delivering the furniture on Friday, is that right? About what time? Sorry? No, your voice has gone very faint ... I can hardly hear you ... sorry, you're breaking up ... shall I ... shall I ring you back? Look, I'm going to call you back. OK? Hello? Hello?

Conversation 2

B: Hello, thank you for phoning Gas Line. You have three options: if you want to enquire about new Gas Products, Press 1. If you have an enquiry about an outstanding bill, Press 2.
Thank you. We're now going to connect you to one of our sales team.

D: Hello, welcome to Gas Line. My name's Andy, how can I help you?

C: Hello, yes, it's about a letter I've just had about a bill I received.

D: Have you got your customer reference number, please?

C: Um ... yeah, it's V290 636K,

D: Okay, just get your file up on the screen. Can I just confirm your name and postcode, please?

C: Yes, it's Christine Ford, and the postcode is MN8 6DK.

D: Okay, that's fine and how can we help you this morning?

C: Well, you sent me a bill which I think I paid three weeks ago, and it says that unless I pay it within seven days, you'll ...

D: Sorry to stop you there. I'll have to put you through to another department as we don't actually deal with invoices which are more than three weeks old. If you'll just bear with me ...

C: Yes, but ...

E: Hello, Customer Service Department.

C: Yes, it's about a letter you sent me. The customer reference is V290 636K, and I sent you ...

E: Can you just confirm your name and postcode for me, please?

C: I've just given all this information to another young man. Do I have to go through all this again? It's MN8 6DK and my name is Christine Ford. Now about this bill that I'm supposed to owe you, now I know I sent you a cheque at least ...

E: Sorry is that M for Michael, N for Nigel ...

Conversation 3

F: Yes, hello, Linda Bates speaking.

G: Hi, it's Jane Markham from Adonis Travel. It's regarding your flights to Istanbul next week. I've just got a couple of queries ...

F: Oh, yes. Hello. Oh sorry, just a second ... No! Not there! Where I told you by the book case ... Sorry ...

G: Yes, I just wanted to know if you'd mind taking a flight a bit later than the one we discussed ...

H: Mum? Mum? Have you seen my trainers anywhere?

F: Please, don't interrupt me when I'm on the phone, yes sorry, you were saying ...

G: No, don't worry … am I ringing at a bad time? I'll ring back later if it's easier for you.

F: Do you mind, it's just that there are some delivery men, and … will you be careful with that please? Sorry …

G: No problem … when would be a good time to ring?

F: Oh, if you give it about an hour things will have settled down a bit … thanks.

G: OK, I'll speak to you later.

F: OK, thanks. Bye.

G: Bye.

Recording 5

1 Am I ringing at a bad time?
2 Could you speak up a bit, please? Your voice is very faint.
3 I left a message earlier.
4 If you'll just bear with me…
5 Sorry you're breaking up.
6 Thanks for getting back to me.
7 I'll have to put you through to another department
8 It's regarding your flights to Istanbul next week.
9 When would be a good time to ring?
10 Can I just confirm your name and postcode, please?

Module 11

Recording 1

The Greeks first cloned plants more than 2,000 years ago.
It is believed that malaria kills around a million people a year, even today.
The most dramatic increases in life expectancy occurred in the twentieth century.
The current average life expectancy for a woman in the developed world is 75.
The quality of human skin begins to deteriorate from the age of about 35 on average.
AIDS first became a major health problem in the 1980s.
Dolly the sheep was born in 1997. She died at the age of six.
The normal life expectancy of a sheep is about twelve.
Genetic engineering of embryos is best carried out when the embryo is only twenty-four hours old. Scientists believe that this procedure will be possible by 2010.

Recording 2

For several years I had wanted a tattoo, but I never liked a design enough to make the commitment. Then, last year, a Japanese student, Yoshi, was doing a course at the college I go to, and we became friends. When he had to leave, he gave me and all my friends a beautifully designed card with the Japanese characters of our names printed on them. My name looked really cool in Japanese script, so I decided to have it tattooed on my shoulder. Everyone said it was the best tattoo they'd ever seen, and I was really pleased … until I went on holiday this April. We challenged a group of Japanese girls to a game of volleyball, and they kept calling 'Sidney' to me, which was odd because my name is Stuart. My best friend's name however is Sidney. Yeah, that's right. The cards had got mixed up by accident and I'd been given Sidney's card. If I'd just checked with a Japanese person before I got the tattoo done! Now I'm walking around with my friend's stupid name tattooed all over my shoulder. I wish I could have it removed, but it's incredibly painful and expensive so I guess I'm stuck with it.

Recording 3

1 Last year, while I was on holiday, I met a guy on the beach and we got talking. Nothing much happened, but on the last day I gave him my e-mail address and phone number and said we should keep in touch. Since I've been back, he's been sending me e-mails – at least ten or twelve a day, saying he loves me and is coming to England to marry me. He's started phoning as well, often very late at night. I've done nothing to encourage this. I'm worried what will happen if he does come over.

2 A few months ago, I got talking to a man at an antiques fair. The man gave me his business card and said that he was an expert on antiques. And because I had an antique mirror at home which I was thinking of selling, I asked the man to come and have a look at it. He did so, but said he couldn't be sure of the value until he'd shown the mirror to a friend. Believing him to be genuine, I let him take the mirror away. I never saw the mirror, or the man, again. The address and phone number on the card turned out to be false. And a few weeks later I arrived home to find that my house had been burgled and several other valuable antiques stolen.

3 Well, I've always been very successful in my career and I set up my own business ten years ago that really did very well. But I'd never really met the right man. That was something that was really missing from my life. So when I met Luke at a friend's party, and he seemed interested in me, I couldn't really believe my luck, to be honest. He was twelve years younger than me and really good-looking and charming, and he seemed really keen on me. In fact, within three months, he had proposed and we were married. I was just totally in love with him and thought we would be happy ever after, so when he came home one day saying he'd walked out of his job, it wasn't a big problem. We just opened up a joint bank account and he was free to use my credit card. That's really where the problems began because he just started spending thousands and thousands of pounds of my money on designer clothes and gambling and expensive nights out … without me. We started having huge rows and then one night he just walked out on me, but not before he'd emptied my bank account. Now he wants a divorce and he's claiming half of my house. I've lost everything I've worked all my life for, just because I fell in love with the wrong man!

Recording 4

1 Mm … it is a difficult one. I think as long as everyone knows exactly what they're letting themselves in for, everyone knows exactly what the situation is, then okay, as far as I'm concerned people should be allowed to do it. I know that many people would say that it's wrong, but if it gives parents who can't have children the opportunity to do so, and no one suffers because of it, then to me. I can't see why not, frankly. I don't have any objection.

2 Definitely. Absolutely, definitely, yes. I'm absolutely convinced that it should be stopped, yeah. Personally, I find smoke really repulsive, really horrible and I really don't see why I should have to endure other people's smoke when I'm at work. It just makes me yeuch, really. It seems that most places have some kind of ban on smoking nowadays, and I think it's to everyone's benefit. It's often said that eighty per cent or something of smokers want to give up anyway, so this seems a good way of helping them to do it.

3 Well, I must say I haven't really thought about it. I think if it's just for unimportant things like cosmetics. They do a lot of testing on animals to see if cosmetics are safe, don't they? I don't think that should be allowed, no, that seems wrong to me, but as for medical research, there might be some real benefit that comes out of it. I haven't really made up my mind about it, to be honest.

4 Actually, I think it can be justified in many cases, but I'd say that it has to be clear that there is some benefit, or possible benefit. I've read that most experiments on animals don't actually have that clear a purpose. I think they should be

allowed, but there has to be very strict control over exactly what experiments are permitted. I know some people believe that all experiments should be banned, but I don't completely go along with that.

5 I think you have a really tricky moral issue here. I know that apparently in the States, there are special agencies that can fix this up for you, if you have the money, of course, and, actually, when you think of it, I don't think that's right. It's like you're treating babies as a commodity, something you can buy, like a new washing machine or something. Frankly, no, I don't agree with it.

6 Erm, it doesn't really bother me. I mean everybody says that smoking's bad for you, and the experts all say that other people's smoke can make you ill, but I don't know really. I don't smoke myself, but I don't have any real objection to other people doing it.

Recording 5

(answers only)
a I'm <u>absolutely</u> convinced
b To be <u>honest</u>
c As far as <u>I'm</u> concerned
d I've <u>no</u> doubt
e To <u>me</u>

Recording 6

A: So, what do you think about this lady in hospital then?
B: Um, I think she shouldn't be allowed to die. I think she should be kept alive.
A: And why do you feel that?
B: Cos it says that her mental abilities are unaffected so she's really conscious of everything that's going on around her and I think they need to find a way of improving the quality of her life within the constraints that she in …
A: But I can see your point but the other side of it is that for exactly the reason you're saying that she can observe what's happening to other people - that everybody else is doing all the things that she now can't do, you're almost condemning her to death by having her just sitting there and … well, I, for me it would be a nightmare if I had to live that kind of life, where I watched people doing things I could no longer do …
B: I know what you mean but I think she … it says that she's depressed, but depression can pass and depression is treatable. I know that she won't recover her physical health but still …
A: Well, you say depression is treatable and it can pass but I … I think in most cases it's with people who can move and do things – to treat somebody who is basically a head that can think and can't …the rest of their body can't move I think it would be very hard to treat …
B: I know but look at what amazing things people have done who are really physically disabled, but who've got all their mental faculties still present – they can write music, they can write novels, you know I mean she … she could live quite a full life, it's a question of helping her to live that.

Recording 7

a I can see your point but …
b The other side of it is …
c I know what you mean but …
d I know but look at what …

Module 12

Recording 2

1 Well the things I don't really look at usually are financial pages, sports pages, things like editorials, because they tend to be very long and quite boring, unless it's a topic that I'm really, really interested in. The things that I do actually read a lot of are things like the arts pages, and reviews of new films, and new books, and that's why I like reading on a Sunday, because the papers that you get on a Sunday are usually full of reviews of the week, and I find that quite interesting, but things like the financial pages just bore me, I just don't understand them and I'm not interested, and sport, I'm just not interested, so I just don't bother.

2 Yeah, the best stuff is on cable and satellite, which I don't have, so I've got to go to the pub to watch it, which is all right, I don't mind, that's a good excuse. But on what I've got at home it's just division two, division three, stuff like that, games which are not very interesting, and then sports which only people who are not really interested in sport like watching – like cricket and darts and um, bowls and things like that. So I just go out on Wednesdays and Saturdays and Sundays, and watch it down the pub.

3 Sometimes I think it's almost impossible to turn on the television without seeing violence, and I never thought I'd feel like that, but maybe it's just because now I've got a little child I feel like that, but I turn it on and adverts seem to be quite violent, and there are cartoons, and it seems to be from seven o'clock in the morning until you turn the TV off at night. On one of the five channels, you're bound to find something which shows people being aggressive towards each other. And I think it's something I've become more aware of since I've had a child of my own, but it's not the thing I'd write to the paper about, but it bothers me quietly, I suppose.

4 Well, the ones that I really, really hate are for perfume, above all others I absolutely detest them, usually around about Christmas time, you're completely bombarded by these things for perfume, and they usually have women in the most ludicrous clothes, doing something really stupid – like, I don't know, wearing an evening dress and stepping out of a shell. They're just absolutely dreadful, they're absolutely dreadful – they're supposed to be really, really sophisticated, and I don't know, the women who are on them are supposed to be really beautiful, but they just look absolutely ridiculous and I loathe them!

Recording 3

1

A = REPORTER; B = ACTRESS; C = PRESS OFFICER

A: Tammy, can you tell us if there's any truth in the rumour that you're pregnant?
B: I haven't got any plans to start a family at the moment. At present, I'm just concentrating on my career.
C: OK, that's enough. Thank you very much everyone.

2

A = MARK; B = SHEILA

A: …. so I'm afraid Rachel isn't here at the moment, Sheila.
B: Well, can you tell her to call me back as soon as she gets in. It's something quite important I need to discuss with her. You won't forget, will you?
A: Of course, I won't.

3

A = MOTHER; B = DAUGHTER

A: Zoë, have you borrowed any money from my purse? I thought I had a lot more than £20.
B: No, I haven't! I haven't touched it! You always think everything's my fault!

4

A = WOMAN; B = MAN

A: A group of us are going out for a meal tonight after work, would you like to come with us?

B: I'm not sure what I'm doing, but thank you. I'll let you know later.

5

A = SON; B = MOTHER

A: I want to go first!

B: Okay, Alex, you can have the first turn, but only for about ten minutes, then it's Rosie's turn. Is that clear?

A: Okay.

Recording 4

A Debbie said she was feeling ill.

B Debbie <u>said</u> she was feeling ill.

Recording 5

a The weather forecast <u>said</u> it was going to be nice today.

b The policeman told us there was nothing to worry about.

c Our teacher <u>said</u> the test was going to be easy.

d Clare <u>told</u> me she was staying in tonight.

e Jonnie said the money was his.

f She said she couldn't afford to come out for a meal with us.

g Nick <u>said</u> he would be home early.

h Alex told me she'd passed the exam.

Recording 6

(answers only)

1	speak	8	speak
2	speaks	9	Talking
3	talk	10	talk
4	talking	11	speaking
5	speak	12	talks
6	talking	13	talk
7	Talk		

Recording 7

1 I use e-mail a lot in my work, and sometimes I use it to look up information for holidays or things, but it's not something I do for pleasure. I would never just go onto the Internet as a form of entertainment. It's definitely a work thing for me.

2 Yeah, I listen to the radio all the time when I'm at home doing housework and things, it's the first thing I do when I go into the kitchen in the morning. I listen a lot when I'm driving, too. It definitely makes the journey go quicker.

3 Everybody enjoys films more in the cinema, don't they? It's just much more of an occasion, isn't it? The special effects are much more exciting on a big screen, and you don't have any interruptions like you do at home. It's just much better in every way.

4 I flick through it every day, but I wouldn't say that I really read it closely. I read the sport first and then the front page news stories, and then probably look at the TV guide, and a couple of other things maybe, but I certainly don't read it cover to cover every day.

5 I find that I watch less and less actually. I usually watch the news at some point in the evening, but to be honest the programmes are getting worse and worse and there are so many repeats and things, that I usually prefer to listen to music or read the newspaper.

Consolidation modules 9–12

Recording 1

Conversation 1

A = HOTEL RECEPTIONIST; B = GUEST

A: Your bill for room 603, madam. How will you be paying – cash or credit card?

B: Cre … just one moment. What's this?

A: What is what exactly, madam?

B: This … $120 … here.

A: That is for your telephone calls, madam. Just here it says 'Telefon' … that means 'telephone' madam.

B: Are you laughing at me?

A: No, madam, of course not.

B: Well, you'd better not be, that's all I can say, because, listen, I am not going to pay this $120, do you hear me?

A: But madam …

B: I phone my husband for two minutes and it costs me $120. It's crazy.

A: I'm afraid the calls were made from your room, madam. You are obliged to pay for them.

B: Listen, I'm not paying anything until I see the manager.

A: I'm afraid the manager is not available at the moment, madam.

B: I said I want to see the manager and I want to see him NOW, you hear, RIGHT NOW!

A: Well, he's having his lunch at the moment.

B: He's having WHAT!!

A: Perhaps you might like to make an appointment to see the manager when he comes back from his lunch. Would two thirty be OK?

Conversation 2

A = ANGRY DRIVER; B = ANDREW CLARK

A: You idiot! What do you think you're doing? You did that on purpose, didn't you? You deliberately backed into me! It's all your fault, you shouldn't be on the road …

B: Oh, no, no. It wasn't on purpose. It was an accident. I didn't see you coming, I honestly didn't mean it!

A: Look at the damage you've done to my car! That'll cost a fortune to get fixed. You're going to pay for this.

B: Well, I think you'll find …

A: Just a moment, don't I know you?

B: Well, you might do. I am quite well-known …

A: You're Andrew whatshisname … Andrew, er …

B: Clark. Yes, that's me. I'm Andrew Clark, yes.

A: I've seen you on television. My wife thinks you're wonderful. I wonder if you'd mind giving me your autograph?

B: Well, I don't normally …

A: Oh go on, go on. Just write 'To Leonora'. She's my wife. She thinks you're fantastic.

B: Well, okay, if you insist. 'To Leonora. Best wishes, Andrew Clark.'

A: Thanks, oh, and sorry I lost my temper just now. It's just that it's not my car. It belongs to my wife, you see.

Pearson Education Limited
Edinburgh Gate
Harlow
Essex CM20 2JE
England
And Associated Companies throughout the world.

www.longman.com/cuttingedge

© Pearson Education Limited 2005

First published 2005
Eleventh impression 2010

ISBN 978-0-582-82525-3

Set in 9/12.5pt ITS Stone Informal and 10/13pt Congress Sans.

Printed in China   GCC/11

Author acknowledgements

We would like to thank the following people for their help and contribution:
David Albery, Helen Barker, David Carr, Rachel Clark, Martin Dewey,
David Evans, Vicky Gemmill, Peta McRedmond, Dennis Murphy, David Todd,
Clare Tyrer, Jacqui Robinson and Penny Reid (Producer) for making the
unscripted recordings. We would also like to thank the publishing team for
their support and encouragement, in particular Jenny Colley (Senior
Publisher), Lindsay White (Project Manager), Shona Rodger and
Rhona Snelling (Editors), Rob Briggs (Designer), Andy Thorpe (Mac Artist) and
Penny Reid (Producer).

The publishers and authors are very grateful to the following people and
institutions for keeping user diaries:
Chris Graveling, EF Int School of Languages, Cambridge; Sally Parry, United
International College, London; Judith Hook, St Giles College, Brighton; Mali
Charlaff, Oxford House College, London; Jason Jerome and Bob Hubbard, Anglia
PU, Cambridge; Emma Metcalf, Chester School of English, Madrid; Amanda Bailey,
Merit School, Barcelona; Graham Sanders, Stanton School, Alicante; Barbara Ortin
Ortiz, Grafton School, Yecla (Murcia); Jose Antonio Alvarez Gonzalez, Trafalgar
Idiomas, Gijon; Howard Evans, English Language Institute, Seville; Małgorzata
Duraj-Czyżewska, University of Lódź, Lódź; Agata Lesińska, II Liceum
Ogólnokształcące, Warsaw; Elżbieta Ciurzyńska, LVIII Liceum Ogólnokształcące im.
K.K., Baczyńskiego, Zespół szkół ogólnokształcących NR 23, Warsaw; Agata
Jagiełło, Progress School, Szczecin; Jadwiga Sowińska, I LO im.B Nowodworskiego,
Kraków; Edyta Frelik, Linguaton, Lublin; Rogerio Sanches, Cultura Inglesa, São
Paulo; Alexander Kouzmin, State Language Courses N3, St Petersburg; Maria
Elova, Kazan State University, Kazan, Tatarstan; Napoleon Mannering, Kanda Gaigo
Gakvin, 2-13-13 Uchikanda, Chiyoda-KU, Tokyo; Alica Hurcak Korojaj, School for
Foreign Languages Kezele, Croatia; Dubravka Sinko, Kezele, Skola Stramih jezike I,
Varazdn; Caroline Nigra Hislop, Hill School, Montelupo Fno; Graham Waters, British
School, Rome; Hugh Moss and Matt Plews, The British Council, Lisbon; Links Team
Links School of English, La Plata; Cecilia Antunia, Laboratorio de Idiomas Faculted,
Buenos Aires; Susana Vidal/Marisa Vidal, 'Smart' Institute, La Saz; Maria Cristina
Castro, Saint Mary's, Paysandu

and the following people for reporting on the manuscript:
Leslie Hendra, Frances Eales, International House, London; Frances Traynor,
Jane Comyns Carr, International House, Sydney; Mike Carter, International
House, Seville; Sally Parry, United Int College, London; Emma Metcalf, Chester
School of English, Madrid; Drew Hyde, Frances King School of English,
London; Agata Lesińska-Domagała, Liceum Ogólnokształcące im. Stefana
Batorego, Warsaw; Pauline Belimova, St Petersburg, Edyta Frelik, Linguaton,
Lublin; Elżbieta Ciurzyńska, LVIII Liceum Ogólnokształcące im. K.K.,
Baczyńskiego, Zespół szkół ogólnokształcących NR 23, Warsaw.

We are grateful to the following for permission to reproduce copyright
material:
Chronicle Books LLC for extracts adapted from 'Lightning', 'Earthquake', 'Leg
fracture', and 'Charging bull' published in *Worst-Case Scenario Survival Handbook*
by Joshua Piven and David Borgenicht © 1999; Johnnic Publishing Limited for an
extract adapted from 'Fame of the game is all too brief' by Justice Malala published
in *Sunday Times, South Africa* 9 December 2001; Reader's Digest Association for
an extract adapted from 'Long at the fair' published in *Strange Stories and
Amazing Facts* © 1975 The Reader's Digest Association Limited; Solo Syndication
Limited for an extract adapted from 'Are you a celeb worshipper?' by James
Chapman published in the *Daily Mail* 14 April 2003; and Transworld Publishers, a
division of The Random House Group Ltd for an extract adapted from *Neither
Here Nor There* by Bill Bryson published by Black Swan © Bill Bryson.

We are also grateful to the following for permission to reproduce copyright
song lyrics:
Screen Gems – EMI Music Limited and Chelsea Music Publishing Company
Limited for the lyrics to 'Always on my Mind', Words and Music by Wayne
Thompson, Mark James and Johnny Christopher © 1971 (Renewed 1979)
Screen Gems – EMI Music Incorporated/Rose Bridge Music Incorporated, USA.
All rights reserved. International copyright secured.

Universal/MCA Music Limited and Windswept Music (London) Limited for the
lyrics to 'Do You Know the Way to San José?', Words by Hal David and Music
by Burt Bacharach © 1967 New Hidden Valley Music Company/Casa David
Music Incorporated, USA. All rights reserved. International copyright secured.

In some instances we have been unable to trace the owners of copyright
material and we would appreciate any information that would enable us to
do so.

Illustrations by:

Adrian Barclay (Beehive) pages 34, 44, 80, 84-85, 119, 128, 132; Melanie
Barnes pages 21, 64-65, 134; Barbara Bellingham (début art) pages 42-43,
138; Emma Brownjohn (New Division) pages 10, 29, 47, 58, 59; Paul Burgess
p116; Stanley Chow (The London Art Collection) p31; Pete Collard pages
32-33, 34, 100; Yane Christensen (Sylvie Poggio) pages 23, 48, 87, 120, 121;
Rebecca Gibbon (The Inkshed) p129; Sarah McMenemy (The Artworks) pp15,
81; Ian Parratt page 110; Jerry Tapscott pages 37, 50

Photo acknowledgements

We are grateful to the following for permission to reproduce copyright
photographs:
Ace Stock for pp74(br), 111; Actionplus for p57(t); Arcaid for p56/57(m)
Richard Bryant; Bananastock / Alamy for p7(t); BBC Photo Library for p126(tr)
© BBC; www.britainonview.com for p67(bl); Bubbles Photo Library for pp11
Frans Rombout, 49 Catchlight; Buzz Pictures for p28(b) Neale Hayes; Camelot /
Newscast for p132; Camera Press for pp63(tr), 86, 88(b), 98(b); Car Photos /
Alamy for p57(m); Capital Pictures for p90(tl); Comstock for p104(br); Corbis
for pp8(b), 38, 67(tr &tl), 67(br), 73(6), 76(tr), 96/97(m); Digital Vision for p78;
Digital Vision for pp25(tr), 92; DK Images for pp36, 76(l); Empics for pp89(t),
41(r), 72(1), 108, 126(tl); Ethno Images Inc / Alamy for p7 (b); Fortean Picture
Library for p97(tl); Geophotos for p28(t); Getty Images for pp6(t), 24(t),
24/25(m), 53(3), 54©, 66, 74(tr), 97(mb), 130; Ronald Grant Archive for p12(b)
Polygram Rowan Atkinson as Mr Bean; Sally & Richard Greenhill for
p24/25(bm); Robert Harding Picture Library for p29(b); Hulton Archive for
pp55(extreme top), 55(t), 56(b), 69(t), 102(l), 103(t); Hutchinson Library for p19;
id8 Photography for p30(l); IPC Media for p126(overlay); Cindy Jackson Ltd for
pp1189tr & tl); Kobal Collection for p12(t) Working Title / David Appleby;
Graham Lawrence / Alamy for p75(5); Life File / The Hughes Collection for
p102(r); Mediscan for pp62, 122(br) Mirrorpix for p107(l); Moviestore
Collection for pp25(b) Artisan Entertainment, 126(m) Columbia / Tristar, 135
Bend It Films / Film Council; www.gianniamuratore.com for p24(bl); NASA for
pp56/579t0; PA Photos for pp53(4), 72(3), 79(tl), 90(tr), 133; Andrew Parker /
Alamy for p57(bl); Pearson Education for pp14, 42/43(m), 42(br, l), 43(t,
b),54(b), 104 (top row, bl, bm), 132(overlay); Photofusion Picture Library for
pp6/7(m) Alamy, 72(2); Photolibrary.com for pp41(l), 96/97(t); Popperfoto.com
for p57(br), Powerstock for pp25(mr), 75(tr); Punchstock for pp75(tl)
Comstock, 40, 75(ml), 97(mr) Digital Vision, 97(tr) Good Shoot, 75(mr)
Hollingsworth, 46, 112 image 100, 75(br) Imageshop; Redferns Music Library
for pp8(m) Mick Hutson, 8(t) Michael Ochs Archive, 9(tl) Bob Verhorst, 9(b)
Christiana Radish, 9(r) Jorgen Angel,74(l) Peter Pakvis; Reportdigital for p30(r)
John Harris; Retna for pp13, 52(1), 68, 73(4), 90(b), 97(mr); Rex Features fo
pp45, 55(b 7 extreme bottom), 103(b), 118(b); Science Photo Library for
pp63(br) E R Degginer, 75(bl) Francoise Sauze, 122(mr) Dr Gopal Murti,
122(tl)Hank Morgan; South American Pictures for p76(br); Timelife / Getty
Images for p88(t); Topfoto.co.uk for pp52(2), 53(5), 57(extreme left), 96/97(b),
98(l), 126(b); Visuals Unlimited / Mediscan for p122(bl); Janine Wiedel
Photography for pp54(a), 69(b); Woodfall Wild Images for p63(bl); Harald
Zoschke www.pepperworld.com for p79(tr). Royalty Free images appear on
pp18, 104(br), 122(t).

The cover photograph has been kindly supplied by Getty Images/Image Bank.

Picture Researcher: Kevin Brown.

Designer: Roarr Design

This book is dedicated to Joseph, Jessica and Isabel.